# THE GOLDEN FORTRESS

## CALIFORNIA'S BORDER WAR
## ON DUST BOWL REFUGEES

### BILL LASCHER

CHICAGO REVIEW PRESS

Copyright © 2022 by Bill Lascher
All rights reserved
Published by Chicago Review Press Incorporated
814 North Franklin Street
Chicago, Illinois 60610
ISBN 978-1-64160-604-2


Library of Congress Control Number: 2022937148


Typesetting: Nord Compo

Printed in the United States of America
5  4  3  2  1

# CONTENTS

# Prologue

# HERE AND THERE, NOW AND THEN

LOS ANGELES WAS AFLAME. It was the end of summer 2019, and a sense of dread spread through the tens of thousands of people in the City of Angels who lacked stable housing. For an increasing number of Americans, the idea of owning or even renting a home felt as inconceivable as hugging strangers, dining at restaurants, and cramming into a crowded subway would feel one year later. Few places seemed to embody the country's widening wealth inequality quite like the Golden State's most populous city, where a series of fires cast a frightening light on what was at stake for people who'd already lost everything.

Those Angelenos who had found a home—or a bed, or perhaps just a few feet under an underpass—sweated through record-setting heat and nervously eyed the tinder-dry hills encircling their city. Wary after massive, deadly wildfires throughout California in 2017 and 2018, which now seemed to occur as seasonally as the flu, they fretted about conditions at nearby encampments of houseless people. The furnace blasts of the Santa Anas, like those of Raymond Chandler's "Red Wind," that sweep across Los Angeles from the Mojave Desert each fall, were looming. The heat of the city's housed residents' complaints about the growth of their unhoused neighbors' camps grew alongside the incendiary weather. Claiming that the camps were multiplying out of control, their own unchecked rage matched the ferocity of the gusts that flung desiccated palm fronds across their yards and whipped single errant sparks into hillside-spanning conflagrations. Fires near these camps seemed to be increasing, and the annual return of the Santa Anas only increased the risk. Public anxiety heightened each time a cookstove ignited a tent here, or somebody lit fireworks in broad daylight there. Worrisome as the stories were, before long they just seemed to pile atop the list of uncomfortable realities that came with the chance to reside in the City of Angels.

Then people started dying.

Sweltering in the relentless heat and wondering whether the next fire was the one that would finally rage through their cul-de-sacs, homeowners in the city turned to a familiar scapegoat—the poor—and a familiar framing for addressing the discomfiting reality that a far greater percentage of the people experiencing homelessness in the United States lived in California than the state residents' share of the nation's overall population. According to figures from the previous year cited in a February 2019 state legislative analyst's report, more than a quarter of people experiencing homelessness in the nation lived in California, but only 12 percent of the total US population were residents of the Golden State.

In our contemporary world of careful political messaging, we've come to address that experience, "homelessness," as a malady of which individuals might be cured and that policy interventions might eradicate. Indeed, on September 25, 2019—the day after Speaker of the House Nancy Pelosi announced President Donald Trump's first impeachment inquiry—Los Angeles City Council member Joe Buscaino invoked a public health framing to insist that homelessness had become so widespread in California that Governor Gavin Newsom urgently needed to declare a state of emergency.

Buscaino was among the most vocal of a number of public figures who claimed that homelessness threatened public safety. (As this book's conclusion will describe, Buscaino would further politicize homelessness in the years to follow.) Homelessness *was* dangerous, but average Angelenos, Californians, or Americans weren't the ones at risk; it was their unhoused neighbors who faced an acute, potentially deadly threat. Those fires breaking out around Los Angeles in the late summer and early fall of 2019 weren't all accidental, nor was negligence at crowded campsites to be blamed for many of them. Instead, arsonists were targeting the most vulnerable residents of one of the most prosperous cities in the United States, if for varied motives in different blazes.

Late that August, two men allegedly torched an encampment of houseless people living in the hills above the middle-class enclave of Eagle Rock, about ten miles northwest of Skid Row and home to Occidental College. As that blaze spread from the encampment into nearby chaparral, frightened neighbors weary from yearly ever-worsening infernos in this parched climate watched anxiously. Their homes were eventually spared, but the encampment's residents weren't so lucky. Campers escaped alive without serious injury, but the makeshift home they'd built was destroyed. Even more frightening, authorities suspected that two men had specifically targeted their community. When prosecutors finally brought a case more than a year later, they claimed the alleged arsonist attacked the camp because he "didn't like the homeless." (In March 2021, prosecutors only charged one of two original suspects with arson because they lacked sufficient evidence showing the other had directly participated in the arson, thus meaning they'd likely be unable to try and convict him.)

Less than two weeks after the blaze in Eagle Rock, flames erupted along Los Angeles's notorious Skid Row—about ten miles southeast of Eagle Rock and adjacent to downtown Los Angeles—after someone set a man's tent on fire. The tent's occupant died of burns suffered in the blaze. Reports of other deadly and damaging fires involving homeless victims on Skid Row and throughout Los Angeles persisted for weeks. Not all of these blazes were arsons, nor did authorities believe the men suspected of torching the Eagle Rock camp were involved in the others that were, but an air of fear permeated the houseless community throughout that fall.

Los Angeles, and the nation, seemed beset by disaster, though an even worse catastrophe was on its way. Before any constructive response to the homelessness crisis outlined by Councilman Buscaino took shape, the new year brought the threefold crisis of the coronavirus pandemic, an economic collapse unseen in the United States since the 1930s, and the eruption of popular anger after police in Louisville and Minneapolis added Breonna Taylor's and George Floyd's names to the long list of Black men and women murdered by law enforcement. Gasping for air amid an ever-thickening miasma of disease, tear gas, wildfire smoke, social isolation, unemployment, and the centuries-deep pain of systemic racism, the nation lurched toward an election so infected by distrust that democracy itself seemed imperiled.

Like the story of our response to the pandemic and our approach to economic recovery, the story that follows is more straightforward than one might suppose. The central challenges of our contemporary crisis and of that dissected in the ensuing pages are similar. Each resulted from tensions between local jurisdictions and the centralized federal response, between unique regional pressures and forces that transcend borders, and between data-driven, reality-grounded analysis and bombastic scapegoating put forth by those who exploit historical inequities, capitalize on fear, and demonize the foreign.

# 1 | THE "BUM BLOCKADE"

A CLOUDLESS SKY BLANKETED ALTURAS as a string of sedans turned off Highway 299.

Temperatures that afternoon had briefly crept above freezing but dipped again as dusk arrived. From atop a three-story brick building at the other end of Main Street, the word HOTEL blazed against the cloudless sky. On an evening as clear as that one in early February 1936, the beacon of the signage must have been a welcome sight to the cars' occupants as they drove those last three blocks from the highway to the Niles Hotel, hundreds of miles, two days, and a world away from home. That those last three blocks also composed the entirety of downtown Alturas said everything about how far they'd traveled.

After the men parked their cars, they might have reflexively shivered beneath their polished leather jackboots and thought of the all-year warmth and sun they'd left behind. If any of the men passed beneath the street lamp at the corner of Modoc and Main Streets, its glow might have glinted across the gold-toned badges they carried, illuminating an eagle's wings spread above the words POLICE OFFICER and LOS ANGELES typed in blue lettering beneath, and the embossed seal that read, CITY OF LOS ANGELES. FOUNDED 1781.

Once inside the Niles Hotel, thirteen Los Angeles police officers waited as their commanding sergeant, R. L. Bergman, checked them into the hotel. The next morning they would officially begin their new assignment here in the seat of Modoc County, six hundred miles away from the City of Angels. Somehow, despite traveling so far, the officers still hadn't left the Golden State.

A cultural distance matched the physical distance. Alturas was Modoc County's largest town and still remote from the nearest settlements of any size. The hotel was at the southern end of downtown, which ended a few hundred feet away at a small bridge over the gurgling Pit River. It was surrounded by the kind of businesses typical of a certain mythologized small town in the early twentieth-century American West: a coffee shop next door, a butcher down the block, a liquor store up the street, and an inn across Main Street with signage advertising BUFFALO BEER on tap. The county courthouse was just a couple blocks northeast of the hotel. A few businesses fronted East and West Carlos Street. The rest of the nearby streets were residential. The surrounding sparse, frigid, mostly undeveloped expanse where the men would work for the foreseeable future dramatically contrasted with the bustling, sun-bathed metropolis they'd left two days prior, but their task remained the same as it had been at home: protect and serve the City of Los Angeles.

Soon after the officers arrived at the Niles Hotel, a primly dressed woman walked in and introduced herself to Sergeant Bergman. She was Gertrude Payne French, the publisher of the *Alturas Plaindealer*. Could she just interview the sergeant for a little bit about why the police had come all the way to Modoc County from Los Angeles?

She could. Bergman knew how highly his boss, Los Angeles police chief James Edgar Davis, valued good publicity. And Homer Cross, Davis's deputy in charge of crime prevention and this operation's key architect, had softened the ground throughout the state in the weeks leading up to the deployed officers' arrival.

French already knew why they were there, of course. Cross had talked to her when he came to Modoc County that January. Even if he hadn't, French may have known, as she prided herself on how plugged in she was to events transpiring all across California. After all, she was one of the Native Daughters of the Golden West, a member of the Alturas Chamber of Commerce board of directors, and, like her husband, R. A. "Bard" French, a former operative in the state Republican Party. Gertrude and Bard were very encouraged, French told Bergman, that someone—Chief Davis—was *finally* doing something about the "penniless itinerants and criminals" plaguing the Golden State. Concerns about how out-of-town police might disrupt Modoc County were already spreading. The *Plaindealer* would diligently downplay these concerns on its pages, but, French told Bergman and would repeat in print the next day, the paper was "reserving our final judgment to see what happens."

Whatever judgment ensued, numerous scenes like the one taking place at the Niles Hotel likely occurred throughout the remotest corners of California that evening. Davis had sent Bergman, the two seven-officer squads working under him, and 120 other Los Angeles police officers—each handpicked by the chief from a larger pool of volunteers—to seize control of the state's borders. Each squad was stationed at one of sixteen entry points around the perimeter of California. Some would patrol highways and set up checkpoints to stop incoming cars, while others boarded trains to look for fare evaders and stowaways. All those entering California who appeared unable to support themselves and likely to become public charges or whom the officers believed likely to be criminals would be stopped. No one was to get through without permission from the Los Angeles Police Department, even if Los Angeles itself was hundreds of miles away.

Los Angeles police chief James Edgar Davis and Los Angeles County superior court judge Minor Moore present Los Angeles mayor Frank Shaw with a Texas-shaped birthday cake on the eve of Davis's rollout of his border blockade. *Courtesy of Los Angeles Times Photograph Collection, Special Collections, Charles E. Young Research Library, UCLA*

Perhaps Chief Davis, originally from Texas, thought of the deployment's launch as a birthday gift for his boss, Los Angeles mayor Frank Shaw. That Saturday morning, Davis sat down with Shaw, not to celebrate his birthday but to discuss the blockade, just as someone wheeled a sixteen-pound birthday cake into the mayor's office. Los Angeles Superior Court Judge Minor Moore—also a transplant from the Lone Star State, and president of the Texas Society of Southern California—was the enormous dessert's likely mastermind. Moore, who called Shaw to wish him a happy birthday just as the cake arrived, had conspired with Shaw's Texas-born wife, Cora; his mayoral counterpart in Dallas, George Sergeant; and officials from the Texas Centennial Exposition, who actually paid for the giant confection.

As mayor and police chief, respectively, Shaw and Davis were among Los Angeles's most prominent public figures. Before becoming mayor, Shaw, a grocery-chain executive and one of California's wealthiest politicians, was a Los Angeles County supervisor who led the county board's efforts to blame Los Angeles's fiscal woes on poor, unemployed migrants. Davis, a former chief of police who'd been re-elevated to the position when Shaw was elected mayor, made arresting homeless and other visibly poor Angelenos a key plank of his policing strategy. Both men could trace their success in part to the city's obsession with drawing tourists (and their money) while simultaneously shunning poor migrants (and their need). Like other California cities, Depression-era Los Angeles treated transients as little more than parasitic threats. Indigent relief was burden enough for these cities' own residents, the argument went. Why should they pay for other cities' discards?

Reliant as their public rhetoric might have been on antimigrant sentiment, neither Davis nor Shaw were truly *of* Los Angeles. Between fleeing his native Texas and arriving nearly broke in Los Angeles, Davis spent many of his early years as a drifter, while Shaw was born in Canada and grew up bouncing around the Midwest. Neither likely discussed those backgrounds when they met at city hall three days before Davis's officers arrived in Alturas.

The day after their meeting, Davis put an exclamation point on declarations that outsiders—or at least, the wrong kind of outsiders—just weren't welcome in the City of Angels. Davis deployed his border patrol, confident in a full-throated endorsement from Shaw. The chief also knew he could count on support from the Los Angeles powerbrokers who helped elect the mayor three years earlier and who for years had decried what they believed were "hordes" of transient "ne'er do-wells" invading the city. Now well into his second stint as Los Angeles's police chief, Davis had Shaw to thank for his job.

Whether Davis conceived the operation as a favor to Shaw or not, the fervor with which he pursued it was hardly surprising. He cared little about misgivings lawmakers expressed about earlier proposed anti-indigent and anti-migrant measures. He also had no qualms that his officers might trample a few constitutional protections in their attack on criminality and the vagrants who he believed embodied it.

And it would make sense if Davis believed he owed something to the mayor. At the outset of 1930 Shaw's predecessor, John C. Porter, had demoted Davis from chief to deputy chief after a series of high-profile scandals involving his department. After Shaw replaced Porter in 1933, one of his first official acts had been to put Davis back in power. In return, Davis carefully crafted his police department to serve as the primary municipal tool to guard the free-market-cherishing, business-friendly forces cherished by Shaw and responsible for his election.

Amid the economic turmoil and labor unrest of the Great Depression, Davis—while also sparking the Los Angeles Police Department's inchoate development into a paramilitary force that would serve as the national standard for militarized policing—reveled in using the department's power to harass and intimidate union organizers, civil libertarians, and political progressives. Now, the chief turned his attention toward the wretched souls washing across California's borders from barren Dust Bowl farms and Depression-shuttered factories. To hear it from the agenda-setting *Los Angeles Times*, the city's chamber of commerce, and Davis himself, these domestic migrants, if not *already* criminals, were likely to *become* criminals given enough time loitering on the streets of Los Angeles.

Davis's plan would neutralize that threat with a phalanx of officers at California's borders ready to block incoming laborers while the rest of his officers scoured Los Angeles's streets for indigent transients and "vagrants." After months of preparation, the plan was finally ready. Beginning that Sunday, February 3—a day after Shaw's birthday—and continuing into the following afternoon, squad after squad of officers piled into personal cars, drove past the city limits, and continued to the farthest reaches of California, where they would assume their duties as the Golden State's first line of defense from the uncivilized masses beyond.

Some newspapers called the deployment Los Angeles's "bum blockade." Others called it Davis's "Foreign Legion." Many described it as the LAPD's "border patrol." However they were described, the Los Angeles Police officers dispatched to California's frontier worked with little restraint. Specifics about who exactly belonged in California were few. It was up to the border patrollers whom to stop and whom to allow into the state. Most detainees exhibited some subjective characteristics of poverty, such as piles of weather-beaten luggage teetering atop a rickety jalopy or bindles sagging behind weary men hiking into the state, but Davis gave the border patrol wide latitude to stop anyone they might simply deem suspicious. In practice, officers tended to wave shiny new Packards through their checkpoints but halted sputtering early-model Fords pulling makeshift trailers and caked with half a continent's dust.

Police also worked closely with managers and detectives employed by Southern Pacific, Santa Fe, Great Northern, and other railroads that transported freight and passengers into and out of California. At railway sidings inside the state's borders, conductors decelerated trains to crawls slow enough for police to walk alongside the tracks, clamber aboard boxcars, climb to their rooftops, and thoroughly check every compartment and hatch inside and outside for stowaways.

Police fingerprinted anyone they stopped, whether they'd arrived by foot, car, or train. (In addition to standardizing the LAPD's policework during his tenure, Davis oversaw the department's implementation of modern techniques like registering fingerprints and two-way-radio linkups.) The policemen also used a state-of-the art teletype system to check whether detainees had criminal records in California or other states. Police gave anyone who wasn't wanted on a warrant the option of leaving the state—some were marched right off westbound trains onto eastbound ones headed out of California—or spending time in jails that might be little more than makeshift cells in rooms rented at off-season hotels in communities near the checkpoints. In other instances, detained transients were brought to penitentiaries as far as one hundred miles from the border and put to work quarrying rock for public infrastructure projects or performing other manual labor.

The deployment opened a new front in the LAPD's yearslong war on vagrancy. Before Davis's return to control of the department and even before the Great Depression, Los Angeles police regularly arrested people loitering in public parks and streets, as a state-commissioned study of transient relief in California found months after the blockade began. That study found many "instances when social workers in local agencies have had to come to the rescue of law-abiding citizens thus arrested and sentenced to terms in the city jail, and instances where people who did not speak English were arrested on the public streets as vagrants, even though they had plenty of money, because the policemen thought they looked like vagrants." After the Great Depression began, unemployment rose, and police departments in many parts of the state relaxed their enforcement of vagrancy laws. But this wasn't the case in Los Angeles, where police often violently enforced such laws.

The blockade was another step for such increasingly strict policing, and it signaled an ambitious power grab by Davis. As an unelected representative of a city hundreds of miles away from the communities where he sent his armed officers, Los Angeles's police chief usurped the authority of these communities' duly elected or appointed law enforcers and public officials. He also circumvented statewide and local institutions under the auspices of a plan that wasn't even devised by his own city's municipal authorities; it was planned by its power-brokering and privately run chamber of commerce. Yet, as Davis invoked the influence and means of California's largest city to close down the state's borders, he didn't simply stanch the flow of unwanted, destitute migrants. He interrupted passenger travel, disrupted interstate commerce, and interfered with local residents' lives and businesses.

In an era when fascist and totalitarian movements around the world used force to achieve political ends, Davis did not hesitate to use armed police like an imperial military deployed to shape California's demographic and economic landscape in his backers' image. To Davis, Shaw, the Los Angeles Chamber of Commerce, multiple newspaper publishers, many Angelenos, and even a sizable portion of other Californians, a statewide emergency justified the blockade. It provided an urgent response to the waves of indigent migrants they expected would inundate the state with criminals if left unchecked, especially after the federal government suddenly pulled its subsidies for relief programs.

Six years after the market crash that set the Great Depression in motion, aftereffects of the gravest economic crisis the United States had ever seen still gripped much of the country. In 1933 Franklin Delano Roosevelt entered the White House promising to reform the country's financial system, create a social safety net, and put Americans back to work with a package of policy initiatives known as the New Deal. By 1935 the Roosevelt administration had added two flagship programs that transformed the federal government's role in society and the economy: the Works Progress Administration and Social Security. These programs gave Roosevelt the foundation upon which he would campaign for reelection in 1936, but they also gave fuel to the populist forces on Roosevelt's right *and* left fretting about the government's intervention in public life.

Meanwhile, an intensifying environmental crisis would complicate the nation's recovery. Mechanized farming techniques and decades of poor soil management worsened the impact of a yearslong drought parching much of the country. As farms failed across a widening swath of the continent that came to be known as the Dust Bowl, sky-blackening dust storms swept across the Great Plains and the Southwest. Year after year, these dark clouds of fine, reddish dirt sliced up lungs, tore paint from cars, and whipped what little topsoil remained across a strained, desiccated landscape.

These storms ate away at the already tenuous footing of agricultural communities bankrupted by collapsing commodities prices, failed investments, and trade restrictions. Tenant farmers had it even worse. Crushed by debt and hungry, they watched what underpriced crops they could still grow wither unharvested. Landowners snatched government subsidies meant to save their tenants. Hopeless farmers walked away from their fields and joined laid-off factory workers, unemployed bank tellers, and hundreds of thousands of others uprooted by the Depression to search for even the meagerest of opportunities elsewhere. For the vast majority of these newly displaced domestic migrants, *elsewhere* meant "west."

Among the New Deal programs meant to help these new refugees was the Federal Transient Service (FTS), which had been established when Congress passed the first New Deal relief program in May 1933. California had been the chief recipient of FTS aid. For a variety of reasons, it's impossible to know exactly how many transients came to or through California at any one time, but what is measurable is how many people applied for FTS relief and where they came from. More aid claims were filed in California than in any other state, and many more of these claims were made by people in California who claimed residency in other states. In any event, aid was short-lived. The White House shut down the Federal Transient Service in September 1935 as it shifted resources to the Works Progress Administration and Social Security.

Suddenly one of California's key sources for funding transient relief evaporated right as the political will to expand such state support dropped. Even before the FTS's shutdown, some legislators had worked to stiffen rules on support for poor transients and aid recipients. Legislation that would have legally enacted some of the restrictions Davis now pursued independently had failed in the spring of 1935, but the FTS shutdown gave him and his allies a new opportunity. Davis gambled that California's public craved order more than it savored constitutional protections or legal consequences, and he believed he could deliver that order by expanding the reach of his power to secure the state's borders.

After the FTS closed, Davis arranged for the creation of a local committee to explore solutions for the transient relief crisis he and other city leaders envisioned in the shutdown's wake. Davis then installed Deputy Chief Cross as chair of the committee, known as the Los Angeles Committee on Indigent Alien Transients, which then developed a raft of proposed solutions to address transiency in California.

The committee was also ostensibly charged with resolving transiency's perceived nationwide cause, but the federal and state officials to whom the committee made its recommendations would not buy into its policy proposals. Frustrated by the outside jurisdictions' unwillingness to cooperate, Davis again turned to Cross. They spent four months mapping out the plan that became the border patrol. Cross then approached executives from railroads operating at California's borders to persuade them to work with the police to limit the number of people who snuck into California aboard freight trains. The railway executives did the police one better: they offered to have conductors slow trains down near border crossings so officers deployed by the LAPD to nearby checkpoints might search their trains for transients (presumably keeping rail companies from incurring the added expense of developing and hardening security measures that might prevent train-hoppers in the first place).

Cross expected that other stakeholders would similarly cooperate with the blockade. As he and Davis solidified plans for the deployment, Cross reached out to each sheriff from the counties along California's interstate borders. He and Davis knew that police couldn't simply travel outside of Los Angeles and continue to enforce the law as they did within the city limits. To be able to operate and avoid jurisdictional conflicts, the deployment's architects needed to be able to provide it with a veneer of legal authority.

Cross assumed he would simply be able to ask border county sheriffs to deputize the LAPD officers arriving in their communities to enforce the blockade. Officers could enforce California's laws in the counties where they were deputized without restriction (although such an interpretation was actually legally erroneous).

Sheriffs in three counties—Siskiyou, Nevada, and Riverside—immediately agreed. (Each borders a different state neighboring California.) Other sheriffs refused, but that would not prevent Davis and Cross from claiming to newspapers writing about the border patrol's first day in operation that every single one had agreed. Davis wasn't going to let the sheriff in some distant cow county get in his way, and who was going to check if a few tried when he said they hadn't?

By the time the papers printed their first stories about the blockade, more than a dozen squads of Los Angeles police officers, clad in their uniforms and wearing the sidearms Davis insisted they learn to shoot so expertly, were at work around the state. Just as readily as they did in the counties that went along with Cross's request, the officers deployed to Del Norte, Modoc, and San Bernardino Counties—each a jurisdiction whose sheriffs had originally refused to deputize them—parked patrol cars at checkpoints, searched trains, and stopped "suspicious" individuals.

Even though he and Cross aimed to validate the blockade via deputizations, Davis didn't actually seem to care if the border patrol had any legal authority or whether locals supported it. Instead, the blockade represented Davis's abiding law enforcement philosophy: what mattered most was order and security and achieving it through any means necessary. Criminals endangered the state and undermined its society, the chief insisted, and only his blockade could stop them. Eighty-five percent of the people his officers stopped, he told credulous newspaper reporters, had criminal records. Or was it half? Or sixty percent? Davis gave different answers at different times to different people, though any answer he gave as likely as not was an imagined statistic made up on the fly. Davis's manufactured data was only made somewhat more credible because he greatly stretched the definition of a criminal. At varying points, he might apply that status to anyone who had spent a night in jail for any reason, who had been arrested (but not necessarily charged with let alone convicted of a crime), or who had been cited for minor violations. The ability to define criminality was powerful, especially in the hands of someone whose career depended on being perceived as helping to reduce criminality.

That first day involved a tremendous amount of such bluster by Davis and his subordinates, but the blockade's outset delivered neither the heroic vanguard protecting the Golden State's way of life that the chief envisioned nor the fascist crackdown his critics feared. Police claimed to detain hundreds of people at California's border in the first sixteen hours of their deployment but made few official arrests. Regardless of how many technical arrests the patrol made that day, more travelers stopped at the border, turned around, and left before encountering the police or after they were given the choice to either leave or spend the night in jail. Davis could therefore argue that by scaring transients away from entering the state in the first place, the operation was having its intended effect.

After they left Los Angeles, some of the police squads traveled across the Mojave to desert towns like Blythe and Needles. Another group followed Highway 101 north to Del Norte County's Lost Coast region, turned east along California 199, and settled amid towering redwoods at a resort closed for the winter. One squad stopped near Truckee at snowed-in Donner Pass, the spot where eighty-nine years earlier the threadbare remnants of a party of settlers seeking prosperity in California turned to cannibalism. Two squads even made their way to Inyo County, where residents were still "extremely hostile toward the city of Los Angeles" three decades after a massive infrastructure project diverted water from farms in Inyo's Owens Valley to Los Angeles. As they stalked highways and counties entering Inyo County from Nevada, these officers visibly manifested the outsized power Los Angeles had seized decades earlier.

Even the closest border checkpoints to Los Angeles were more than two hundred miles from the city. The farthest was a crossing along the Pacific Coast Highway between Brookings, Oregon, and the tiny settlement of Smith River, California. Other checkpoints were scattered from the Siskiyou Mountains along the Oregon border to the alkali wastes of northwestern Nevada, through the pass that damned the Donner party, and south to the desert banks of the Colorado River along California's border with Arizona. The force consisted of three divisions: one comprised the California-Oregon state line and the northernmost part of the Nevada border, one centered near Lake Tahoe that supervised the rest of the Nevada state line, and one focused on the Arizona border.

However far police were stationed from Los Angeles, municipal coffers continued to pay their salaries. Other expenses—like rooms at the Niles Hotel or meals at local restaurants—came out of a separate fund outside of payroll and not easily trackable by city officials. The fund even paid for regular travel home to Los Angeles so officers could see their families.

All of this was still to come when the fifteen members of Davis's Foreign Legion stationed in Modoc County settled in at the Niles Hotel. Modoc County was and still is a world apart from Los Angeles. Today, the quickest route there from the City of Angels takes drivers out of California through Nevada before returning north of Lake Tahoe. The 641-mile trip crosses the Mojave Desert, weaves past five national parks, and traces the length of the Sierra Nevada mountain range. With modern vehicles and highway infrastructure, the trip would likely take more than ten hours without stops. On the way, travelers pass such memorable places as Viewland, Likely, and Dogtown. Should they opt to stay in California for the journey, drivers might cover anywhere between two-thirds and the entirety of the San Joaquin Valley. That could mean traversing the almond orchards, feedlots, and megafarms of the Golden State's breadbasket or winding along the valley's eastern flank, threading the main streets of mining towns that bustled when California first struck its gilded reputation. That's just to get to Alturas, Modoc County's population center. The city's 2.8-square-mile chunk of the county is just a pinprick of the more than four thousand square miles of mountains, lava beds, grazing land, alfalfa fields, rice patties, and reed-filled wetlands covering the rest of it.

Whatever route taken to get to Modoc County, one must travel a tremendous geographic, and perhaps mental, distance. This is the case now, just as it was when the predecessors of the indigenous population that gave the county its name—the Modoc People—first arrived thousands of years ago, and as continued to be true in the nineteenth century when the first American explorers reached Modoc land. It was also the case during the Depression-era migrations that set off this tumultuous chapter in history, when one reporter from Reno, Nevada—about 170 miles southeast of Alturas—described Modoc County as "wild, mountainous country," whose "inhabitants still follow the spirit of the old west."

In February 1936 Modoc County Sheriff John Christopher Sharp was just such an inhabitant, and given the size of the territory where he was charged with enforcing the law, it was his opinion of Los Angeles's Foreign Legion that mattered, not that of Gertrude French, nor the residents of Modoc County, nor Alturas's tiny chamber of commerce, nor even the town's solitary municipal policeman. Like the Del Norte and Plumas County sheriffs, Sharp refused to deputize the police Davis sent to his home, Modoc County.

Immediately after Bergman and his officers arrived, Sharp resisted their presence, telling reporters that he didn't think the blockade "[held] water by either United States or California Constitutions." He and Davis were both veteran lawmen by the time their paths crossed, each certain of his personal philosophy of law enforcement and convinced of the lunacy of the other's approach.

The sheriff was not quite a David to the Los Angeles Police Department's Goliath, but over time, their dispute would put remote Modoc County on the front pages of newspapers throughout the county, render Sharp as the face of Davis's opposition, and transform this rural corner of California where he grew up into a major flashpoint in the battle waged by the bombastic, headline-loving police chief hundreds of miles south to keep transients out of the Golden State.

# PART I

# FUSE

We're sorry, said the owner men. The bank, the fifty-thousand-acre owner can't be responsible. You're on land that isn't yours. Once over the line maybe you can pick cotton in the fall. Maybe you can go on relief. Why don't you go on west to California? There's work there, and it never gets cold. Why, you can reach out anywhere and pick an orange. Why, there's always some kind of crop to work in. Why don't you go there? And the owner men started their cars and rolled away.

—John Steinbeck, *The Grapes of Wrath*

# 2 | CHILDREN OF THE GOLDEN WEST

ROUGHLY THIRTEEN THOUSAND YEARS AGO, near the western edge of the North American tectonic plate, molten basalt and rhyolite erupted from the northern flank of a million-year-old volcano. The fiery slurry spread across a broad, shallow caldera, rippling the soil with rough stone and black, glassy ribbons of obsidian as it cooled over an 850-square-mile expanse. Millenia passed as range grass and scrub brush crept through fissures in the igneous rock covering the caldera. Nurtured by the volcanic soil, a thriving ecosystem evolved. Soon, animals, both large and small, wandered into this emerging world, spreading across the caldera and into a rich landscape that covered thousands of square miles bound by snow-capped volcanoes, rippling hills, and forbidding, desert expanses of alkali. Abundant with life, the land teemed with possibility.

Bands of hunters and gatherers trickled in from the north. If the first of these wanderers arrived on a cloudless day, they might have watched the sun sink over the world's western edge, its light gilding the rich landscape as darkness chased after it.

More people came upon this land, lured by the potential and opportunity it promised. A transient people no longer, some of those who came stayed, thriving on the acorns, fish, and other sustenance they found here and sheltering in the now-dormant caverns that led to the darkness beneath the mountain and, somewhere far, far below, a world churning in flame. As age passed into age, they built a society while the world continued to take shape.

These people, the Modoc, chronicled their exploits and recorded their legends on the land that provided life and shaped their home. They sketched

17

stories on the caldera's sprawling rock fields and drew tales on the cavernous entrances of the volcano's dormant lava tubes. Generation after generation, century after century, millennium after millennium, the universe in which the Modoc's story took place largely contained only them and neighbors like the Hewisedawi, the Astarawi, and the Paiute.

Fourteen millennia after the volcano's eruption—an instant in the Modoc's history—Spanish sailors led by Juan Rodriguez Cabrillo left a port on the West Coast of present-day Mexico and explored northward. Sailing up the coastline, Cabrillo's fleet observed a land in many ways strikingly similar to their Mediterranean home, yet one unexplored (by Europeans), untouched (by Europeans), and untamed (by European standards).

Though Cabrillo would die on this voyage, word of the land his fleet spied reached Iberia. The sailors' descriptions recalled an early sixteenth-century Spanish novel about "Califia," the pagan, griffin-riding, black-skinned queen of a wild, gold-filled island east of Asia. In the tale, Califia joins Muslim armies besieging Constantinople and, with it, Christendom. Ultimately defeated, she marries one of Constantinople's defenders and converts to Christianity. With the abundance of the land explored by Cabrillo and his fleet reminding them of the fable of Califia, the Spanish dubbed it "California."

Spain would dispatch soldiers and sailors to the lands Cabrillo and other explorers "discovered" in the Western Hemisphere. Armies of priests sailed with the Spanish colonizers, a robed vanguard sent to "civilize" these lands. Two hundred years after Cabrillo's arrival, a Franciscan monk named Junípero Serra (recently canonized as a Catholic saint) brought this civilizing zeal to California and strung a series of religious missions along the length of California. The missions facilitated the Spanish Crown's claim by coaxing—or forcing—the land's indigenous inhabitants into its sphere of influence.

The Spanish told the people living in California that they came from a land called "Europe," a distant, exotic place so far away as to seem almost imagined. Spain's alien and inscrutable culture was matched in its strange ways by that of its neighbors. Just as Spain had, these neighboring tribes—the British, French, Dutch, and Portuguese—also dispatched navies and armies in search of lands to colonize in the "New World."

Spain and its neighbors justified their spread through California and other lands as service to the strange god they worshipped. Their actions revolved around performative devotion to their deity expressed through elaborate, heavily choreographed rituals. Elders chanted and sung during ceremonial retellings of their sect's founding mythologies. During these ceremonies, worshipers crossed their bodies with their fingers, sipped from communal potions, and offered tributes to their god.

The Modoc and other indigenous Californians eventually learned that while Spain's neighbors worshiped the same god as the Spanish, some belonged to sects whose rituals diverged significantly from those practiced in Spain. These differing superstitions so inflamed Europe's restive tribes that they sometimes went to war over their divergent interpretations of spiritual mythology. Despite their violent sectarian conflicts, all the tribes seemed to agree that only their god could grant "dominion," a sort of supernatural control of the land they believed their deity had given them, and only them. Once Europeans reached Modoc territory, including the area surrounding what's now known as the Medicine Lake Volcano, they would even insist that their dominion reached this land that had never known their god, just as they insisted it did throughout California and the lands that seemed to stretch beyond imagination to the north, south, and east.

The first Europeans who arrived at Medicine Lake had once been subjects of a place called Great Britain and lived in colonies established by the British far to the east of Modoc territory. A few decades before arriving, these British subjects rebelled against their rulers and set up a nation of their own. The new nation, the United States of America, then spent a century and a half stretching its influence ever westward, conquering the land its people entered as they subdued—and often eliminated—any resistors. The newly independent "Americans" pushed across the continent in pursuit of their own sense of dominion. Along the way they fought, destroyed, tricked, dispersed, and eradicated societies, cultures, and nations whose own histories stretched into ancient pasts yet, to the Americans' eyes, remained "uncivilized."

By the early nineteenth century, exotic-looking Europeans finally appeared in the Modoc's world. Within decades the first Americans appeared in small numbers, haggard and worn from strenuous travels. With each season larger groups of these newcomers came, each wave better fed, better supplied, and more heavily armed.

The Modoc soon recognized that these invaders posed a danger to their society. Wave after wave of Americans washed from the East, borne over the horizon by a menacing tide of destruction, theft, and pestilence. They threatened to upend Modoc society, erode its foundations, and steal its abundance.

Should the Modoc have afforded these migrants the slightest generosity or succor, it would have removed the dams holding them back.

The flood was too strong to contain. In washed the barbarians to inundate the Modoc's society. They swept away their heritage and drowned their traditions. Soon the Modoc were submerged and rendered invisible by the waves crashing upon them.

The newcomers brought whatever they could carry to the land, loading belongings anywhere they could fit them on their ramshackle, road-beaten wagons. They lugged with them as many remnants of their distant world as they could bear and used them—especially guns, oxen, and horses—to recreate their home on the Modoc's land.

They weren't staying temporarily until they found better places to go. They were *settling* here. Once here, they lived wherever they pleased, never considering upon whose land they squatted. They sowed foreign seeds in the remnants of the volcano that had given shape to the Modoc's world. They broke apart the soil's surface, plowed and planted it year after year until, finally, barley and alfalfa brought from their distant shores took hold, grew, and sprawled in dun and emerald seas.

It wasn't long, only a few years really, until the invaders told the Modoc that the land that had always been the Modoc's home was not the Modoc's home. Instead, the occupying hordes insisted, the Modoc and all their other ancient neighbors did not belong upon the only land they'd known. The interlopers told the Modoc that the Modoc themselves were unwelcome, dismissible interlopers in this place they called California.

## Gold and the Modoc War

The warlike societies of Europe may have worshipped and bickered over their god, but no spirit kept them in thrall quite as completely as gold. Nothing brought out the Europeans' savagery so quickly. Gold was everything. Spanish, British, Mexican, American—their rituals, tribal bonds, and folkways never mattered quite so much as how much gold an individual could acquire, process, transfer, or store, or how well one could help others acquire, process, transfer, or store gold.

Gold, pursuit of gold, management of gold, movement of gold, handling of gold, trading of gold, stealing of gold—that's why California mattered. It was

The Founders of Los Angeles. *Courtesy of the Miriam and Ira D. Wallach Division of Art, Prints and Photographs: Picture Collection, New York Public Library Digital Collections, 1883-12*

and would always only really be about gold, or at the very least the promise or temptation of gold. It became all but synonymous with California.

Before California's association with gold was made complete, Spanish colonists founded El Pueblo de Nuestra Señora la Reina de los Ángeles on September 4, 1781. Its name often informally shortened to Los Angeles, the settlement was founded while the British and their breakaway American subjects fought on the other edge of the continent. It remained part of Spain's dominion for thirty years, until the Spanish empire faced a rebellion of its own from subjects in America, some of whom lived in Los Angeles. The rebels won, established a new nation known as Mexico, and made Los Angeles the capital of a territory they called Alta California.

All the while, the United States continued its westward spread. The new nation competed with its European progenitors and its "new" neighbors in Mexico for claim to dominion over the land. In 1846, as the Americans approached

California, that competition turned to war. Mexico and the United States fought for two years. The United States won, and shortly before the fighting ceased, Mexico signed the Treaty of Guadalupe Hidalgo, which transferred control of Alta California, among other territory, to the United States. With California came Los Angeles.

As Mexico and the United States fought to the south, European immigrants and other "settlers" came to California in search of opportunity. One was a bankrupt Swiss man named John Sutter. Sutter abandoned his family and built a trading post along a creek in the foothills of the Sierra Nevada mountains, more than four hundred miles north of Los Angeles and nearly as far south of the Medicine Lake caldera. Granted land for the compound by the Mexican governor of California, Sutter enslaved indigenous people to labor at the compound while welcoming and employing European migrants, traders, and craftspeople as part of his new community.

Less than two weeks before the signing of the Treaty of Guadalupe Hidalgo, James Marshall, a carpenter hired by Sutter to build a saw mill, discovered gold flakes in a nearby creek. News of the discovery changed the world. Lured by the golden promise, masses of settlers came to California from the eastern United States and far beyond. Most came by sea and began their new lives in San Francisco, a rapidly growing settlement built on a peninsula at the entrance of a well-protected bay.

California became a state two years after Marshall's discovery. Ever larger numbers of migrants arrived, craving either the gleam of the state's gold or the richness of its soil. The land now *belonged* to America, to its people. Now that California was part of the United States, the Modoc and their neighbors were deemed *trespassers* upon the very land where they'd always existed but that they were now repeatedly told the United States owned. They were told not only that their land was not theirs but also that the Modoc were, the Americans insisted again and again, *savage*, less than human, beast-like.

The Americans dismissed the Modoc's claim to the land as they had the claims of countless other peoples throughout California and the United States. Even then, the Americans who came to the lands around the caldera felt threatened by the Modoc's ongoing presence. As they had throughout the lands the United States conquered, its people formed armed militias that roamed the land to enforce and defend their control of it, regularly turning to force and killing hundreds of Modoc over the ensuing decades.

Finally broken by the slaughter, surviving Modoc accepted an offer to leave the land they'd always known and relocate to a distant "reservation." In exchange, the Americans offered peace. The Modoc found anything but that on the reservation. For millennia, they had occasionally gone to war to protect their land from invading neighbors like the Klamath. Now they were forced to live alongside their sometime enemies. Unable to keep any distance from one another, old tensions resurfaced, and new conflicts erupted.

Unhappy with this and other untenable conditions of being pushed to a world far from their home, a band of Modoc left the reservation and returned to northeastern California. Growing impatient with the Modoc's resistance, the American settlers who'd replaced them demanded action from their leaders. In 1872 the US government responded and dispatched soldiers to quell the insurgency.

The US soldiers and the volunteer fighters who joined them had successfully silenced previous uprisings with little opposition. This time, the Modoc proved challenging opponents. The same volcanic landscape that had nurtured their society for millennia aided the Modoc. The holdouts fighting back against the American soldiers deftly exploited their knowledge of lava tubes that countless generations of their ancestors had explored. This network of caverns provided the Modoc resistance bases from which they were able to repel the invading army far longer than anyone expected, forcing the Americans to expend an outsized toll of blood and treasure in their effort to subdue the Modoc.

However, even this resistance ultimately failed. The Modoc could capably defend themselves against the US soldiers despite imbalances in weaponry and resources—less than one hundred Modoc fighters resisted ten times as many heavily armed US soldiers for months—but they could not hold out after a breakaway group of resistors approached the American troops and offered to lead them to the hideout of the Modoc resistance's leader, Kintpuash, or Captain Jack.

With the hideout pinpointed, the army seized Kintpuash and five other Modoc leaders. All six received death sentences, though President Ulysses S. Grant later commuted three of these sentences to life in prison. However, Kintpuash and three others were convicted as war criminals and hanged in Klamath Falls, Oregon, on October 3, 1873.

After the executions, nearly all of the remaining Modoc were forced onto trains and relocated. This time, the US government sent the Modoc far from their homeland, thousands of miles away, to a place the Americans designated as "Indian territory": Oklahoma.

Oklahoma—in six decades' time this place would become synonymous with despair. Its people would come to personify a continental tragedy as twin disasters of economic depression and catastrophic drought wracked the United States. Amid these calamities, White men with power would collectively refer to White men with no power as "Okies"—whether they came from Oklahoma or not—and attempt to keep their powerless brethren from the land and riches they, in turn, had wrested from the Modoc and *their* brethren.

The Modoc War would become one of Northern California's (and Southern Oregon's) foundational myths. Over the ensuing decades, the Americans who made homes in Modoc County lionized the US soldiers and militias who fought in the Lava Beds as patriots rather than enforcers of empire. Despite the persistent fighting between US troops and Modoc resisters, American soldiers continued to come to northeastern California. Yet more came once the land was "cleared," thus allowing them to build homesteads that solidified claims to the land and "settle" this remote corner of the United States.

These claims required collective acceptance of the myth that settlers and their armed defenders had tamed an uncivilized, threatening wilderness. The soldiers who died fighting the Modoc would be cast as heroes, especially Major General Edward Canby, the only US general killed in a war with Native Americans. Memorializing the US soldiers and volunteers who died at the site kept the Americans' version of history present for each succeeding generation. In turn, the sons and daughters and grandsons and granddaughters of those who found success in their new home could defend their status by reinforcing the myths that elevated their families to power.

## Inheriting the Myth

One such descendant was Gertrude Payne. Born in 1886, Payne was the second child of Henry Gustavus "Harry" Payne and Laura Ann Wood. In turn, Harry was the son of Parthenia Hayes. When Harry was born, Hayes lived in Yreka, west of present-day Modoc County. Her brothers and cousins had established the town of Dorris Bridge (with the town named after Presley Dorris—one of the first two White settlers to reach the town site—and his cousin, James, with whom Presley built the bridge) along the Pit River in what would become Modoc County. Hayes moved to Dorris Bridge after Harry was born and lived in one of the first houses in the town, which, in 1874, became the seat of Modoc County and, two years later, was renamed "Alturas."

These details of her predecessors convinced Gertrude Payne that she *was* Alturas heritage. As a direct descendant of the Dorrises, Gertrude celebrated her inclusion in what local historians now call "the founding family of Alturas." Gertrude—Gertie to her family—took this lineage seriously. Growing up steeped in lore about how her family and other "pioneers" established Modoc County, Gertrude also heard many tales from Harry and other relatives about the Modoc "renegades" they'd defeated in the 1870s (though Harry claimed at least one friend among Kintpuash's allies and often told a story about how that man had saved his life while he was herding cattle through Modoc land as a young man).

Product of such prominent Alturans as she may have been and proud of her lineage as she was, Gertrude did not have an easy upbringing. Her mother died unexpectedly when she was just seven years old. After his spouse died, Harry, who'd worked for his uncles as a cattle hand, decided he wasn't prepared to raise five children—three of whom were younger than Gertrude—on his own. Harry's cousin, Rachel Cyrus Dorris, took Gertrude in and raised her as her own child.

Dorris—whose own father had been one of Alturas's original founders—unquestioningly supported Gertie alongside her four biological children (two sons and two daughters). Gertrude repaid her foster mother's care with deep pride in her lineage as an adult. She would also be unquestioningly devoted to her own children and spouse. That devotion would not falter, even when severely tested during the final years of the Great Depression.

Over the decades, the mythology surrounding Gertrude's family's role in Alturas led her to perceive herself as an inheritor of what might be interpreted as a sort of Californian purity. Gertrude felt a sense of duty toward that legacy as she grew up. She began to see herself as a "native" daughter of California.

In identifying with Modoc County's founders, Gertrude also felt a sense of belonging among California's founding families, which made Gertrude an ideal candidate for membership in a growing statewide sororal organization, the Native Daughters of the Golden West. Established in 1886, the same year Gertrude was born, the Native Daughters and its counterpart Native Sons of the Golden West emerged loudly among California's ascendant "nativist" voices. Club members were required to prove lineage from families residing in California prior to its statehood. They also had to commit themselves to four principles: "Love of Home," "Devotion to the Flag of Our Country," "Veneration of the Pioneers of California," and "Abiding Faith in the Existence of God." Often the members also belonged to an overlapping mesh of social clubs, fraternal orders, and semisecret societies that reinforced White, Anglo, Protestant community identities and informal but powerful social networks. These societies appealed to those expressing antiforeigner and nativist hostility with increasing fervor throughout the United States but especially to such in California at the turn of the twentieth century and into its first decades.

Gertrude felt strong connections to Modoc County's heritage aside from her family's role in its history. When she was seventeen years old and still a year from graduating high school, Gertrude went to work for Colonel William Thompson. Thompson was a colorful, hard-drinking Modoc War veteran who founded a string of newspapers in Oregon, then moved back to Modoc County in 1896 to launch one more paper: the *Alturas Plaindealer*. Under Thompson's tutelage, Gertrude did everything at the *Plaindealer*. From writing stories to editing copy to setting newsprint, she impressed the publisher with her "rare intelligence, discretion, and conspicuous ability." Writing about Gertrude later, Thompson paid what he believed was the "highest compliment that can be paid a woman—that she represents the highest and purest type of American womanhood—honest, upright, self-reliant, intelligent and noble."

The colonel became one of Gertrude's dearest friends, and his newspaper was the center of her life. She worked for the paper through graduation all the way into 1908, when, that August, a courtship with Bay Area insurance agent Robert Angus "Bard" French evolved into marriage. French, whose ancestors were pioneers who "settled" parts of Nevada and San Francisco, was not unfamiliar in Modoc County. Two of Bard's sisters had married into prominent Alturas families, and he frequently visited them for extended periods. When he and Gertrude wed, they held a small, family-only ceremony in Alturas, then returned to the Bay Area to begin their life together.

The following summer, Gertrude and Bard's first child, Harry, was born. Two more children, Dorris and Ruth, eventually followed. Before Harry's first birthday, Colonel Thompson enticed the family back to Alturas with a business opportunity. The colonel's business partner, L. G. McDowell, wanted to depart the newspapering life and was willing to sell his stake in the paper to Bard and Gertrude. The couple bought McDowell out, moved to Alturas, and went to work as the colonel's partners. Though Bard joined Thompson atop the masthead as the *Plaindealer*'s business manager, Gertrude *was* the paper. Originally serving as assistant business manager to Bard, Gertrude was—as Bob Sloss, a Modoc County publisher who inherited his position from one of Gertrude's competitors, Robert M. "Gop" Sloss, later described it—"unquestionably its guiding force."

The newspaper was Gertrude's calling. Bard continued to handle business and mechanical aspects of printing the paper, but as a regional insurance agent, publishing wasn't his only focus. Gertrude, on the other hand, used the *Plaindealer* as a springboard into public life and as the platform from which she'd set Modoc County's agenda for three decades.

Colonel Thompson retired from running the *Plaindealer* in 1915. The colonel's retirement left Bard as the paper's publisher while Gertrude became its editor in title as well as practice. That role and Gertrude's membership in the Native Daughters of the Golden West put her in an instrumental position after President Calvin Coolidge proclaimed the Lava Beds National Monument at the field of volcanic rock in northeastern California where the United States had fought the Modoc people five decades earlier. After the monument's fall 1925 designation, Gertrude and two other members of the Alturas Native Daughters chapter spent months planning a memorial to General Canby at the site where the general and a US negotiator sent to broker a deal with the Modoc were killed. Gertrude and her committee members also arranged for the restoration of a cross that had been planted there to mark the site.

Built from volcanic rock found at the national monument, the memorial to Canby embodied an inverted mythology about California history. It recast the story of whose land the war had been waged upon, who had been the attacker, and who had defended it. That reversal of history is clear in a 1926 *Sacramento Bee* article describing the memorial's installation as "topped by a bronze bear wounded with an Indian arrow, typifying California invaded and wounded and defending herself against the onslaughts of her savage foes."

More than one thousand people came to the monument's June 13, 1926, dedication. The following week, Gertrude dedicated the *Plaindealer* to veterans of the Modoc War. By helping the Native Daughters shepherd the memorial's installation, Gertrude positioned herself further as one of Modoc County's chief propaganda brokers and reinforced the officially accepted narrative of Modoc County's history. In turn, she influenced who would be commonly accepted among the county's founders and who might be excluded from the region's establishing legacy.

Though Modoc County comprised a remote, sparsely populated corner of California, the Alturas narrative exemplified the foundational mythmaking of the entire state. Right down to the membership credentials required by the Native Daughters, Gertrude French committed her life to defining what it meant to be a Californian and who was eligible to make such a claim. The monument to Canby served as a tangible and enduring reminder that the Californians who openly proclaimed themselves "native" had replaced the Modoc.

French's one-time employer and partner, Colonel Thompson, spoke at the monument's dedication in a speech that also reinforced the Native Daughters', and by extension French's, central role in building the myth of who could lay claim to being the true inheritors of Queen Califia's legacy:

> It has been said, and truly, that the history of vanished civilizations is written on the monuments and their tombs. That patriotic band of women, the Native Daughters of the Golden West, have here written OUR HISTORY in enduring letters of stone and bronze and to them we bow in gratitude and admiration.
>
> On the spot where we are now assembled was enacted one of the last as well as one of the greatest tragedies attending the conquest of the wilderness.
>
> —Colonel William Thompson, 1926

In the decade that followed the monument's installation, French continued to frame state, local, and even familial challenges as threats originating from without. By the outset of 1936 it would be poor migrants headed toward California via frontier communities like Modoc County who endangered the state.

A "native" Californian, French would become Los Angeles police chief James Davis's primary local defender. It wouldn't even seem to matter for her that Davis himself was not originally a Californian, unlike the Los Angeles police chief's local foil, a sheriff who grew up in Modoc County.

## Son of a Filibusterer

That sheriff was as much a product of Modoc County history as Gertrude. In the 1860s a New York–born adventurer and soldier named Christopher Thorpe "C. T." Sharp arrived in Modoc County by way of Central America. Sharp had been part of an ill-fated 1855 expedition in which "Walker filibusterers," as they were called, attempted to establish English-speaking colonies in present-day Nicaragua. Only two members of that expedition survived. One of them was Sharp, who, after other adventures, wound up in the Surprise Valley, the easternmost stretch of what is today Modoc County.

Wedged as far northeast as one can get in California and separated from Alturas by the green spine of the Warner Mountains—an eighty-five-mile-long range jutting south from Oregon—the Surprise Valley flattens as one heads eastward into alkali flats washing far across the Nevada border. Today, hippies, ravers, and artists know the valley's largest town, Cedarville, as the last stop for fuel and supplies on their annual pilgrimage to the Burning Man festival in Nevada's Black Rock Desert, a destination beloved by attendees precisely because of how removed from "civilization" it is.

Christopher Sharp built the first home constructed by Americans in the Surprise Valley, helped establish Cedarville, and became one of the valley's wealthiest residents. He even made it possible for the region's first American inhabitants to vote. In 1864, shortly after his arrival, the Surprise Valley was still part of Siskiyou County. That year, Sharp drew straws with other early residents to decide who would deliver the first presidential ballots cast in the Surprise Valley to Yreka, Siskiyou's county seat. Sharp, who supported Abraham Lincoln's reelection, evaded Modoc ambushes and other hazards as he rode on horseback for 150 miles to deliver the ballots on time. (Lincoln won the majority of local votes.)

As Sharp settled into the Surprise Valley, Dorris Bridge was established on the other side of the Warner Mountains. Dorris Bridge was founded next to the Pit River, a 207-mile-long tributary of the Sacramento, and originally was part of Siskiyou County, which spanned the length of California's northern border at the time. In 1874 California legislators split Siskiyou County into multiple counties, including one they called Modoc in a nod to the people whom the Americans had ejected from the land. The legislature also made Dorris Bridge (with the name soon to change to Alturas) the new county's seat.

Eight years after Christopher Sharp arrived in the Surprise Valley, he met and married Christina Higgins, who'd migrated from Illinois to Modoc County in a covered wagon. Christina gave birth to their first child, John Christopher Sharp, in 1876.

C. T. Sharp taught John and his brother Jake everything he could about ranching. Jake would later become a lawyer who would serve a term as Modoc County's district attorney while John was its sheriff. When not helping at the ranch, the children explored the thick forests of the Warner Mountains, familiarized themselves with the broader Surprise Valley, and listened raptly to their father's tales of ill-fated exploits in Central America, friends and enemies among the Modoc—C. T. often warned his children about the dangerous "Indians" they might encounter while hunting and fishing in the Warners—and other adventures.

John lived at home in Cedarville until 1901, when a fire destroyed the house his father had built. Just four weeks after the fire—from which John narrowly escaped—he married a woman named Annie Lee. Scant records survive about the marriage or even about Lee, who died from an illness just six years later.

Lee passed before she and John ever had children. Left with no one to look after, John focused his attention on tending his ranch. He also established and grew a blacksmithing business.

Even in remote Modoc County, automobiles were quickly gaining widespread acceptance. John did well enough in business that he bought one of the county's first cars, and by June 1912 he partnered with John Wylie, another local scion, to open a garage in Cedarville. The garage—Cedarville's third—signified local boom times.

"The suprise [sic] Valley farmers are so prosperous that all are getting automobiles, and consequently a garage at Cedarville is just as good as a gold mine," reported the *Alturas New Era* in a brief on the garage's opening. Sharp's life wasn't suddenly gilded by the garage's opening, but it nurtured community stature he'd inherited from his father and continued building as a rancher and blacksmith.

In 1912 John met Harriet E. Essex. On September 11 of that year, they were married at Harriet's family ranch in the Modoc County town of Canby. Harriet—also a member of the Native Daughters of the Golden West—was similar in age to John. Her thirty-seven years were many more than the typical bride's during that era and far beyond the typical child-bearing age of early

John Christopher Sharp photographed with a family dog circa 1930s or 1940s.
*Courtesy of John Boyle*

twentieth-century American women. Though the Sharps did not have biological children, they adopted two daughters.

John continued his ranching, blacksmithing, and garage running in Cedarville while Harriet worked as a telephone operator, and at one point in 1919 he even filled in as postmaster when the permanent one's wife was ill. John's business thrived. His family was stable. Though already in his forties, his life only just seemed to hit its stride.

In 1918, John entered politics, running as a candidate for county supervisor, representing Modoc's 2nd District, which included Cedarville. After winning the August primary, he beat opponent John Patterson by a nearly three-to-one margin in the general election.

It was a bittersweet win. The 1918 election took place as influenza swept through the globe. The pandemic spared few places, including Modoc County, where one newspaper described Alturas as "about as lively as a graveyard." As the outbreak's threat became clear, the city's board of supervisors passed a mask mandate for all citizens. The new requirements took effect just one day before the election. Anyone caught without a mask in the city was subject to arrest and fines.

"Most of our citizens, however, have [already] complied and the town looks like it was overrun by burglars, vigilantes, and such," wrote the *New Era*. "However, they are the good kind and strangers need fear no bodily harm."

The epidemic disrupted life throughout the county, including for many candidates running for office in Modoc County that year. County coroner and public administrator candidate Frank Kerr stopped public appearances shortly before the election after contracting influenza. Reuel Laird, who was running for district attorney, ceased door-to-door campaigning after the flu's arrival in Alturas. He won the election anyhow. Sharp's brother, Jacob, had been one of Laird's opponents in the primary elections. After failing to secure the nomination, Jake suffered another blow: his wife contracted influenza the week John won his race for county supervisor.

Four years later, reports of flu again appeared in Modoc County as an election approached. In May 1922 John Sharp's wife, Harriet, suffered "considerable flu" as the disease swept through Cedarville. Harriet survived, and soon thereafter John prepared for the upcoming ballot. Opting not to seek another term as supervisor, he instead ran for county sheriff. He won and never looked back. (Jake also ran, and lost, for district attorney again that year.)

Sharp took his responsibilities seriously but tried to avoid the more ceremonial trappings of his office. He preferred to keep his badge in his pocket. Whenever possible he avoided a uniform in favor of a business suit and a deep-crowned hat, its brim pulled low enough on his forehead to shade his bushy eyebrows and round, wire-rimmed glasses. The suit jacket John typically wore helped him avoid standing out and concealed a .22 caliber Hopkins & Allen double-action revolver he kept in an interior pocket. Because Sharp began his law enforcement career in his late forties, his gaunt, age-lined face gave him a grandfatherly countenance that belied the seriousness with which he approached his work.

In January 1919 the Eighteenth Amendment to the US Constitution was ratified, and Prohibition became the law of the land. The federal ban on alcohol sales meant that Sharp began his career as sheriff enforcing prohibition. In the same election that made Sharp Modoc County's top law enforcer, voters in Alturas overwhelmingly supported a related prohibition law.

Modoc County's position near the Oregon and Nevada state lines and its remote, rural, sparsely populated geography made Sharp's jurisdiction an attractive waypoint for alcohol smugglers. He spent much of his first term pursuing and apprehending rumrunners and distillers. When yet another campaign cycle arrived in 1926, Sharp decided to run for reelection as sheriff. That year, shortly before the election and just a few months after Gertrude French helped unveil the Canby Cross, her *Plaindealer* praised Sharp's "summer roundup" of bootleggers and other liquor purveyors.

"Sheriff Sharp and his wideawake deputy [Frank Van Horn] are to be congratulated," wrote the *Plaindealer*. "They not only catch the law violators but wait until they have perfect evidence, ensuring a conviction, thereby saving expensive trials, with doubtful results. John and Frank are sure on the job."

In a decade's time, French wouldn't look so favorably on Sharp's cautious, methodical approach to law enforcement when it ran against the brash, blunt, and sometimes legally sloppy crimefighting campaign that would bring Los Angeles police officers to Modoc County. But she welcomed Sharp's discerning nature for now.

One notable case Sharp handled began when a shopkeeper outside the Modoc County community of Adin killed a federal agent after the G-man caught the shopkeeper selling homemade booze. After the killer fled to nearby woods, the slain agent's partner asked Sharp to help apprehend him. Sharp employed the considerable knowledge of Modoc County's wilderness that his father had instilled in him and his siblings to begin his hunt for the killer. He also drew on the network of community members he built over his decades as a rancher, businessman, and politician to help. Sharp finally located the suspect's trailer thanks to a Modoc tracker he enlisted to aid the search.

Sharp may have been raised on a ranch and may have enforced the law in one of the state's most sparsely populated counties, but his garage and blacksmithing businesses also made him a successful twentieth-century entrepreneur with a number of lucrative real estate investments to his name. Sharp's ongoing investments underscored his law enforcement ethos, which he hinted at in 1926, when a candidate for sheriff in California's Sonoma County asked Sharp to contribute a letter for a full-page newspaper discussion of whether business acumen had a place in sheriff's departments.

"A sheriff should be a business man," Sharp wrote. "The better business man he is, the better sheriff he will be."

Sharp's savvy, modern skills coupled with his intimate familiarity of rural Modoc County life would prove valuable when the police chief of the state's largest city, the powerful business interests aligned with him, and the media and political machines that supported those interests took aim at Modoc County and Sharp himself.

# 3 | CITY OF DREAMS

ONE WONDERS WHAT MELISSA Howell would have thought that mid-March Friday morning in 1926. What would she have made of her son, James Edgar Davis, astride a horse, gazing toward the center of California's largest city? How might she have reacted to the cheers erupting from a crowd of Los Angeles's most powerful people watching her son, his hand thrusting from the sleeve of a sharp business suit straight into a mountain of ham and eggs?

How would she ever square such ridiculousness with the way she'd raised him? Would she think him ostentatious in his suit or chastise him for sullying it in such an embarrassing manner? Might she call him blasphemous for swearing upon such an "altar," however humorously it may have been intended? Or would she let that moment be and praise her son for the sobriety that led him to that moment and the sense of purpose that placed him in a position to serve the "white spot" that had become a beacon for the Protestant values she treasured?

In 1911 James Davis had stepped out of a Southern Pacific train at Los Angeles's Arcade Depot. He had just finished two years of army service, during which he deployed to the Philippines as an army corporal with a mountain artillery battery. A nobody who could barely afford to buy clothes that weren't his army uniform, James Edgar Davis scraped up enough cash for a room at the Golden State, a hotel for transients just down Fifth Street where human traffickers, elderly office workers, and poor job seekers like Davis intermingled.

A decade and a half later, Davis was about to become chief of police in the same city he'd stumbled into after his time in the army. First, he would be anointed as one of Southern California's ruling elites. That morning, March 19, 1926, three hundred of Southern California's top political, business, and social figures turned out for Davis's initiation into the city's informal but influential Los Angeles Breakfast Club. A Texas farm boy who couldn't even get a spot in the army the first time he tried was now rubbing elbows with mayors, bankers, merchants, actors, studio heads, publishers, and manufacturers and about to become the top cop in California's biggest city. (Davis's counterpart, San Francisco Chief of Police Daniel J. O'Brien, who was visiting Los Angeles that morning, was also inducted as an honorary Breakfast Club member, ham and eggs and all.) Once more in a land of make-believe, the fantasy of opportunity had been rendered tangible.

## Imagination Made Manifest

There's an American dream. There's a California dream. Then there's Los Angeles. The City of Angels is dreamlike, a geography of imagination made manifest.

Though there may not be an explicitly expressed Los Angeles dream, the city is in many ways a transitory, ethereal embodiment of turn-of-the-twentieth-century ideals viewed through tinsel, lens flares, and cellulose, then repeatedly reimagined, recast, relaunched, and rebooted all the way into the twenty-first century's third decade. It is a manufactured utopia fringed by crashing waves, sewn upon arid plains, draped over sagebrush hills, tucked into oak-speckled canyons, and laced with concrete-encased waterways.

With each wave of new arrivals to California, that golden land at the edge of the Pacific—wild, full of potential, and set apart from the world—repackaged and resold itself. Nowhere was this truer than in the half-desert, mountain-encircled expanse comprising Los Angeles, where each wave remade the land, the city, and itself. Arriving as colonizers, immigrants, settlers, industrialists, dreamers, opportunists, grifters, and drifters, all staged Los Angeles in their own image, then billed themselves as the city's original cast.

Like present-day Modoc County, Los Angeles is among California's twelve largest counties by size. It even encompasses a little more land than Modoc does, but the two counties' demographics differ dramatically and always have. As of 2020 more than 10 million people packed Los Angeles County; that same year, fewer than nine thousand lived in Modoc County.

Without a natural deepwater port and far from the gold-rich foothills of the Sierra Nevada, Los Angeles at first held little allure for immigrants. The community grew slowly for nearly three decades, but that changed in 1876, when the Southern Pacific railroad linked San Francisco to Los Angeles.

More rail lines followed. They first connected Los Angeles with other California cities, then they linked the city with the rest of the United States. Real estate investors seized upon these new connections, snatched up land around Los Angeles, and packaged Southern California as an as-yet-untapped opportunity to grab a piece of the golden West. They planted citrus orchards to sweeten the deal, then marketed the land with tales of abundant, favorable growing conditions.

The full sales pitch was still half a century away when the promise of "empty" land enticed the first of these speculators. Among those hoping to become the first to cash in on Los Angeles was Edward Doheny, who in 1892 quite literally struck upon another selling point for the city: oil. Doheny realized that abundant tar deposits in the Los Angeles area and other natural conditions suggested the city might sit upon significant oil reserves. His hunch paid off after he drilled a series of exploratory wells in the hills just west of Los Angeles's still sleepy downtown.

The timing was auspicious for Doheny. He'd made his discovery just as the age of the automobile began. Doheny quickly became the wealthiest person in Los Angeles. His good fortune inspired a new wave of speculators eager to try their luck in Southern California. The investors who once sold Los Angeles as an oasis now had a chance to sell its promise as an oil town.

The ensuing boom only deepened the already-parched land's thirst. Enter William Mulholland and Fred Eaton. Backed by Los Angeles's ascendent business class, Mulholland and Eaton orchestrated a massive infrastructure deal that diverted water from the verdant Owens Valley in Inyo County, about two hundred miles northeast of Los Angeles. Though interpreted as outright theft by many in the Owens Valley, water diverted by the deal helped irrigate places like the San Fernando Valley and transformed Los Angeles into the country's top agricultural county, a status it would maintain for decades even as its population continued to boom. By 1920 the city surpassed San Francisco as California's most populous municipality, a status it's never lost.

Los Angeles had finally become a land of plenty. At least, that's how the Los Angeles Chamber of Commerce, the Merchants and Manufacturers

Association, the region's citrus industry, and the region's new crop of real estate tycoons marketed the newfound abundance they'd engineered. They never looked back.

## Keeping the "White Spot" White

As Los Angeles's population boomed, the city's elites turned from boosting the city to protecting the power they'd seized. They faced new challenges to their interests and shifting demographics that might impact public perceptions of their legitimacy. Immigrants from outside the United States arrived in increasing numbers, joined by domestic migrants—including a sizable number of Black residents descended from enslaved populations in the South—who increasingly sought opportunity in Southern California. Meanwhile, labor movements agitated for improved working conditions, though, thanks to pushback from the city's ruling class, with less success than in other parts of the country.

Early-twentieth-century Los Angeles distilled more than a century of California xenophobia. Spanish missionaries had first used the guise of "civilization" in God's name to concoct the idea that certain people deserved a place in the Golden State, while others must be excluded. Spain's Mexican successors continued to stir this toxic brew, followed by the Americans, who'd cleared a continent of indigenous societies in the name of Manifest Destiny.

After California's 1850 entry into the union, the state's founders deepened and broadened its exclusionary policies. Though California's first exclusionary act as part of the union was an attempt to constitutionally prohibit African Americans from residing in the state, much of the ensuing xenophobia targeted Asians. Self-described "native" (read, White) Californians deployed decades of legal, rhetorical, political, and physical attacks against Asians. Well into the twentieth century, California's so-called nativists championed restrictive immigration policies meant to exclude Chinese, Japanese, and other Asian immigrants from American life.

These policies explicitly excluded migrants originating from Asia and the Pacific Rim from entering the United States for any purpose. They also prevented anyone already in the United States descended from people who'd emigrated from these parts of the world from claiming citizenship, or any other legally protected status. Though technically statutory, the exclusions stemmed from nativist hostility, which often turned violent. Sometimes it was even murderous.

Even as Asian migrants navigated the violence and legalized racism, Jewish émigrés began arriving in Los Angeles from Europe in the second half of the nineteenth century, and their numbers continued to increase over the first few decades of the twentieth century. Aided by their European features, many Jewish immigrants assimilated into Los Angeles society. Still, their acceptance within the city's carefully orchestrated and staunchly defended White, Anglo, Protestant society was constrained and complex.

The development of a Jewish commercial class in Los Angeles coincided with the emergence of a new industry that would come to define Los Angeles to the rest of the world by the second decade of the twentieth century: motion pictures. The film industry's ascendence challenged Los Angeles's existing Anglo-Protestant power centers, as many of Hollywood's early business leaders were Jewish.

Civic and business elites in Los Angeles recognized the powerful persuasive tool that film could be. Eager to exploit that power in their ongoing campaign to promote their vision of Los Angeles, they grudgingly accepted emergent Jewish film moguls into their circles, to a certain degree. They could now turn to movies to help sell Los Angeles as a place where newcomers—but only the right kind of newcomers—would find abundance and year-round opportunity.

Flush with wealth and power extracted from their new land, Los Angeles's power brokers used film, magazine articles, and even produce cartons to spin yarns about the city's golden promise. Their effort began before the motion picture industry's incarnation, but the new medium helped them compose establishing shots of the Southern California dream they could use to sell ensuing quasi-official schemes. This continued until 1921, when *Los Angeles Times* publisher Harry Chandler and a cabal of fellow chamber of commerce members formalized the mythmaking in the All-Year Club.

Bankrolled by Los Angeles County taxpayers, the new club advertised Los Angeles, and California, as idyllic destinations replete with literal and spiritual wealth. The spoils of this marketing campaign further reinforced the club's backers' positions atop the the city's power structures. Nothing seemed able to tarnish their message, not the tumult of Prohibition-era violence, not a series of vice and corruption scandals, not even, perhaps, the first tremors of approaching economic turmoil.

The All-Year Club promised year-round splendor, but it was a qualified promise. The song of the Golden State and the fertile, season-to-season riches

Southern California offered was meant only to be heard by those who could afford a first-class railway ticket and a fine hotel, and who accepted the city as a beacon for White, Protestant transplants. But it sounded just as sweet in the ears of tens of thousands of bedraggled souls scratching their way across the continent even before the approaching financial storm struck and sent tens of thousands more toward Los Angeles. Desiring only the former to hear its song, the All-Year Club implicitly and explicitly warned the latter that *they* would find no riches here. The dream had its limits.

Los Angeles's founders began to set those limits in 1869, when they established the city's police department to defend the status quo amid the city's accelerating growth. In practice, that protection meant quashing labor agitation, harassing minority communities, and rooting out vice (or, as it would turn out in actual practice, vice from which they could not profit).

In 1924 Los Angeles civic leaders formed the Greater Los Angeles Association. They envisioned the association as a business alliance that might one day become a twenty-five-thousand-member, $50 million behemoth. They also gave it a stark, explicitly stated slogan: "Keep the White Spot White."

An advertisement for the Greater Los Angeles Association featuring its Keep the White Spot White campaign. *Los Angeles Evening Express, March 29, 1924*

In part, the slogan invoked California governor William Stephens's 1922 reelection campaign, in addition to ads for everything from real estate to grocery stores to automotive parts retailers that regularly included variations on the theme of keeping the white spot white. This theme wasn't overtly or solely about race; *white* in these ads and the association's aims also referred to Los Angeles as a place of unmarred industrial and commercial activity free of the kind of labor strife (read, successful labor action) that in its eyes plagued other parts of the country.

The Greater Los Angeles Association's White Spot campaign nurtured the LAPD's aggressive antivagrant law enforcement. The department's "vagrancy squad" was even led by an officer who called unemployed men "the scum of the earth." After an unemployed World War I veteran killed himself trying to escape a vagrancy arrest, and similar tragedies, an outraged public demanded policing reforms and criticized the Greater Los Angeles Association, the All-Year Club, and other civic boosters.

Despite the public's anger, LAPD leadership continued to support the vagrancy squad. At the time of the killing, the department was led by a temporary chief, August Vollmer. Often lauded as the "father of modern policing," Vollmer was brought in by city leaders for a one-year term to reform and professionalize the department in the wake of earlier scandals. Nevertheless, after the veteran's killing, Vollmer's first inclination seemed to be appeasing Los Angeles's business community by blaming the victim.

"It is not our duty to support people who migrate to California with the idea that they can get rich quick here," Vollmer wrote in a press release. During the same period, the *Los Angeles Record* reported on the city council's appropriation of $10,000—matched by $10,000 from six movie studios—to pay unemployed Angelenos $2 a day to dig a drainage ditch in Hollywood. It was an abysmal rate, even in 1923. Just a few weeks earlier, noted a labor advocate who called the plan a "crime," the city had established a $16 weekly minimum wage for women working in the city.

Los Angeles's city council justified the low pay because it planned to staff the project with "undesirable" laborers who might otherwise be charged with vagrancy crimes. Police would round up these laborers with raids at "pool halls, railroad yards and downtown assembly places of unemployed," reported the *Record*. Foreshadowing the blockade of California's state lines that would begin exactly thirteen years later, anyone detained in these sweeps would be offered the choice of taking the job, leaving town, or going to jail.

Aside from signaling to local leaders that his policing reforms wouldn't upend the city's status quo, Vollmer may have also influenced how a young subordinate rapidly rising through the LAPD's ranks would lead that future blockade. That man had spent a decade mired as a patrolman, but he'd begun quickly ascending the department's command structure shortly before Vollmer's arrival. His name was James Edgar Davis.

## "Soft-Spoken and Hard-Fisted"

Back in February 1911, when Davis stepped off that train from San Francisco, he'd only just marked his twenty-second birthday. Barely able to stay afloat long enough to find work, he spent the last of his army salary on his hotel room and new clothes to replace the uniform that was to that point his only outfit.

Davis arrived in Los Angeles amid a yearslong effort to break almost completely with his past and establish himself as the man who would one day

Chief James Edgar Davis, center, shooting target practice with visiting Mexican dignitaries circa 1935. *Courtesy of Los Angeles Times Photograph Collection, Special Collections, Charles E. Young Research Library, UCLA*

become the most visible defender of the purely distilled, orderly, business-friendly city that the All-Year Club and the Greater Los Angeles Association were selling.

Davis, who'd since jettisoned any attachment to the hardscrabble circumstances that surrounded his February 8, 1889, birth, started life as a Texan, but just barely. Just a dozen or so miles spared him from origins as an Okie. His parents lived in the northern Texas town of Whitewright, just south of the Red River, which separated the Lone Star State from Oklahoma. Davis's father, who died before James Edgar was old enough to remember him, was an Englishman named William. His mother, Melissa Haseltine Howell, was the conservative daughter of a strict Methodist family with pre-Revolution roots in Kentucky and Pennsylvania.

Davis might not have been an Okie, but his early life was about as spare and unpleasant as the rough-spun origins of many of the Dust Bowl migrants he'd one day vilify. From what few sources survive, Davis's beginnings seem not to have quite equaled the poverty his future targets would endure, nor did they indicate that his path would lead to the power and influence he'd enjoy three-and-a-half decades later. Instead, Davis's joy-parched upbringing appears to have been a product of his mother's strict religiosity. Always circumspect about revealing too much of his background, Davis would spend much of his adulthood muddying what was known about his past. Thus, accounts of Davis's early life appearing in the few newspaper profiles written about his upbringing differ from one to another.

One telling profile presents the transformative moment of Davis's life as taking place when he ran away at sixteen years old to escape his mother's strictures and his stepfather's acquiescence to them. Drifting between various unskilled labor and farmhand jobs, Davis never settled into any work. Continuously unsatisfied, he eventually enlisted in the army in 1908. After training in Wyoming, Davis shipped out to the Philippines, where he was stationed at Camp Keithley on the island of Mindanao, and, later, at Luzon's Camp Stotsenburg.

Ten years earlier, the United States had defeated Spain in a war that helped cement the United States' position as a global power. Among the spoils of victory in the Spanish-American War was control of the Philippines. Long Spain's only significant colony in the Eastern Hemisphere, the Philippines became the United States' primary gateway to Asia. Though officially a commonwealth of the United States, in practice the Philippines remained a colony, only now one controlled by the ascendant power in North America. For nearly half a century, the United States would enforce control of what was arguably its most valuable colonial possession while simultaneously protecting its foothold in the Eastern Hemisphere by stationing thousands of American soldiers and sailors in the Philippines, Davis and many other future Los Angeles leaders among them.

Davis's position among those leaders was still many years away. For the moment, he just needed a job, though the thought of becoming a policeman appealed greatly to him. Just three weeks after getting to L.A., he took an examination required to join the police department and passed. Another few weeks on, Davis began his career stationed out of the LAPD's 77th Street division, located just south of downtown Los Angeles.

The opportunity with the LAPD evaporated almost as fast as Davis had found it. Just a few days after he was hired, the young patrolman was walking the beat near the University of Southern California when he passed a house where a young woman and her mother were sitting on their porch. The women got Davis's attention, and, as he later described the incident, invited them up to their porch to chat. Davis claims he assumed it was an innocent invitation that might also give him a chance to get to know the people who lived along his beat.

Whatever his or their reasoning had been, Davis accepted the invitation. He didn't know that a neighbor noticed. Thinking the visit by a police officer to the nearby house was peculiar, the neighbor mentioned it to the older woman's husband that night. Angered to learn of the visit, the husband complained to Davis's supervisors, who fired him for an action they said violated protocol and reflected poorly on the department.

After stretching the last of his army pay until he was hired by the police department, Davis didn't have any financial buffer. He needed a new job immediately. Unable to find one in Los Angeles, he looked further afield. Finally, he found an opening at a railway in Arizona.

Despite the new job, Davis remained upset about his dismissal. He wrote to then-LAPD chief Charles Sebastian to explain what had happened and to plead for another chance as a patrol officer. Sebastian agreed to allow Davis back on the force if he retook the civil service exam and passed it again. Near the end of 1911 he returned to Los Angeles and did precisely that.

True to his word, Chief Sebastian rehired Davis, who began his second chance as an officer in July 1912. That was Davis's only break for many years.

He spent most of the next decade in the doldrums. His career only caught wind in 1921, when he was first promoted. After that, Davis proceeded to storm up the department's ranks, receiving promotion upon promotion over the next five years. Finally, in early 1926, Davis reached the zenith of the Los Angeles Police Department.

That February, R. Lee Heath—who later admitted to teetering precariously close to a nervous breakdown—surprised Los Angeles by announcing plans to retire as police chief. At Heath's urging, Los Angeles police commissioners provisionally appointed Davis to succeed him. The commission hoped that by elevating the young head of the department's vice squad as the next chief, it might avoid disrupting the department significantly. Despite his early-career tests, Davis would again have to pass a civil examination for his appointment to become permanent.

Though that requirement was meant to help prevent corruption at the police department and other city management positions, it was largely a rubber stamp. Thanks in part to Heath's support, many institutions in the city already treated Davis as its new chief. After he made his surprise announcement that he was stepping down, Heath even orchestrated the Breakfast Club event that welcomed Davis as the club's newest member. In passing the baton to the thirty-six-year-old Davis, Heath also helped name as his successor a man who, when officially appointed, would be Los Angeles's youngest ever police chief (no one has since been appointed at an earlier age). It was a provisional appointment at first, but by July 1926 the police commission officially named Davis Los Angeles's new chief of police.

"Quiet and unobtrusive, soft-spoken and hard-fisted, this is the picture that his friends will paint to you of the youngest Chief of Police in the history of the city," wrote the *Los Angeles Times* in a profile of Davis accompanying its coverage of Heath's resignation.

Upon being elevated to chief, Davis denied that he'd sought the position or that he suspected ahead of his appointment that he might be named for the post. "This appointment is such a surprise to me I have had no opportunity to formulate any policy," he told a reporter from the *Los Angeles Evening Express*. "Of course, I intend to enforce the law without fear or favor, but I will have to think it over before I could say whether I contemplate any changes. I can say at this time, however, that I consider the Los Angeles force one of the best, and that it will be a pleasure to work with such a fine body of men."

Despite his claim to the *Evening Express* that he didn't have plans for the department, let alone his claims that he would enforce the law without fear or favor, Davis quickly overhauled it upon becoming chief. Even people described by newspapers as "friends" of Davis suggested that nothing about his rise to the chief's office had been improvisational. Writer A. M. Rochlen portrayed the new chief as subdued and controlled in a glowing 1926 profile published by the *Times* after his appointment. Rochlen, a Hearst reporter, would later become a vice president and spokesperson at the Douglas Aircraft Company (a position that would later prove beneficial to Davis), and a close friend of Davis's. Aside from suggesting Davis's ability to cull favor in Los Angeles's reactionary press or Rochlen's ability to cultivate allies for the city's powerful publishers, if not both, the profile provided an early example of the false modesty Davis often invoked and the myths he and the city's fourth estate jointly devised about how he led the police department.

If there was anything about Davis's promotion of which his mother would have been especially proud, perhaps it would have been how little enthusiasm Davis publicly expressed, whether about his appointment as police chief or even a recent victory in a major marksmanship competition. Davis appeared in dozens of newspaper photos that busy spring. Just as would be the case in hundreds of photos for the next two decades, whether winning marksmanship trophies, posing behind bars in goofily staged photos with police commissioners and other city officials, or addressing luncheons hosted by influential right-wing women's clubs, Davis never seemed to display satisfaction or pleasure. He certainly didn't express joy. If Davis ever felt joyful, he did not typically let it show publicly.

Instead, in photographs, Davis typically appears alert, perhaps a little wary, and almost always either in or feigning control. James Edgar Davis cherished control more than anything. He treasured restraint. He valued precision. Once he became chief, Davis required that officers serving under him exude control while performing their duties with military precision. Control and order were so important to Davis that he expected it of the public as well. The citizenry he wanted to protect was an orderly, peaceful, law-abiding citizenry. If Melissa Haseltine Howell had wanted anything from her son, it would be that he grow up to become a man who eschewed the sins of excess and frivolity. Aside from that moment with his fingers immersed in his breakfast, it appeared that he had.

Even one of Davis's first orders as chief was about appearances. A month into the job Davis ordered his officers to start taking greater care of their public appearance. If the police were to ensure that Los Angeles remained an orderly city—and if he wanted to show those in power who helped him become chief that he could control their city—he needed his subordinates to *look* as professional as the public wanted them to *act*. Davis told officers that they would lose a day's pay for every button on their uniform coats left unfastened. These rules, the *Los Angeles Evening Express* told readers, were laid out by "Los Angeles' immaculate and polished chief of police."

Davis fervently honed that immaculate image once he started ascending the department's ranks. Now he wanted those he commanded to look just as polished. The new acting chief told the *Evening Express* that he wanted the Los Angeles Police Department to become known as the "best dressed and neatest" police force in the world. His officers, he told the paper, would "look as well as a naval officer on dress parade."

It might not have even been an accident that Davis used the navy as his department's model. After his years of youthful drifting, Davis had attempted to join the navy, but a recruiter in Oklahoma City thought he wasn't fit enough. Davis said that was because he'd bicycled all around the city before his appointment with the recruiter and arrived out of breath. His dreams of being a sailor never died. When Davis finally retired from the police department decades after his attempt to enlist, Los Angeles area newspapers reported that one of the first things Davis did was join the crew of the tuna trawler *Sea Boy* for a seventy-five-day voyage (photos from which are among the few where Davis wears a natural smile and appears relaxed).

However extensively the navy may have contributed to Davis's professional ideals, he loathed unruliness, whether in his officers' uniforms, the manner with which civilians behaved on the street, the way laborers worked on a factory floor, or how longshoremen unloaded cargo ships. Every Halloween, Davis even made statements to Los Angeles newspapers sternly warning the city's youth against rowdy pranks and other mischief.

"We mean to see that your All Hallow's Eve is properly observed, but we don't stand for too much enthusiasm," Davis told a *Los Angeles Times* columnist in 1933, explaining how he had to extend daytime police shifts into the night to ensure he had enough officers on duty to handle complaints of petty vandalism on Halloween.

The unblinking, serious expressions that filled Davis's face in the many public appearances his duties as chief required didn't suggest stiffness on the chief's part, nor did they betray any doubts he might have been trying to conceal about his rapid elevation to the Los Angeles Police Department's top office. Instead, Davis presented his public image with the kind of discipline that one might argue made him an expert marksman, even when he was newly appointed. Perhaps when making public appearances, speaking to city council, or talking with reporters, Davis drew from the same well of reserve that he did when shooting a target on a pistol range. At least at this early point in his career, he seemed to approach the press with caution and intention, as if choosing his comments like he might have chosen his shots and only speaking when he had a clear target in mind.

A common thread wove through the media depictions of Davis that emerged over the years since he became chief. Davis wasn't just a clean living, pious man who believed passionately in "law and order." He was effective. His nickname—"Two Gun Davis"—was well deserved. He'd won multiple shooting championships in both left- and right-handed pistol competitions, but it was more than his firearm aptitude that earned him the nickname. The moniker also referred to Davis's readiness to employ that aptitude on the job.

Davis revered firearms and their role in law enforcement. Early in his career, he encountered a murder suspect during his regular patrol, and the ensuing shootout helped make Davis locally famous. Afterward, his marksmanship skills kept him in the public eye. As he started climbing the LAPD's ranks, Davis continued to improve his shooting and encouraged other cops to do so as well. Once he became chief, he immediately made firearms training one of his department's absolute highest priorities. On one hand, police working under Davis would get pay bumps for high marks on shooting ranges; on the other, they'd be docked for underperforming.

Two Gun Davis lacked any interest in due process. From his perspective, it was the police department's job to discipline anyone who disrupted the city's order. Any infraction, however minimal or significant, represented a smoldering threat that must be extinguished. "To make crime unpopular by the certainty of punishment," Davis told Rochlen in his 1926 profile, "is the surest way to combat it."

Davis was an early proponent of what we've come to recognize as broken-windows policing. No crime was too minor to address. Los Angeles's new chief refused to spare any tool he believed his department could use to fight crime. This didn't just mean the use of force—though Davis wasn't shy about aggressive policing. It also meant completely retooling the machinery of justice.

Davis tried to speed up criminal trials soon after taking office. The new chief told the *Times* that he planned to ask Los Angeles County courts help him identify "courageous" judges. In Davis's assessment, "courageous" judges were ones who were willing to incarcerate anyone accused of using a weapon in commission of a felony within two weeks of arrest. Challenging Los Angeles's judiciary to get tough on sentencing gave Davis one of his earliest chances to use local newspapers to exploit Angelenos' fears to further his own agenda as chief. "If it goes through, I believe it will make Los Angeles the safest city in the world," Davis said of his plan to hasten prosecution of armed suspects, though he did not further detail the plan.

Throughout his career, Davis used his unfazed affect to lend unwarranted credibility to outrageous claims and invented numerical figures about crime and police work. Despite the chief's controlled mannerisms, his self-assured reliance on misinformation and manufactured data maintained a tinge of bluster, especially when he wanted to target a specific demographic. In those instances, he'd couple invented statistics with declarations about one societal bogeyman or another and declare it as the current root of all of Los Angeles's crime.

Even before his position as chief was made permanent, Davis outlined plans to end narcotics crimes in Los Angeles. Davis told reporters that the LAPD would aggressively and unapologetically pursue drug addicts while pushing prosecutors and courts for harsh sentences. He even claimed that 40 percent of all criminals in Los Angeles were addicted to one drug or another, some arrested numerous times and all at "enormous expense" for the city.

"These narcotic addicts have no economic value," Davis told the *Los Angeles Times*. "They are a source of danger and a sore or blot on civilization."

Without citing any evidence beyond his own certainty, Davis insisted that punishing drug users would significantly slash Los Angeles's crime rates. Only the harshest responses would suffice. "I am determined to eliminate these misfits from this city," he said. "I'm going to make it so uncomfortable for them that they will not want a second sentence, and I intend to make this community too hot for them to tarry in. I'm sorry they have to take their slime into some other community, but we're going to get rid of these misfits."

*Misfits.*

*Slime.*

*No economic value.*

*Blot on civilization.*

Los Angeles's soon-to-be chief of police characterized drug users the way he, his new Breakfast Club companions, and the rest of Los Angeles's elites would characterize any group they chose to cast as undesirables. Through such characterizations, crime and disorder in Los Angeles became forces not borne of Los Angeles itself but rather brought to the city by unwanted, foreign actors and influences. To be a criminal was to be an alien, and, in many ways, to be an alien was to be a criminal.

The following year Davis would laud the Narcotic Detail's work in the police department's annual report. The chief would even claim that cooperation between the drug squad, courts, and other agencies was so successful that it cleared local courts and jails of repeat drug offenders and swept them from the city's streets. The "apparent elimination" of "police problem drug addicts" from Los Angeles had, in turn, reduced property crime in the city.

In the same annual report, Davis bragged about police using vagrancy charges as a tool to investigate other crimes. The chief was candid with the board of police commissioners about the pretext; his department's new policy of rounding up "suspicious characters" was central to its "determined attempt to prevent as many crimes as possible." Again, Davis thanked courts for cooperating, this time for letting the police detain the alleged vagrants until they were able to gather their fingerprints.

Spurious and politicized as Davis's claims may have been, he acted decisively as chief. He more than doubled the size of the police department's narcotics squad from nine to twenty officers after becoming chief. Publicity about the augmented squad's frequent drug raids and arrests further buttressed the department's image and Davis's record of accomplishments.

James Davis's initiation into the Breakfast Club hadn't only allowed Los Angeles's new chief of police to indulge in the group's morning gluttony; it also anointed him as an unofficial member of the city's ruling class. Hurdles remained, but a bevy of influential figures were ready to help him clear them. Sooner than he expected, he would need to lean on them and the record of accomplishments he'd manufactured as chief.

# 4 | REGIME CHANGE

SIGNS OF MISERABLE CONDITIONS spreading throughout the country since the fall were starting to appear in Modoc County by the middle of 1930: a family of six riding out the Modoc County winter in a part-tent, part lean-to shack, sustaining themselves on some sacks of cornmeal and a few large bags of beans; men discretely coming to neighbors' back doors to ask for something, even just a little, to eat; a couple with six children huddled against the cold inside a converted woodshed.

At first, the crash had seemed abstract, distant—something that happened in New York to people in over their heads, to people who'd borrowed far more than would ever be sensible, to people with nothing backing their investments.

It's true that the first dramatic scenes of distress came from distant New York, but tickertape-strewn trading floors and despairing brokers were only symptoms. The disease was nationwide (worldwide, really). The 1920s' clamorous finale woke countless Americans from the reverie of easy credit promises and sure-thing, gravity-defying returns. Worthless investments collapsed in on themselves. Borrowers discovered they couldn't borrow anymore, and everything they'd borrowed against all that they'd previously borrowed against was now due. A decadelong roar gave way to sobs.

Markets shut down as politicians hastily erected trade protections. Goods and commodities piled up in warehouses. Factories and other firms shuttered as revenue sagged. Layoffs followed. Savings evaporated. Banks failed. Misery spread.

Still, the people of Modoc County thought they were safe, that they didn't have any reason to worry. The *Plaindealer* assured the county in the first piece

51

of local writing it published after the crash that the financial jitters on the other side of the continent would not reach them. Gertrude French made sure that the paper echoed this sentiment. For months, little mention appeared on the *Plaindealer*'s pages that the crisis was engulfing much more of the country than lower Manhattan. Then, with increasing frequency, words like *depression*, *scarcity*, and *unemployment* started appearing.

By May 1930, Alturas's other paper, the *Modoc County Times*, claimed that for one month the previous winter Modoc County officials had issued more building permits than their counterparts in far more populous Alameda County (originally home, as it happened, to Bard French). That didn't really mean that Modoc County was in the clear; it just meant that things were worse in the Bay Area. Even so, Modoc County residents no longer could deny what was already happening around them, as evidenced by the *Times*'s description that same month of locals building makeshift shelter, scrounging questionable meals, and, as was increasingly necessary, swallowing their pride to go next door and beg in order to feed their families.

"At that, however, Modoc having gained a place in the sun we have had a chance sometimes recently to witness some of the actual hardships resulting from national unemployment," the column's author, identified only by the initials B.S.B., wrote.

Most Southern Californians were similarly unconcerned when Wall Street's troubles began. Financial and business circles in the region were still celebrating the October 21 opening of the Los Angeles Stock Exchange's new building when reports of the financial calamity in New York broke. These reports would soon eclipse news of the opening, but Los Angeles residents first paid little attention to the news from the East Coast. Even after news of the crash appeared, local business prognosticators quoted by the *Los Angeles Times* took what historian Leonard Leader later called the "traditional view" and forecast a financially promising 1930.

"Earlier economic setbacks such as drought, flood, bank failures and even an epidemic of hoof and mouth disease among livestock had been surmounted," Leader wrote. "In their time, massive population increases, sunny skies, crop cultivation, discovery of oil, the film industry and land development and sales, had come to the local economy's rescue."

Angelenos were instead engrossed by yet more turnover at City Hall. Earlier that year, allegations of corruption in Mayor George Cryer's administration mounted until Cryer announced that he wouldn't seek reelection. The surrounding scandal even seemed poised to engulf James Davis, who was already scrambling to contain the fallout of a botched kidnapping case that began the previous year.

## The Wrong Boy

How Davis Solved Murder Mystery
Davis Tells of Crime Battle
Why Liberals Hate Davis

For three weeks at the end of 1929, the *Los Angeles Record* filled wraparound covers of its daily extra editions with lengthy stories that delved into every aspect of James Edgar Davis's life and career history. Meanwhile, the chief's job was on the line barely two years after his official appointment. First, Davis had angered Los Angeles's war veterans after age requirements included in new LAPD hiring policies Davis implemented led some who'd fought in the World War to believe he was discriminating against them. Then a woman sued Davis for allegedly mismanaging her son's high-profile kidnapping and gruesome murder. Like other papers throughout the city, the *Record* joined the fray weighing the chief's fate, but each piece of breaking news about the scandal was obscured by the *Record*'s daily newsstand wrappers affording Davis a far softer touch.

The botched kidnapping case began in early 1928 when a boy named Walter Collins vanished. Police investigating Walter's disappearance turned up few leads. Finally, months after Walter's mother, Christine, reported her son missing, she heard from the LAPD. Walter had been found! Two officers were headed to Illinois—where he'd been located—to get him and bring him back to Southern California. Collins was elated.

Then the officers returned to her home with the boy. Disappointment and confusion washed over Collins. The kid standing in front of her wasn't her son.

The officers were furious when Collins rejected the boy. They weren't even confused that she'd said they'd misidentified the child. They didn't treat this like a logistical mix-up. The police simply insisted that Collins was the one who was wrong. Why wasn't she grateful for the police finding him?

Aghast, Collins held firm. This wasn't her boy. She was a mother. She knew her son. This boy was not him.

Collins's anger made the officers angry. Instead of reuniting her with the boy, whoever he was, the officers arrested Collins after she kept resisting. They had her committed against her will in a mental health ward at Los Angeles County Hospital and put a psychiatric hold on her so she could not get out of the hospital. She would remain an unwilling patient for nearly a week.

Then authorities in Canada arrested a man named Gordon Stewart Northcott just days after Collins was released. Northcott, a Canadian who'd fled to his home country after evidence of grisly murders were discovered at a Riverside County chicken ranch, was suspected of killing and molesting numerous boys there. Walter Collins, whose remains were never found, was believed to be one of Northcott's victims. Northcott, whose own mother helped him commit some of the murders (she later confessed to killing Collins), had also beaten and sexually abused his nephew, Sanford Clark. He forced Clark to watch the abuse and killings and even compelled a terrified Clark—who believed he'd seen the Collins boy among the victims—to take part in some of the murders.

The grotesque ordeal outraged Southern California. As Northcott went to trial in Riverside County, Christine Collins sued the City of Los Angeles, the officer who'd had her committed, and Chief Davis. Some members of the public demanded that Davis be fired. In a precursor to scandals that would again place Davis's career in jeopardy a decade later, he originally claimed he knew nothing about the shocking circumstances surrounding the case and its handling but admitted otherwise after intense legal pressure. Davis survived, if barely, when the case against him was declared a mistrial.

Scrutiny of Davis's career intensified over the ensuing year as Collins's case and other controversies intensified. By December 1929 Davis faced the very real possibility that he'd be fired. The Los Angeles Record continued its serial biography for twenty-three days as if nothing had happened. The series appeared daily except for two holidays, profiling Davis the man and his career.

Perhaps conceding he was unlikely to survive the inquiry, Davis may have sensed that he needed to humanize himself to Los Angeles's news-reading public. Whatever the reason, Davis's ordeal finally ended on December 26, as the end of the year—and the decade—approached. Instead of firing him, newly elected mayor John Porter offered to demote Davis to deputy chief while deputy chief Roy Steckel took Davis's place.

Davis narrowly avoided another trial by agreeing to the demotion. As deputy chief, Davis remained involved in the ongoing battle against the disorder and undesirable forces he so loathed. Moreover, his ill-fortune might turn out to be short-lived as the Roaring Twenties shuddered to a close and the city's attention turned from reshuffled top brass at the police department to more cataclysmic matters.

## Unhoarding

Voters in Los Angeles had elected Porter in part because of his reputation as a puritanical reformer. Los Angeles, at least from certain vantage points, seemed like it was emerging from years of corruption and scandal just in time for the approaching decade. But the new year also brought a new reality. Try as it might, Hollywood could not script its way out of the Depression.

Nor could Herbert Hoover. Hoover hadn't even completed a full year as president when the US economy collapsed; when it did, his administration and its Republican allies in Congress refused to shift from his predecessors' light regulatory touch. Instead of unified federal aid to individuals, a patchwork of community-based relief efforts emerged. Often, these localized responses didn't come from state, city, or county governments. By design, private citizens and nonprofit organizations organized ad-hoc responses to fill the vacuum left by the public sector through what President Hoover termed "money unhoarding."

Still, little changed. Underutilized land and abandoned worksites throughout the nation's cities began filling with jobless men (mostly) who built homes out of scrap metal, wood, and whatever else they could find. The numbers of unemployed grew as the months progressed, and these shantytowns soon became makeshift communities, some of which even formed their own shadow governments and microeconomies. Eventually, most Americans—whether city dwellers or country denizens—encountered one, if not many, of these encampments.

By the end of 1930, residents of one such encampment along the shores of Lake Michigan near Chicago began referring to themselves as "Hooverville" denizens, a sardonic nod to the then-president. Before long, the term Hooverville became an era-defining bit of verbal baggage that heavily weighed on the president's slumping political ambitions.

Hoover was not a passive victim to clever wordplay and circumstances out of his control. His distaste for federal relief did not mean his administration hadn't tried to address the worsening Depression in its own manner. Still, the

White House's approach reinforced societal divisions and cemented conservative narratives about the role government should play in the economy for the next decade, if not for decades to come. Instead of experimenting with economic remedies, conservatives turned further inward. They rejected any suggestion that existing institutions needed to change and dismissed calls for government intervention and reform as risky schemes that threatened democracy itself.

Many members of Hoover's administration and politicians and business leaders in his orbit also refused to accept, at least publicly, that any threat the United States faced could have originated from within the country and been exacerbated by existing conditions unique to the United States. Such denialists instead made spurious claims about foreign meddling in the nation's economy. Their protests repeatedly devolved into insistence that alien agitators were undermining the United States at the behest of foreign powers aiming to manipulate the country's recovery.

Xenophobic but more general and nuanced assessments of this sort expressed by members of the Hoover administration gave cover to more explicitly nativist responses that tapped into racist, anti-immigrant sentiments that had peaked in the 1920s. In 1931, for example, Charles Visel, head of Los Angeles's Citizens Committee on Coordination of Unemployment Relief, concocted a protectionist, anti-immigrant scheme ostensibly meant to protect American workers from competition, even as it contravened core American principles.

Visel turned to two Hoover appointees tasked with coordinating his administration's response to the unemployment crisis: Colonel Arthur Woods and William Doak. Woods chaired the president's recently created employment commission. Doak was Hoover's labor secretary.

Visel, Woods, and Doak enacted the scheme that put Mexican immigrants to the United States as well as US citizens with Mexican backgrounds (as well as other immigrants and non-White citizens) in their crosshairs. Through what the trio euphemistically dubbed "self-deportation" and "repatriation" drives, they ejected hundreds of thousands of people of Mexican descent, regardless of whether they were in the United States temporarily or were permanent residents, whether they had violated immigration laws to enter the country or were here legally, and even whether they were United States citizens.

Though packaged as voluntary, these deportations were coercive in practice. They were enforced through racist roundups and raids that selectively targeted non-White immigrants and citizens. Under Doak, the US Department of Labor—then tasked with enforcing federal immigration policy—empowered its agents to stop, detain, and even deport anyone who "appeared" to be an alien. Defining those to be deported by physical appearance meant federal agents swept up many American citizens who happened to have Mexican parents or ancestors. Though the deportation drives were primarily aimed at Mexican immigrants, they also targeted people of Asian descent, who were already excluded from legally migrating to the United States, let alone becoming citizens.

"Some may say to deport these people is inhuman, but my answer is that the government should protect its own citizens against illegal invaders," Doak said. "This I propose to do with every weapon in my power. Law is law, and I intend to enforce it as long as I hold my office."

Los Angeles might have been the country's "white spot," but it wasn't the only place that supported repatriation. Nativists throughout California were among those who welcomed the policy. In Modoc County, for example, Gertrude French's *Alturas Plaindealer* praised tightening of US government immigration enforcement after federal authorities asked local law enforcement to detain a Mexican man who had been accused of illegally entering the United States. Local officials (though not named, this meant John Sharp, who, as sheriff, ran the Modoc County jail) kept the man jailed at the feds' request. French welcomed the event.

"The change in attitude is said to be having the most salutary effect," opined a *Plaindealer* item about the arrest. "Not only are many undesirable aliens being deported, but the news that one is no longer safe after he gets into the United States, circulating among the peons below the border, is making the adventure of sneaking across the Rio Grande look much less attractive than it did."

While not atypical of nativist attitudes, the unbylined story's inclusion on the *Plaindealer*'s front page as well as the pejorative dismissal of Mexicans as "undesirable" and "peons" made clear that Gertrude French—who the previous year was still a member of the state Republican Party's central committee—readily endorsed the Republican administration's xenophobic policies. (Many Democrats unapologetically shared that xenophobia.)

Its printing was made more notable by another piece in the same edition of the *Plaindealer*. Just a few inches away, French ran a column by her friend and mentor, Colonel William Thompson. That piece excoriated Peter

Schonchin—the son of one of the resistance leaders executed with Kintpuash during the Modoc War—for an article Schonchin had written about the war, printed in another paper. Thompson insisted that Schonchin had botched his history. "As all know, the Modoc tribe was the most savage, bloody and cruel encountered by the immigrants of early days, hundreds of men, women and children having been butchered in attempting to pass through their country," Thompson wrote, insisting that he needed to set the record straight.

French assisted her mentor's argument. She wrote an editorial noting that the paper repeatedly refused Schonchin's requests to print the piece in question because "no one believed it." Printing it, she insisted, would be an "insult to the memory of the Modoc County pioneers who took part in the war."

In a single issue, the *Plaindealer* reinforced the myths White Californians held deeply about who belonged in the Golden State (Thompson called it the "true history"), who could rightfully tell the state's story and record its history, and who should be kept from sharing in its bounty.

## Aliens Within

While Doak, Visel, and Woods orchestrated the deportation of hundreds of thousands of foreign immigrants and non-White Americans, other authorities at all levels of government agitated against communities supporting their newcomers. When Colonel Woods resigned in the summer of 1931, Hoover replaced him as head of the newly created President's Organization on Unemployment Relief with AT&T president Walter S. Gifford.

Gifford continued the theme of promoting individual Americans, local communities, and the private sector as essential for the economy's recovery. With unemployment still lagging, Gifford offered guidance for local relief programs, but not funding. Meanwhile, politicians and business leaders in Los Angeles—deploying increasingly vile characterizations of migrants—saw Gifford's appointment as a chance for the federal government to assist attempts to interdict domestic migration to Southern California.

In November an unnamed railroad police investigator alleged in an interview with the Associated Press that thousands of unemployed men were stowing away on trains entering California or hopping onto boxcars to wander within its confines. The railway investigator claimed that these men refused to work, opting instead to take meals from soup kitchens and other charities despite being capable of finding a job. He also alleged that significant numbers of these interlopers were criminals.

In Los Angeles County, a grocery-chain executive who also served as a member of the county's board of supervisors noted this and other antimigrant fervor and sensed a political opportunity. At a November board meeting, this supervisor, Frank Shaw, who also chaired the Citizens Committee on Employment, warned that an "employment mirage shimmering in southern California and apparently visible all over the nation is beckoning 2000 men across the state line daily" creating what he called, as recorded by the *Oakland Tribune*, a "disturbing economic problem" in Los Angeles County.

Shaw's colleagues resolved to ask broadcasters to air radio ads warning people in other parts of the United States not to migrate to California. At their meeting, unidentified members of a previously unknown group that called itself the Unemployed Voters' Association urged supervisors as well as California Governor James Rolph to prohibit unemployed people from entering the state.

Later in the month, Shaw, Gifford, the chamber of commerce's managing secretary Arthur Arnoll, California Attorney General Ulysses S. Webb, and other prominent Los Angeles, state, and US leaders met to discuss the possibility of dispatching California Highway Patrol officers or other law authorities to bar migrants from crossing the state line, using force if necessary. Though that plan never materialized, it informed future attempts to restrict domestic migration.

The Depression deepened as it entered its fourth year and an election approached. President Hoover knew his chances to remain in office were narrowing, but he refused to shift his course even as his laissez-faire economic policies failed to spark a turnaround.

The job losses mounted. It was difficult enough for healthy young men to find work but even harder for those whose physical condition might prevent them from performing manual labor. Men who'd lost limbs or were otherwise injured in the World War or the Spanish-American War haunted soup kitchens and charity offices. Even veterans not maimed were anxious about their economic prospects. In 1924 they'd been promised bonus payments, but those were not scheduled to be paid until 1945. Then a cannery worker living in Portland, Oregon, persuaded veterans there to march on Washington, DC, with him to demand immediate bonus payments.

Word of their march spread and inspired similar marches from throughout the country. Tens of thousands of veterans and their families convened on Washington. They squatted in abandoned buildings and built a massive Hooverville on the Anacostia flats. The House of Representatives passed legislation to pay the bonuses, but the bill failed in the Senate.

The veterans pressed their demands. Then six people died in a violent standoff after local police tried to evict marchers from some buildings owned by the Treasury Department. The deaths gave Hoover and his allies justification to clear the larger encampment. Army Chief of Staff General Douglas MacArthur, Colonel Dwight Eisenhower, and Major George Patton ordered one thousand soldiers, cavalry, and light tanks to dismantle the camp. The active-duty troops crushed their veteran counterparts' structures and used bayonets and tear gas to force holdouts away. A twelve-week-old baby died in the ensuing chaos after inhaling tear gas.

The baby's death, the image of thousands of maimed, haggard war veterans climbing the Capitol steps to implore Congress for help, and an American general deploying active American soldiers against American war veterans hung over the approaching election. Hoover would have to contend with the summer's deadly consequences if he wanted another four years in the White House.

Despite the Democrats' surfeit of advantages, their party's return to the White House was not guaranteed. Regional and ideological differences split the party, whose leaders sought a presidential candidate who could unify voters and carry large electoral prizes. Finally, late that summer in sweltering Chicago, New York Governor Franklin Delano Roosevelt emerged from multiple ballots and significant deal-making as the Democrats' standard-bearer against Hoover.

Roosevelt charged into the race promising to bring to the entire country the kind of wholesale administrative reforms and public relief programs he'd implemented in the Empire State. Voters overwhelmingly welcomed that pitch and sent Roosevelt to the White House.

The economy had cratered yet further by the time Roosevelt was inaugurated in March 1933. One quarter of the country's eligible workers were unemployed. An imminent banking crisis threatened to explode any reforms the new administration planned. Elsewhere in the world, dictators and demagogues consolidated power as they seized upon economic uncertainty. To counter similar movements brewing in the United States, Roosevelt and his allies needed to act quickly and decisively to wrest the nation from the Great Depression's deepest abyss.

## Relief

A whirlwind of executive actions and legislative flurries followed. Roosevelt's frenzied first one hundred days in office—a benchmark for future presidential activity and initiative, arbitrary though it may be—deployed the first volley in a barrage of economy-steadying initiatives known as the New Deal.

These initiatives marked a decisive and clear break not just with Herbert Hoover but also with Hoover's Republican predecessors, Calvin Coolidge and Warren G. Harding. For more than a decade, Republican presidents kept the federal government at arm's length from private business. First they cheered as the '20s roared, then they washed their hands of the mess left by the decade's catastrophic finale.

Beginning with such new bureaucracies as the Public Works Administration, the Civilian Conservation Corps, the National Recovery Administration, and the Agricultural Adjustment Administration, New Deal initiatives deployed millions of Americans—and millions of public dollars—throughout the United States. They modernized infrastructure, reformed agriculture, electrified rural America, and otherwise overhauled the character of American geography while retooling its economy.

In May 1933 Congress passed and Roosevelt signed the Federal Emergency Relief Act. Through FERA, the US government provided aid to states to pay for both direct aid to residents and work relief programs. The act also established the Federal Transient Service, or FTS, which established a single, centralized federal program that managed relief for domestic migrants who moved frequently from city to city, county to county, and state to state throughout the nation. This meant, in part, that the US government shouldered the burden that internal migration placed on state destinations popular with migrants and reimbursed those states for food, shelter, and economic relief.

This mattered immensely. Access to relief was often based on one's residency status in a particular jurisdiction. The cost of relief was a major reason why migration and transient aid were such divisive subjects. Few in California, or elsewhere in the country, wanted to pay to support *any* indigent populations. Even fewer wanted public dollars to assist relief seekers who didn't reside locally. County and state jurisdictions already struggled to meet aid demands. Economically disadvantaged migrants made for particularly easy targets.

Such migrants could easily be depicted as outside burdens piled atop already excessively burdened local aid operations. Not all opponents of migrant relief were against relief itself—many claimed they opposed assisting migrants and transients because they wanted to help local neighbors—but complicated state residency requirements and other bureaucratic obstacles often made it difficult to establish one's eligibility as a local. Usually the obstacle-strewn path to establishing residency in one jurisdiction or another was by design.

The terms *migrant* and *transient* are not interchangeable, either in general vocabulary or in their legal implications. Migrants can be transient, but many permanently relocate. On the other hand, transients are definitionally impermanent.

Regardless of such distinctions, Depression-era authorities often managed migrants and transients interchangeably, and the obstacles they placed in front of migrants often made it harder for them to avoid becoming transients (or enduring the same treatment). For example, a state might lengthen the amount of time migrants needed to live in a particular jurisdiction before officially becoming residents. Without status as residents, they'd be prevented from accessing the kind of assistance and resources that would allow them the stability to stay in their new home long enough to become residents in the first place. Unable to remain, migrants would be forced into transient status, which in turn would limit the financial or work relief opportunities open to them. This was absolutely the case in California, which hardly welcomed its status as a beacon of opportunity.

Anxious California legislators scrambled to insulate the Golden State's budget from the New Deal's impact. Rather than look inward, the state endorsed claims that the biggest danger to Californians was poor non-Californians. That May, the legislature criminalized aid to indigent nonresidents. The state had already extended residency requirements in 1931. Now lawmakers made it illegal for Californians to help nonresidents who couldn't afford to support themselves to enter the state, access relief, or otherwise try to survive in the state while they waited to become residents.

## Dealmaking at City Hall?

State legislators debated the kind of hardline antimigrant measures that Frank Shaw had championed for years as a Los Angeles County supervisor. Now, only half a year after the landmark election that sent FDR to the White House, Los

Angeles voters were back at the ballot box deciding whether to make Shaw their next mayor. As the New Deal launched, they made it abundantly clear that they were as fed up with Porter as they had been with Cryer and were ready for another change atop the city. Shaw, who supported the New Deal despite his protectionism and antimigrant sentiment, won.

The new mayor's earlier attempts to keep destitute migrants out of the Golden State may have helped him over the finish line, but he entered the 1933 election opposed by some of the city's most powerful people and institutions, including Harry Chandler and the *Los Angeles Times*, whose opposition at first lingered after Shaw's victory.

Chandler nearly destroyed Shaw's chances after a *Times* reporter turned up a glaring detail about the candidate's legitimacy: he wasn't technically an American. Shaw was born in Canada in 1877, about thirty miles east of Port Huron, Michigan, in the Ontario town of Warwick, where he lived until he was five years old.

When the Shaws relocated to Detroit, the future Los Angeles mayor still did not become a US citizen, nor would he in the ensuing years as his family moved first from Michigan to Colorado, then to Kansas, and, finally, to Missouri. Never in all those years did the Shaws take the time or effort to properly naturalize Frank, whose brother Joseph would eventually become his chief political advisor. When questions about Shaw's citizenship emerged, he swore he never knew about his parents' oversight.

Shaw had always considered his upbringing rather typically American. In 1909 he and his wife, Cora—a Texan whom he'd married four years earlier—moved to Los Angeles from Arkansas. In California, Shaw worked in retail and wholesale, moving ever higher up the ladder at Haas, Baruch & Company, a prominent Southern California grocery distributor. Later identified by the *Los Angeles Times* as one of California's three wealthiest politicians, Shaw was elected to the Los Angeles City Council in 1925 and the Los Angeles County Board of Supervisors two years later. The same Frank Shaw who wanted stricter prohibitions against work-seeking migrants had himself migrated to the Golden State to begin a career.

A deft political team navigated Shaw toward electoral success. One member was Joseph, his campaign secretary and, once he was elected, his private secretary. The other was his field secretary, James Bolger. Bolger and Joseph Shaw masterfully packaged Frank's candidacy for broad appeal. Joe Shaw had his brother campaign as a New Deal Republican. Shaw could also draw from that favorite well of Los Angeles mayoral candidates: after more than a decade of popular discontent in Los Angeles, he insisted he would finally reform local government, reduce crime, tamp down vice, and clean up corruption.

To show that he was serious, Frank Shaw also promised to shake up Los Angeles's police department just four years after the reshuffling that led to James Davis's demotion. Labor discontent stirred up by Depression-related events made some in the city nervous. The *Times*'s Chandler was at first particularly anxious about labor organizing in his oasis of the open shop, but then he realized he knew the perfect person to help him do something about it: the labor-hating, red-baiting one-time chief of police James Davis.

Davis's dogged pursuit of subversives and loathing of anything that even whiffed of an association with Communists appealed to Chandler. Davis would be an effective ally. Chandler called off the *Times*'s reporting on Shaw's eligibility and convinced Shaw to swap Davis and Steckel once again. Shaw didn't like this idea at first but relented and accepted Chandler's deal. "Davis will have no strings tied to him," Shaw told the Los Angeles Police Commission when Davis's reappointment was made official.

What began as a compensatory trade with Chandler grew into a three-way symbiosis between mayor, police chief, and publisher that lasted for years. It wasn't just Chandler whom Davis had to thank. Joseph Shaw was largely responsible for convincing his brother to accept Chandler's deal. Joseph orchestrated the deal, as he would many future deals once Frank became mayor. Though Frank Shaw held the office, it was Joe, as personal secretary to the mayor, who was city hall's real power broker, and it was Joe whom Davis typically dealt with.

Just as promises of reform from Mayors Porter and Cryer had led to little change when it came to City Hall corruption, under Shaw little about the favor-trading, kickbacks, and other glad-handing that he campaigned against shifted once he and his brother arrived. Money and influence remained the driving forces behind Los Angeles municipal affairs. Backroom deals and favors drove every aspect of local government, as they had throughout Los Angeles's history.

Davis's appointment might very well have been the first such deal. One Friday night soon after Frank Shaw officially became mayor, he and a number of other local figures met secretly at a Los Angeles hotel to discuss the future of the police department. Timing their meeting to take place when Steckel was on a trip to Chicago, the power brokers unofficially anointed Davis days before a newly constituted Los Angeles Police Commission met to discuss the position.

Four years after Davis's ignominious departure from the chief's office, his name again filled Los Angeles front pages. Unlike where it had fallen by the end of 1929, the current publicity was mostly laudatory. Much of the negative attention that had surrounded Davis had petered out since his demotion. In its place were incandescent profiles that praised the old new chief and his approach to urban law enforcement. Hard questions about Walter Collins and veterans were out. In was praise of Davis's gunplay, promises to attack vice and gangsterism—the returned chief coordinated with the district attorney and sheriff on county-wide public-enemy warrants targeting gangsters—and warnings about courts being too lenient on "moochers," making it harder for police to prosecute them.

This time, the public appeared to welcome Davis's aggressive approach as he, the Shaws, and Chandler worked together to give their machine a shiny new polish. Davis's action-first, unapologetic, labor-hostile leadership pleased institutions like the Merchants and Manufacturers Association and the chamber of commerce. Renewed threats to Los Angeles's business-friendly open-shop labor environment made the chief an ideal avatar for the puritan, free-market-loving, orderly city that they sold.

He delivered almost immediately, dispatching hundreds of cops armed with tear gas, batons, and shotguns in October 1933 to break up a march of unemployed people on downtown Los Angeles that he claimed was led by a Communist-controlled organization.

Los Angeles and California would continue to reckon with transiency, disaster, unemployment, and crime through the end of 1933. That October, rapidly shifting winds drove a wildfire through the sycamore-covered hills of Griffith Park, trapping in its parched canyons scores of inadequately trained transient workers hired by the county to fight what had been a smaller fire, killing more than thirty of them.

By the end of November, the lynching of two suspects in the kidnapping and murder of a San Jose department store heiress sparked a heated debate about crime and punishment in California. Among the Los Angeles figures responding was Louise Ward Watkins, president of the influential Friday

Morning Club and a figure increasingly prominent in the city's conservative circles. "I am not defending lynching, but if we were sure of speedy and effective justice, there would be no necessity for lynchings," Watkins cautioned.

Watkins's comment expressed a worldview that closely resembled Chief Davis's. In the new year, she and Davis would forge an ever-stronger alliance, crusading for public vigilance against subversive elements that, they said, were plotting to upend the social order. Davis, meanwhile, was far from subtle in his thoughts on vigilante justice of the sort that occurred in San Jose. "The lynching symbolizes the desire of all citizens for immediate and adequate punishment for all heinous crimes," Davis said.

---

Just after Davis's reappointment was official, he sat down with *Los Angeles Times Sunday Magazine* contributor Mary June Barton for an interview. Barton's resultant profile described a string of well-wishers interrupting their interview as they dropped into the chief's office to congratulate him.

"It was one of the rare occasions when his reserve was down—he was smiling," Barton wrote. "Anyone could see that he was riding on the crest of the wave, thrilled to be back in power again, and to have people tell him how glad they were to have him back. He acted as if he were teeming with a thousand ideas, and could hardly wait to put them in force."

Published a month after Davis's return, Barton's words—like those of her press contemporaries—portrayed Davis as a man of self-control, discipline, and sobriety significantly matured by his service to the city. In Barton's telling, Davis had found a sense of discipline that he'd lost when he first left home.

"You can see he was a restless youth," Barton observed. "It's just chance that he is Los Angeles's Chief of Police rather than the hard-boiled commandant of the French Foreign Legion today—or perhaps of the Canadian Northwest Mountain Police." Only Davis's 1915 marriage and the five children who followed kept him from pursuing dreams of joining these institutions.

"There was no way out then, for his ambition, but up—up through the ranks of the police department," wrote Barton. "He took it one step at a time. He learned ordinances, effective police measures, regulations, everything a good patrolman should know."

Barton celebrated the chief's teetotaling, nonsmoking manner. She meticulously detailed his developing plans for a hardline traffic safety campaign aimed at slashing alcohol- and speed-related deaths. Barton also cheered the chief's nickname: Two Gun Davis. Some might see negative inferences in the sobriquet, but Barton's fawning profile illustrated how Davis understood how to exploit it for his own benefit.

"Physically, he might be the writer's ideal of a chief of police," Barton marveled. "Big. Powerful. Broad-shouldered. Eyes blue and keen; thick wavy hair, turning slightly gray, although he is only forty-four. He gives orders crisply and unhesitatingly. You know he is running things."

## A Self-Educated Man

Just a week before the *Times* published Barton's profile, Davis met with Leon Lewis, a lawyer who founded the Los Angeles Jewish Community Relations Committee, and launched a network of private spies investigating anti-Semitic movements and subversive, sometimes violent plots involving Nazi agents and sympathizers in Southern California. Introduced by another Jewish activist, Lewis visited the chief at his office to apprise him of his investigation. There, he formed quite a different opinion of the chief than Barton. He wasn't impressed.

"He is a self-educated man who likes to hear himself talk, uses long sentences and unnecessarily big words," Lewis said in a memorandum he wrote immediately after leaving Davis's office. "What literature or communications he may have received in regard to Hitlerism were undoubtedly of Nazi origin. He has no true conception of the reasons for the development of Anti-Semitism in Germany; and has no true conception of the dangers to the community of an aroused class hatred."

Lewis hoped Davis would see the seriousness of the Nazi threat. He wanted the chief to understand that German agents were engaged in subversive activity in Los Angeles and other nearby cities and asked that he be allowed to coordinate with LAPD Red Squad Captain William "Red" Hynes, who, Lewis had learned, was also investigating suspected Nazi activity in the city. (Hynes was himself notorious for his sometimes violent, legally questionable pursuit of suspected Communists, and he was believed sympathetic toward far-right extremists.)

Davis immediately stopped Lewis and told him that not only would he make no progress with the police but also Davis could even understand Adolf Hitler's reasoning. After he interrupted Lewis, Davis prattled on about how it was the police department's duty to protect both life and property. Germany, Davis said, had been "forced" to turn to Hitler because the Nazi leader understood, in Davis's interpretation, that "the Germans could not compete economically with the Jews in Germany."

Davis continued to lecture Lewis but never committed himself one way or another on the question of police assisting his investigation. Lewis eventually secured access to LAPD files about a Nazi-aligned group known as the Friends of New Germany through other means, but that morning he could not prevail upon Davis's sense of patriotism, even though he was a former US Army captain who had served in Europe and chaired the local American Legion's Americanization committee. Lewis told the chief that the information he was ready to share with the police would make clear "the anti-American purposes of the leaders of the Nazi group both here and generally throughout the country, and that their efforts to create fascist action in the U.S. *was* an attack on life and property."

Davis didn't want to hear it. "He replied that there was a far greater menace to life in L.A. from the Communists and that is why they had to have a Red Squad," Lewis reported.

Two Gun Davis had barely been back at the chief's desk before making his agenda clear. Nothing would be more important to him than stopping the Communist threat, real or imagined—not even stopping Nazis.

# PART II

# FUEL

In 1933 America was in an expectant mood: great urgencies of the hour were expected to break forth at any moment as political miracles. The atmosphere was charged with Utopian excitement, and many strange economic and political revelations bubbled to the surface of American life.

—Carey McWilliams, *It Can Happen Here*

# 5 | RED DUST, RED MENACE

THE SKY DARKENED. DESICCATED topsoil swept skyward from fore-closed farms. Useless barns and rotten lean-tos groaned, rattled, and cracked against blasts of dirt, dust, and debris. Deep maroon clouds whipped across hundreds of miles of prairie, roiling and churning as they towered high enough to veil the sun.

Radios fell silent. Anyone brave, foolish, or unlucky enough to be on the road turned on their headlights. It didn't matter if it was the middle of an April afternoon. It could have been midnight.

Houses quaked. Women and children inside stuffed wet towels under doors and along windowsills. Still the dust entered. Men spat. A gritty paste cut their tongues and scoured their lips. City dwellers saw dust rip the paint off cars. Country farmers watched emaciated livestock suffocate. Parched crops withered.

"Our cotton would be about five or six inches tall, and it looked like a fire had gone over that field of cotton," Vera Ruth Woodall Criswell said about her and her family's experiences in Texas and Oklahoma and their migration to California via Arizona, as part of a 1981 oral history project.

A decadelong drought that began in 1930 became a nearly continent-wide environmental catastrophe. Though worsened by the dry weather, the disaster largely emerged from industrialized farming practices that radically altered the agricultural landscape of North America's Great Plains in the late 1910s and 1920s. The World War had ravaged European farms, especially those in France and Belgium. After it ended, fields that had been fertile before the conflict were

71

left gouged by trenches, laced with barbed wire, and polluted with lead and spent gas canisters, to say nothing of bodies and blood.

As Europeans recovered, Americans saw opportunity, but it came at a cost. From the Dakotas to Texas and the Ozarks to the Rockies, American farmers mechanized their operations. Instead of plowing their fields with draft animals, they used tractors that could more quickly cover far larger areas. Able to cultivate more land than ever and enticed by skyrocketing prices for annual crops like wheat and cotton, farmers changed the very nature of the land they tilled. First, they removed the region's native perennial grasses so they could plant even larger fields, then they stopped rotating crops each season. Their harvests were commodities now. To keep the most valuable of these producing year-round, they even stopped regularly letting fields lie fallow so they could plant and plant and plant the same crops as fast as possible.

Without the reparative time such fallow periods enabled, the land recovered fewer nutrients each season. Never particularly deep to begin with, the topsoil thinned. Tractors and harvesters flung it around with each pass. Each new layer of dirt exposed to the air oxidized what phosphorous, nitrogen, and potassium that layer contained.

Then came the drought and a series of heat waves. Voided of nutrients and loosened by the continual turnover, the soil baked into a powdery dust. Once upon a time, stands of trees and other vegetation blocked the wind; now, with the land having long since been cleared to make way for more farms, nothing stopped the wind from roaring across the plains, carrying with it the now rootless dust that tore and gouged and scoured the exposed land. Each windstorm, each season worsened the cycle.

Less productive than ever, farms grew costlier to operate. It became nearly impossible to generate a profit. Those farmers who did still own land sold it at a fraction of what it had cost them to manage it. The tractors and other modern farm implements were also far more expensive than horses and donkeys. Farmers took out loans or mortgaged their farms to pay for the new equipment. Some sold their property and then leased back the land. Those who turned to leasing their farms could not turn enough of a profit from their crops to afford the rent, while those who'd mortgaged their farms could not keep up with payments. Just as reckless and predatory financial practices preceded the economic collapse, these storms were neither inevitable nor wholly unpredictable. Their ravages were not felt equally at all levels of society.

Farming practices and technology that once seemed innovative intersected with inopportune climatological conditions to create a geographically—if not socially—enormous disaster that rendered North America's midsection into the infamous Dust Bowl.

Punishing winds further stripped the threadbare prairies, scoured already battered farms, and swept what little soil remained into black, churning towers of dust. The otherworldly clouds barreled through Midwestern cities and blanketed a swath of the country so wide that, in some cases, skies darkened above cities for more than a thousand miles.

If the storms happened early enough in the year and the cotton was still young, farmers could plant new crops in place of the dead plants, but the window was narrow. Crisswell remembered seeing entire fields destroyed. Local storms were enough to destroy crops, but they were nothing like the calamitous ones that whipped across the Oklahoma and Kansas prairies into Texas. The dust left behind was inescapable.

"You'd try to eat and you'd find grit in your food," she said. "It was terrible, really. Sometimes this would wipe out a whole month's work. When it was gone, you'd have to start over."

Drought and dust intertwined as an environmental catastrophe unparalleled by any yet experienced in US history and made tangible the disastrous maelstrom of forces roiling America. They further eroded the nation's economy, upended livelihoods, and scattered hundreds of thousands of people throughout the continent. Conditions only worsened as desperate farmers worked the already overstrained land yet further, leaving only when they'd coaxed the very last bit of productivity from the soil. If not a wholly human-caused calamity, this disaster was accelerated by society and, in turn, made those who fled the Dust Bowl some of the twentieth century's first environmental refugees.

## The Cultured Farm Boy

While California reluctantly absorbed tens of thousands of these and other refugees and migrants, Claude McCracken planned a move to Alturas, about three hundred miles north of McCracken's current home in Sacramento. A publication that billed itself as "A New Deal Newspaper" needed a new editor, and McCracken, a diehard Democrat and lifelong newsman, thought it sounded like a perfect fit for him. McCracken's decision would prove fateful and, ultimately, fatal.

McCracken was born in North Carolina but grew up in Omholt, Montana, just south of the Marias River on the northwestern edge of the Great Plains. He was the kind of kid who organized a literary society with other teenage farmhands and won debates about the role of religion in civilization, but though he was once praised by the *Conrad Independent* as "a fine example of the cultured type of farm boys," he also knew his way around his dad's hog farm, where to hold his catcher's mitt when a leftie was at the plate, and how to deliver a punch in a boxing ring.

Whereas Gertrude French reveled in her family's Modoc County roots, McCracken left Montana as soon as he was old enough and started a life of near-constant movement. French built her identity as a "native" Californian. She was a Native Daughter and also involved with pioneer societies, the chamber of commerce, women's groups, and even the local and state Republican Party central committees, all of which tightened her California ties. McCracken, by contrast, spent much of his life and career bouncing from town to town, assignment to assignment, job to job.

However, McCracken and French shared a passion for newspapering. McCracken helped out at a community paper as a teen in Montana and then spent much of the 1920s and 1930s reporting, editing, or otherwise contributing to a number of newspapers throughout the country. Where French proudly worked at the *Plaindealer* her entire career, McCracken never seemed satisfied staying in one place too long. After high school, his byline appeared on news articles, sports pages, and mastheads throughout the western United States and beyond. He was also a lifelong Democrat who coordinated the Carbon County, Utah, office of New York governor Al Smith's 1928 presidential campaign, worked as the *Salt Lake City Tribune*'s news correspondent in the city of Price, and edited the local *Price News Advocate*.

McCracken stayed in Price long enough to meet and marry Frances Edna Dunn, a nurse who frequently traveled to western Nevada to treat patients on the Goshute tribal reservation. When other assignments beckoned McCracken, she stayed behind, at least in the beginning. She was as committed to nursing as McCracken was to reporting.

New gigs took McCracken to Wyoming, Sacramento, and, for six months in 1931, El Paso, Texas. There, he frequently traveled across the border to Juárez,

Mexico, to help set up a local English-language radio station and interview former Mexican guerillas for a book he was writing about early-twentieth-century revolutionary Pancho Villa. None of that, though, would impress Gertrude French. Instead, she treated her fellow journalist's rootless path as one of many reasons her beloved Alturas community should not trust him.

Though McCracken was still based in Sacramento when he was offered the job in Modoc County, he contributed to newspapers in other parts of the western United States. His multicolumn stories covered such urgently important subjects as the Grand Tetons' endemic coney, related to the rabbit; hitching a ride on the first airplane flight out of Jackson Hole, Wyoming—"Jackson to Victor in thirteen minutes! Victor to Jackson in the same time! Dreams come true"—and the moment he nearly severed his thumb while chopping wood. The breezy, slightly humorous style that included himself tangentially was fairly typical of McCracken's style.

McCracken detoured from newspaper work for a few years in the 1920s when he played catcher for the Ogden Gunners, a baseball team that played in the independent Idaho-Utah League, and then traveled around the Midwest as the minor league Indianapolis Indians' publicist, but despite his sports experience and light feature writing, McCracken was unabashedly political. He didn't presume the kind of reportorial distance and studied objectivity that became journalism's norm as the twentieth century progressed. Instead, he exemplified a vanishing iteration of journalists open with their political inclinations and affiliations. In that, McCracken was of a piece with French, though their inclinations and affiliations seldom, if ever, overlapped.

In early 1934 *Modoc County Times* editor and publisher R. R. Anderson sold his stake in the paper to Charles Fitzpatrick, and Fitzpatrick, in turn, gave ownership to his son Delbert as a twentieth birthday gift. Delbert lacked newspaper experience, so he looked out of town for an editor to help him run the *Times* and, that April, hired McCracken.

McCracken quickly emmeshed himself in Modoc County society. Bringing along his unapologetic loyalty to President Roosevelt and the New Deal, he also quickly joined various county boards affiliated with the administration's new programs. McCracken even organized a regional baseball league with Jake Sharp—Sheriff Sharp's brother and Modoc County district attorney—and other prominent Alturan Democrats (including A. K. Wylie, who would run against and defeat Jake Sharp in the upcoming district attorney race).

McCracken's arrival coincided with a particularly difficult period of French's life. Colonel Thompson, French's friend and mentor, was on his deathbed and would die by the end of May. French was among those by his side when the colonel passed. Afterward, French coordinated tributes from the colonel's friends to print in the paper she'd inherited from him, but the most glowing reflection that appeared in the *Plaindealer* arguably was her own.

"There was no better nor more eloquent writer in the United States, according to the opinion of the editor of this paper than Col. Wm. Thompson," French wrote in her announcement of Thompson's death.

Earlier in the piece, French described Thompson as "a true builder of the west" whose newspaper pieces "were all meant to convey a message." Naturally, that included the colonel's 1931 rejection of Peter Schonchin and Thompson's exhortations about the "true history" of the Modoc War and the "savage" people the army quelled to pacify the region. French lamented Thompson's passing by quoting what she called the "literary beauty" of a memoir Thompson wrote about the war. Tellingly, the excerpt she chose was a florid concluding passage describing the murder of General Canby as a "demonic" betrayal of Canby's civilized peace mission.

"There lay the noble Canby, prone upon his face, cold and still in death; having breasted the storm of many a well fought field to fall at last by the treacherous assassin hand of a savage to whom he had come on a mission of peace and friendship," Thompson wrote, as quoted by French.

Twenty years earlier, when he sold his stake in the *Plaindealer* to Gertrude and her husband, Thompson had already passed the baton of conveying the message of Modoc County's origins and place in America to her. Now, in memorializing Thompson alongside reminiscences from other "men of the Old West" who were, one stressed, "bound by ties, by traditions, often stronger than those of blood," she implicitly bound herself as well in a responsibility to shape Modoc County's sense of itself.

Thompson departed just as McCracken drifted into Alturas. Gertrude had lost her mentor and a link to her heritage even as this utterly unknown newcomer arrived and immediately elbowed into the local newspaper business. Who would protect Modoc County's legacy by distilling its true identity if someone else was, as she saw it, actively trying to redefine that legacy?

McCracken's headfirst dive into civic life in Modoc County—which included his own bylined tributes to the colonel—rankled French. At first the *Plaindealer* covered its competition diplomatically, but within a month of McCracken's arrival French started publishing columns and editorials attacking the *Modoc County Times*'s coverage of local (and sometimes national) politics. The attacks often obliquely (and later directly) targeted McCracken and took on personal tones not reflected in the *Times*, which throughout 1934 never mentioned the name of its more established competitor.

French seemed to believe the strength of the forces holding an individual to a place or community indicated the value society placed in that individual. It indicated trust in that person, or a sort of social credit. If you were known, you were accountable, and if you were accountable, you were less likely to threaten those around you.

On the other hand, the rootless, unfamiliar, and foreign were inherently untrustworthy. If you were not known, how could you be *known*? How could you be trusted if there was no one to vouch for you? This didn't mean one had to be known literally. Established institutions and organizations as well as informal associations—ties and traditions stronger than blood—served as proxies for direct interpersonal relationships.

Family bonds *did* still matter. In a sense, by adopting Gertrude after her mother died, R. C. Dorris thus maintained Gertrude's legitimacy within Alturas's founding family and underscored for Gertrude the weight one's familial bonds could carry if cultivated. It was a lesson that may very well have informed French's commitment to the Native Daughters of the Golden West, whose entire existence was based on heritage and inheritance. Similarly, Colonel Thompson's employment of French at the *Plaindealer* had been a sort of professional adoption of the young woman. Gertrude, in turn, committed herself to the newspaper, to newspapers as an institution, to the community of Modoc War veterans of which Thompson considered himself a member, to Alturas's early-twentieth-century business community, and to the idea that Thompson and the Dorrises and everyone else who had been involved in "taming" the Modoc people and the land where they lived, then building a new and prosperous civilization, were the truest and most deserving of California's multitudes.

It's conceivable, therefore, that French saw the combination of Claude McCracken's arrival atop the *Modoc Times* masthead and the colonel's death as interconnected tragedies that threatened *her* Alturas and *her* California. Having worked at so many different newspapers in so many states, McCracken was himself a sort of drifter—perhaps even worse, a drifter of his own making, not unlike a train-hopping hobo vagabonding from city to city—whose outspoken political views only heightened his contrasts with French. These contrasts would only sharpen in the coming years as French attacked McCracken, McCracken counterattacked, and each wound up on different sides of a battle over who was, and who wasn't, allowed to seek the California dream.

## Two Gun Davis's Second Shot

At the other end of California, James Davis was all but settled into his new old job. He realized he could combine his love for firearms, his insistence that officers serving under him knew how to shoot well, and the police department's need for favorable publicity by enhancing the Los Angeles Police Revolver and Athletic Club. Davis had helped establish the club, nestled in the hills of Elysian Park just northwest of downtown Los Angeles, in the late 1920s as a private recreational facility and shooting range.

Now that he was back atop the department, Davis transformed the club into his department's primary training facility. After Los Angeles hosted the Olympic Games in 1932, buildings that had been part of the Olympic Village were even transferred to Elysian Park for the facility's use. Davis would eventually make it the home of Los Angeles's West Point for law enforcement training, the Los Angeles Police Academy. Meanwhile, the clubhouse—whose rooms Davis offered as meeting space for civic groups like Los Angeles's Native Daughters organization and other groups—became the epicenter for Davis's effort to cultivate powerful allies for his fight against subversives.

Even with all the other uses Davis found for the clubhouse, it was still first and foremost a shooting range. True to his nickname, Two Gun Davis had made firearms training one of his first priorities for the LAPD after he originally became its chief. Besides instituting the aforementioned bonuses and fines based on officers' marksmanship performance, he also made the shooting ranges a de facto stage for various PR stunts that involved shooting, such as holiday turkey shoots and the same kind of high-profile marksmanship competitions of which he and his department's best shots were frequently champions. The most memorable stunts, though, involved trick shooting, especially one favorite gimmick.

Chief Davis—or another of his crack shots—would place a lit cigarette into a subordinate's mouth (though occasionally a nervous public figure), walk across the range, raise a loaded pistol, and aim it at the smoldering cigarette.

Then the shooter waited.

The audience fell silent.

The volunteer stood still.

No one moved, not even the volunteer, not even as glowing embers approached his lips. Everyone waited. The only thing that seemed to move, if only slightly, was the cigarette's tip, the glow of its red ash pulsing with each breath the volunteer took.

Finally, the shooter's finger flexed.

BAM! The bullet struck. Out went the flame. Up went the cheers. The smoldering cigarette disintegrated in one explosive but controlled instant. Not so much as a smudge appeared on the smoker's lips.

Mary June Barton vividly described one of these sessions. It wasn't simply a trick, she wrote. Davis was demonstrating his exacting precision as well as illustrating to the public the kind of precision he exacted from his subordinates. "Davis did not become a crack marksman for stage purposes; he became an expert because he knew it would make him a better policeman," Barton wrote.

True as that may have been, the cigarette trick and other shooting demonstrations exemplified a subtle theatricality underlying Davis's public persona of disinterested restraint. Over the next four years, Davis would cultivate a visage of power coupled with the kind of reserve and propriety he believed would prevail in an orderly society. Such a society was unsullied by the misfits, vagrants, and subversives Davis detested. Through breakfast talks presented to women's groups meeting at his club, fervent keynote addresses at policing conventions about the intersection of crime and subversion, and dramatic busts orchestrated to capture headlines, the chief demonstrated a new appreciation for how his image as a law enforcer was as important, if not more so, than the substance of policing actions. A well-trained, uniformed policeman blasting a cigarette to shreds without singeing the man smoking it, while society women gasped in awe, powerfully distilled that image.

Two Gun Davis's police department was powerful. His police department was orderly, meticulous, and controlled. His officers were protectors of a civilized "white spot" constantly threatened by barbarians in every direction. They kept a vigilant watch, aware these enemies could strike at any time and certain they would exploit any subversive tide that Davis and his guardians of peace and security could not stem.

## "The Enemy Within Our Gates"

One evening at the end of February 1934, Louise Ward Watkins finally returned to her Pasadena, California, home and reflected on a long, event-filled day. She was surprised to realize how invigorated she felt after yet another day racing here and there through Los Angeles, getting what felt like very little done.

A busy schedule was typical for Watkins. Her father had moved the family to California so he could serve as a vice president of Los Angeles railway pioneer Henry Huntington's firm. By the mid-1930s she had become a powerful Los Angeles conservative activist and speaker in her own right. With that power came frequent tedium. Most days felt like a blur of luncheons, meetings for various club boards of directors upon which she sat, and a cycle of obligatory social functions that never seemed to actually accomplish something. In a time when President Roosevelt and his administration seemed to be unraveling everything Watkins believed in and everything the country had built while imperiling freedom itself, Watkins felt increasingly frustrated.

Watkins loathed inaction, especially now, when the specter of Communism stretched ever more ominously toward California. Ill omens were appearing all over the country in 1934, especially in the Golden State, where unions were organizing, a former socialist (Upton Sinclair) was talking about ending poverty and running for governor as a Democrat, and California taxpayers seemed to be paying to feed and house what seemed like an ever-higher share of other states' castoffs. It could feel taxing to constantly warn other citizens about the Red threat and other ills and to make sure that the groups she served stayed solvent and on track, but Watkins knew it had to be done.

Watkins had spent February crisscrossing Los Angeles for various engagements and finished the month with a board meeting of the Friday Morning Club, where she was president, before a driver raced her across the city to Hollywood. There, Watkins was slated to speak at a lunchtime banquet at the Spanish-style headquarters of the Women's Club of Hollywood.

Busy as all that had been, when the day was over, Watkins filled every bit of the brief six free lines her Ward "A Line a Day" diary afforded. One thought captured how she felt best. Events that afternoon had left Watkins feeling a sense of "unexpected pleasure" that still lingered at the end of the night, when she finally picked up the diary and started writing.

Getting yet another chance to speak to Tinseltown women about pervasive Communism and "The Enemy Behind the Gates" probably wasn't enough to produce such satisfaction in Watkins. Maybe it had something to do with the man with whom she'd shared the stage: a man, Watkins knew, who seemed as certain as she was that California seethed with Red interlopers: James Edgar Davis.

The Hollywood Women's Club had invited Chief Davis to talk about automobile safety, but once he was on stage he couldn't avoid talking about Communists, his favorite bogeymen, especially now that he could amplify Watkins's comments. The pair already knew one another. They frequently shared appearances at Southern California civic events throughout 1934 and 1935 as each railed against Communist designs on California and the United States.

Davis *did* have a keen interest in traffic safety to accompany his politics, but even though that was the subject the club wanted addressed, Watkins had teed him up perfectly to veer off script. Revolutionaries, Davis cautioned that afternoon, aimed to turn the country's "high born women" into "playthings." He knew his audience, and, like Watkins, he implored them to act, lest they become Communist prey.

"Americans are asleep," he warned. "They should not forsake the principles on which this country was founded."

Davis pleaded for Hollywood's leading ladies—at least those women who spent their mornings and luncheons on Los Angeles's club circuit—to help save democracy. A year earlier, the *Los Angeles Times*'s Harry Carr had again lauded Los Angeles as the "white spot on the map." Riff-raff now blemished that reputation, Davis lamented. The chief appealed to the audience's sense of civic duty and patriotism to enlist their help cleaning up the city—and America.

Watkins shared Davis's aggressive, fear-stoking style. Castigating pacifist sentiments in a rearming world—not to be confused with her belief in a defensive but isolationist foreign policy—Watkins labeled "Sovietism" as "the greatest danger at hand." In an earlier iteration of the anti-intellectualism dominating twenty-first-century conservatism, Watkins told the Hollywood clubwomen that this danger was spreading "through the schools, on the lecture platform and through organizations of superior-sounding names" and that "too much attention has been given Henry L. Mencken, Sinclair Lewis, and others of the 'intelligentsia' and not enough to the principles of the constitution."

Each speaker impressed the other. After clubgoers, as Watkins reflected, "grilled" the pair, Chief Davis offered her a ride back to downtown Los Angeles for a visit to his office. Watkins sent her driver home, then joined Davis in his car.

Perhaps they followed Hollywood Boulevard eastward to Los Feliz, turning onto Sunset Boulevard and cruising through Silver Lake and Echo Park until climbing the hills above the city center. Or maybe they wove northeastward through the neighborhood streets, tracing the undulating spine of the Hollywood Hills before connecting with Sunset. Regardless, the two titans of Los Angeles antiradicalism had an important stop to make before Davis's office: the police pistol range in Elysian Park.

The facility was deeply important to both driver and passenger. Watkins frequently lamented days she couldn't get there to fire at least a few rounds of target practice at the range, which sometime seemed like Davis's sixth child. Watkins and Davis each believed well-armed civilians would be necessary as a bulwark against the imminent Communist threat they perceived.

Watkins enjoyed Davis's company and his shared ideals, but it turned out the true thrill of that day was still ahead. He had a surprise for Watkins in his office at the Hall of Justice. They left the range, traveled downtown, and went up to Davis's office. There, the chief cemented Watkins's status as a fellow defender of Los Angeles's social order: a real LAPD badge to go along with his and the city's Board of Police Commissioners' designation of Watkins as an honorary policewoman.

Davis frequently presented such honorary police titles and badges to influential locals in recognition of civic service, or, more often, in exchange for social and political favors. He also purportedly sold these badges for patronage. Nevertheless, that afternoon, Davis clearly recognized Watkins's shared commitment to his antiradical cause. That recognition pleased her.

Watkins's pleasure seemed to linger the next day. When she returned to the diary that night, she wrote of the day as a "summery" beginning to March. She'd exhibited little haste to start her usually overcrowded schedule and instead "sat and dreamed a good deal," finished little work of any significance, then went shopping in the afternoon, had clothes mended, and stopped in for tea with her mother, who was ill. Despite her fellow Americans possibly being asleep to the menace of Communism, Louise Ward Watkins did not seem especially stirred to service on that, her first day as an honorary policewoman.

Watkins made up for her respite in the months and years to come. In speech after speech, she and Davis repeated claims of Communists hiding around every corner, preying on schoolchildren and masking criminal plots in progressive agendas. Aside from stopping Communists and quelling labor uprisings, Davis prioritized appealing to influential women like Watkins for their support of him and his department. Mary Barton's profile of Davis in 1933 had been one piece of that effort. Regular speaking engagements like the one at the Hollywood Women's Club, where he could address and maybe impress the wives, mothers, daughters, and sisters of Los Angeles's business and political leaders, were also integral.

Many clubs gave Davis speaking time in exchange for him allowing them to use space at his police clubhouse in Elysian Park, though he also addressed events elsewhere. As had been the case at that event alongside Watkins, these talks were usually billed as addressing more pedestrian topics like traffic safety or protecting oneself against theft and other crimes, but they almost always turned into sermons about dangers like the "threatening menace of radicalism." At least as far as events at the pistol range's facilities were concerned, the talks also gave Davis and his officers frequent opportunities to show off to the women attending, either by demonstrating tricks like Davis's beloved cigarette-shooting stunt or hands-on instruction in how to shoot competently.

"The police really take unusual pains with the untrained civilian when he comes to their firing line," remarked writer Gordon Ray Young in a 1936 piece for the National Rifle Association's monthly *American Rifleman* magazine about how Davis's police department was encouraging the "right kind of citizens" to learn how to properly use firearms. "National title holders and other expert marksmen often come up to the baffled beginner, and without introducing themselves show him what is wrong with his hold and position . . . and often as not, the civilian doesn't know that he has received instruction from one of the best shots in the country."

Davis didn't reserve his warnings about Red plots for speeches at women's groups, but he enjoyed the moments when the wives and daughters of Los Angeles's political and business elites focused on him. He might show off his own shooting prowess or, as was often the case, use subordinates' skilled marksmanship to underscore the training and discipline he prided himself for instilling. Then there usually was a chance for Davis or whatever top marks-man was performing on a given day to let the clubwomen fire some shots of their own, which often meant actually placing the women's hands on gun stocks and positioning their bodies to best absorb the concussive force of their weapons' recoil.

These events may have given Davis credible excuses to spend time in intimate proximity with women who were not his wife, but they also stoked the nativist fires that aligned with his and Mayor Shaw's political agenda. These clubs were perfect venues for Davis, Watkins, and their allies to mask their reactionary pushback against migrants, civil libertarians, government watchdogs, labor groups, and any other critic by labeling it as "Americanism" or "patriotism." Further, Davis simultaneously cultivated future vigilantes, as long as they were well trained and had the proper character.

"However, permission to use the police range does not by any means permit a man to pack a gun," concluded *American Rifleman's* piece. "That is given only when a man is qualified by character, and the nature of his work requires

Police Captain R. R. McDonald with Barbara Whittaker, Louise Ward Watkins, Elizabeth Kromer, and Mable Patton at a shooting range in Los Angeles, 1935. *Courtesy of Los Angeles Times Photograph Collection, Special Collections, Charles E. Young Research Library, UCLA*

it. Chief Davis recognizes the fact that in the nature of things each and every citizen is himself something of a peace officer, in that under the law he is empowered to arrest any person detected in the act of committing a felony."

Long the influential Friday Morning Club's president, Watkins insisted that her club's members shared the sense of urgency she felt about the imminent subversive threat and arranged for the organization to hold its weekly meetings at the Elysian Park police clubhouse. Watkins believed that skillful, armed self-defense was nothing less than a civic necessity. She wanted club members to practice shooting after each week's meeting. Many LAPD officers were recognized as some of the best shots in the world, and, aside from the various shooting demonstrations, it was common for any marksmen who happened to be around to offer informal pointers to club members.

Watkins believed an armed showdown with Communists was possible, perhaps even likely. Patriotic women had to be ready to fight. It was these women's duty to fight if called to do so. Far too much was at stake for the families who built Los Angeles, or for that matter, anyone who cared about the city, California, or America, to count solely upon police to protect them.

"The society women of California are not leaving all the shooting to the veterans," wrote J. B. Matthews and R. E. Shallcross in their 1935 *Partners in Plunder: The Cost of Business Dictatorship*, adding the observation that "vigilante activities are commonplace affairs in the State of California today whenever organized labor attempts to win for itself tolerable living conditions."

Labor was indeed making such an attempt in 1934, which naturally concerned people like Watkins and Davis. Then, that June, California's state of affairs was further upended by Governor James Rolph's sudden death. Republican Lieutenant Governor Frank Merriam of Long Beach—a coastal metropolis just next door to Los Angeles—succeeded Rolph. Merriam instantly became a leading candidate in the upcoming gubernatorial race. He also faced a crisis almost immediately.

Merriam became governor right as a simmering conflict between San Francisco waterfront workers and shipping companies exploded. After their union was unable to come to satisfactory contract terms with their employers, the dockworkers went on strike. Other unions launched a broader general strike in support. The ensuing work stoppage paralyzed the Bay Area.

Pressured to act before labor unrest spread throughout the state, Merriam deployed National Guard troops to San Francisco to end the strike. Cargo operations in San Francisco soon resumed, but a divided California prepared for more drama. An already chaotic election cycle was about to get more dramatic.

That summer, Democrats voting in California's primary elections would surprise the nation by nominating Upton Sinclair, an author who'd previously run for the US Senate as a Socialist but was now running as a Democrat and promoting a movement known as End Poverty in California, or EPIC.

Sinclair's candidacy deeply divided the state's Democrats. Sinclair lost, but not necessarily because voters preferred Merriam. Nearly 13 percent of voters instead opted for Raymond Haight, a more moderate candidate running on the Progressive Party ticket—enough that, if combined with the almost 37 percent share Sinclair claimed, Merriam may have lost.

Despite his loss, Sinclair's EPIC movement drew extensive support throughout California and highlighted green shoots of progressivism growing throughout the state yet still obscured by the conservative forces controlling power centers in Sacramento, San Francisco, and Los Angeles. EPIC supporters even won many down-ballot races, including two in Los Angeles: City Councilor Parley P. Christensen and State Assemblyman Augustus Hawkins.

None of the potentially transformative events of 1934 that so worried police, right-wing orators, and conservative leaders had come to pass. But to justify their alarmism, those individuals still pointed to the mere potential for strikes and insurgent campaigns to cause disruption, even as the ongoing Dust Bowl conditions and lingering Depression remained a far more tangible, more immediate threat to the United States. Nevertheless, Louise Ward Watkins and Chief Davis sensed an opportunity in the heightened sense of alert.

# 6 | STATE OF EMERGENCY

CHIEF DAVIS AND HIS SON saw so many boxcars overflowing with hobos that they almost lost count—train after train after train, with 100, maybe 150, people packed inside. And those were just the people they could see in the open boxcar doors. Who knows how many more vagrants were onboard those trains? There were thousands upon thousands altogether, and Davis knew they were all going exactly the same place he was: California.

In late September 1934 Davis took his son along on a trip to Washington, DC, where the elder Davis was to attend the annual conference of the International Association of Chiefs of Police. There, Davis wasn't a planned speaker, but he hoped he might get an opportunity to join other big city police chiefs in advocating for a nationalized system of policing that did away with small town departments altogether and implemented a more military-like set of standards for law enforcement throughout the country.

Meanwhile, right up until election day, Frank Merriam's surrogates alleged that if Upton Sinclair were to win, huge numbers of unemployed migrants from throughout the country would descend on California with their hands out. Even the mere potential of a Sinclair victory had lured many, they warned, as did the possibility of other midterm election results that might give Roosevelt more sway in Congress. As the election approached and he was back in California, Davis made a series of presentations using the migrants he'd witnessed to warn of dire days ahead.

Late that October, Louise Ward Watkins invited Davis to speak to an audience of three hundred Friday Morning Club members assembled at the

Elysian Park shooting range about the Communist threat. "This is the most strategic point in all America just now for the Communist and all other kinds of radicalism and they are coming here by the hundreds," Watkins said, with the *Times* adding that Californians "must protect the State now from a continuance of the influx."

Davis, who'd brought a treasury of Communist paraphernalia seized by his officers to show club members, told them about seeing so many boxcars on his drive home that he estimated that 150,000 indigent migrants would come to the Golden State that winter in search of jobs and may turn to crime if they couldn't find any. Davis also agreed to an interview by an anti-Sinclair group called the California Crusaders (a meeting of whose Watkins urged Friday Morning Club members to attend after Davis's presentation), in which he warned of a migrant invasion already taking place in California.

"The numbers of people invading Southern California this fall exceeds anything known in the history of our police department," Davis said in the interview, as quoted by the *San Pedro News-Pilot*. "Let me explain—in good years and bad, we have normally 40,000 so-called shiftless migratory indigents, harmless, harmful, and occasionally vicious men flocking to California for the winter. This year the numbers of this type already are several times that amount."

Davis claimed that rapidly increasing numbers of transients were causing crime to rise in every major California city. When Davis had called for nationalized policing at the conference he attended in Washington, he'd claimed that doing so would limit political influences on law enforcement. Now Davis was on a speaking circuit (among other presentations Davis gave that week was one titled "Treason from Within"), fearmongering about the possible impact to California if its voters elected the wrong person as governor.

Despite Merriam's victory, Democrats had gained ground nationally. Concerned that Roosevelt's plans to expand on his New Deal program might soften the ground for Communist activity, Louise Ward Watkins got to work. In December she returned to the Elysian Park range, having assembled fifteen like-minded women to found a new explicitly anti-Communist woman's organization, Americans Incorporated (though press about the organization's launch in late 1934 uses that name—which was also used by a national far-right organization that shared many of the same anti-Communist talking points—future references describe Watkins's organization as American Women, Inc.).

The new group wouldn't simply be another stop on the luncheon and lecture circuit; instead, it was a militant, almost paramilitary response to the Communist encroachment Watkins feared. Aside from regular shooting practice, the new club required members to learn how to shoot and defend themselves and their country.

"This is not a social organization, for we are engaged in something dangerous and women elected to membership must be prepared to be on the firing line," she stressed.

Not unexpectedly, the new club antagonized progressive figures in Southern California. One was Kate Crane Gartz, a San Gabriel Valley heiress with Socialist leanings who sent Watkins a letter dismissing the new club. Gartz described the pistol range as "a very appropriate place for belligerents to meet."

Watkins welcomed Gartz's characterization of her and her new club. Instead of ignoring the criticism, she read Gartz's letter at the club's introductory meeting. She was unapologetic about Americans Incorporated's purpose in her public reply to Gartz.

"We are belligerent," Watkins said, "and we are fighting to protect our youth. We feel there should be a close connection between the youth of this country and this group."

The club launched with Watkins as its new president, with other prominent women joining its roster of officers and charter members. There were also three honorary founding members: Margaret Kerr, who led a Communist-hunting organization known as Better America Foundation; Dr. Frederick Woellner, a University of California, Los Angeles professor of education and "Americanist" whose anti-Communist speeches and appearances often shared the same bill as Chief Davis and Watkins; and Davis, who also spoke at the group's inaugural meeting. The last two, being men, were otherwise ineligible for membership.

Watkins launched Americans Incorporated as ascendant dictatorships in Europe and Asia closed 1934 by revving their war machines. Regimes in Italy, Germany, and Japan shared anti-Communist fervor, mythologized visions of glories past, and authoritarianism masked as appeals to law and order. Steeped in militaristic pageantry, these regimes seized upon popular anxiety, solemnly promised to protect and sustain anxious citizens, then deftly crafted propaganda that defined who were citizens and who should be excluded from citizenry, forcefully if necessary, to protect that citizenry and their institutions.

All shared passionate, almost messianic visions of an approaching all-out war on Communism.

The bylaws of Americans Incorporated shared a similar vision. They detailed the club's purpose as "advancement of Americanism through patriotic education and by exposing, and aggressively opposing, Communistic and other seditious activities which are determined to undermine and eventually destroy this nation." That term *other seditious activities* meant the club had significant room in the future for determining its enemies, depending on how it might later define *sedition*.

Governor Merriam began his new term with welcome news for Chief Davis: an invitation to elected officials and law enforcement professionals from throughout the western United States to a region-wide anticrime conference to be held in Sacramento in 1935.

The proposed conference was envisioned by the California Peace Officers' Association (CPOA), which was led by Chief Davis, Los Angeles County Sheriff Eugene Biscailuz, and chiefs of police from the Bay Area and Sacramento. That meant that the organization was especially effective in lobbying for the kind of big city law enforcement priorities Davis had promoted when he went to Washington. It also left smaller, rural California jurisdictions—especially most of the state's sheriff's departments—resentful of the CPOA.

The CPOA promoted an anticrime agenda that echoed Davis's antimigrant, antisubversive fearmongering. Though the organization presented itself as a professional association, its officers and members shared Davis's extreme anti-Communist politics. Much of its 1930s-era literature framed law enforcement as California's front line in a war on Communism already underway. Thus, its leaders and their political allies envisioned the Western States Anti-Crime Conference as much as an opportunity to identify, recruit, and inspire collaborators in their antisubversive war as a politically disengaged strategy session for better protecting the West's residents from criminals.

The earlier annual conference of the International Association of Chiefs of Police notwithstanding, *this* proposed CPOA event was designed to position California as a counterweight to Washington, with Merriam at the forefront. Its organizers wanted the conference to dovetail with concerted efforts by California and its neighbors to preserve law and order, which, they believed, were under assault by forces nurtured by FDR's New Deal policies. Throughout 1934, public clamoring for decisive action on crime grew, as widely publicized, often brutally violent crimes were covered by newspapers that tended to focus on high-profile gangsters.

Newspapers stoked the outrage with this coverage even as they demanded decisive action to stop crime. Editorials decried politicians and activists who slowed police down by dithering over constitutionality, legal complications, and jurisdictional issues. The press continued to churn out articles filled with dramatic, gory details of violent crimes alongside stories about public demands to end them. As Merriam's call for the conference solidified into actual planning, papers endorsed the streamlining of law enforcement, which was expected to be the event's focus.

One such paper was the *Bakersfield Californian*, published in the inland oil and agriculture boomtown at the southern end of California's fertile San Joaquin Valley. The *Californian* urged readers to fully support Merriam's plans and "every movement to reduce crime." It argued that state lines and jurisdictional restraints gave criminals "gateways of safety" that were made more accessible by modern automobiles' faster-than-ever transportation. The conference, the editorial continued, could inspire western states to work together to reduce red tape and "see to it that these gates are closed, or that they do not become the entrance to safety zones."

Bakersfield was the seat of Kern County, a major destination for Dust Bowl migrants, and its leading newspaper was clamoring for measures that might strengthen the Golden State's porous borders. Support from such a community for the planned anticrime conference and associated measures promoted by Los Angeles and San Francisco emboldened people like James Davis as they prepared for the conference. The conference and the publicity sure to accompany it would allow them to define a different kind of criminal threat to the Golden State.

The year foreshadowed a dark future and set the stage for a global war against fascism, but it began with Davis and his colleagues still using the specter of Communism, not fascism, to spook Californians. The enemies they saw over the horizon were Communists. They were coming to California under the guise of indigency and desperation, demanding relief, better working conditions, and "civil liberties" while hiding criminality, pestilence, and disorder in ever-swelling numbers. Davis insisted that he and the police force under his command must be ready to stop this perceived enemy infiltration even if nobody else was willing to help.

A bust of Theodore Roosevelt, an idiosyncratic metal duck, and a miniature suit of armor atop Davis's desk, as well as a wall full of shooting trophies won by the LAPD pistol team, all spoke to a subtle shift in Davis's work by the outset of 1935. In his first stint as chief, he might have tried to maintain the modesty and selfless sobriety of his upbringing, but his office decor now suggested that he was relaxing into his lofty position. The scattershot arrangement of his desk spoke to a disorder for which the ever-in-control chief might have fined other police officers. Some of the knickknacks cluttering his office were probably even souvenirs of patronage paid by local business and civic leaders, but the patronage helped Davis feel comfortable about pressing them for support as he began work on his and the California Peace Officers' Association's plans to launch a statewide anticrime campaign alongside their proposed conference.

That January, Davis hosted the CPOA's board at the Elysian Park pistol range as they planned the Western States Anti-Crime Conference. They planned to maintain the event's ostensible focus on reducing crime in the eleven states they asked to participate, but they also made it clear that they intended to use the conference as a springboard for a targeted assault on Communism. The conference would be a venue for law enforcement to legitimize and justify even their most outrageous attempts to target subversive influences as well as to strategize on effectively fighting crime.

Though many in California shared Davis's loathing of the left, sustaining his campaign against it would still cost political capital. To earn that capital, Davis needed influential Californians on his side. While most public power in the Golden State was still wielded by men, the chief turned again to swaying the women he knew could influence the men he wanted to sway. This time, he asked the Native Daughters of the Golden West—the same organization of which Alturas's Gertrude French was so proud to be a member—to plan a luncheon at the range scheduled to coincide with the January planning meeting.

Involving the Native Daughters reengaged this still-prominent nativist group's statewide membership and particularly its many chapters north of Los Angeles. Davis's inchoate plans for a statewide anticrime campaign arguably required buy-in from organizations like the Native Daughters and its allied Native Sons of the Golden West. Native Daughters chapters weren't significant forces in Los Angeles and the rest of Southern California, unlike Watkins's Friday Morning Club and similar institutions, though such groups included members who also belonged to the Native Daughters. But the Native

Daughters and Native Sons chapters still actively participated in Northern and Central California's civic life, and their statewide reach made them more likely to influence distant corners of California than the CPOA could independently.

The rest of California resented Los Angeles's seemingly outsized influence in state affairs. Some who resided outside Los Angeles were even openly hostile toward the city and its institutions, regardless of which political party's members represented Los Angeles–area voters in Sacramento or Washington, DC. It didn't help that many of California's most powerful government posts were held by people from Los Angeles or its immediate vicinity, like Governor Merriam.

There was one other problem, especially where the question of migration to California entered the discussion. Merriam wasn't just a Southern Californian; he wasn't a native Californian at all. The governor had grown up in the Midwest. Then there was Frank Shaw—the mayor of Los Angeles was an erstwhile Canadian. He might not have even been in office legally, despite the hastily arranged recognition of his citizenship that the *Times* had facilitated. How could any of these people really have California's interests in mind if they weren't even from the state?

Nevertheless, Davis could still count on the Native Daughters' fear of Communism. Even the Native Daughters believed that Communists threatened California's safety even more imminently than the barrage of outsiders trying to move to the state. Davis of course could also effectively exploit their xenophobia by suggesting that foreign Communists were infiltrating the state to foment revolution.

Davis's pitch to the Native Daughters and elsewhere was simple, if repetitive of warnings to other groups at other times: Danger loomed over California. Only loyal patriots willing to cooperate with law enforcement could stop the Communist agents who planned to subvert the state, the nation, and democracy. Nothing short of a war against radicalism could save the Golden State.

Davis shifted the Los Angeles Police Department's tack in 1935. The previous year, he'd sanctioned LAPD Red Squad commander Captain William "Red" Hynes from the police department to work as a private antiunion enforcer (albeit one paid in part through a confidential and untracked police secret fund) and other strategies targeting Los Angeles's labor movement. Davis certainly did not soften on labor, but this year he reinforced the LAPD's role as an antimigrant, antipoverty vanguard protecting Los Angeles.

Part of that shift meant he and his department continued their emphasis on fighting back the migrant invasion Davis had claimed he'd seen on its way that fall when he drove back from Washington, DC. It also often involved justifying aggressive policing with overtly racist rhetoric, wildly inflated statistics about Communism's spread, and poorly substantiated claims about subversive influences in schools and other public institutions. In part, the anticrime conference operationalized and amplified years of right-wing rhetoric about the risk migrant aid and other public relief posed and the criminal tide surging toward California that at best masked revolutionary infiltrators and at worst was part of a larger conspiracy.

Meanwhile, in courting the Native Daughters ahead of the anticrime conference, Davis aligned himself with an organization that promoted a racialized ideal of Californian purity. The Native Daughters and its counterpart Native Sons of the Golden West linked citizenship tightly with ethnic identity. By the 1920s these groups had honed decades of anti-Asian hate into advocacy for xenophobic restrictions that specifically excluded immigrants from around the Pacific Rim.

A decade later, the *Grizzly Bear*—the official publication of both Golden West organizations—amplified nativist fears of what the magazine warned in a headline would be a FLOOD OF 100,000 ASIATICS if the United States granted statehood to the territory of Hawaii. Through an essay submitted by the California Joint Immigration Committee, which lobbied against Asian integration into California society and civic life and of which the Native Sons was a member, the *Grizzly Bear* said Congress's preliminary discussions of potential Hawaiian statehood threatened national security due to Hawaii's large population of residents from Japan or of Japanese descent. The committee and its allies alleged that these residents were secretly plotting to infiltrate America and that if allowed to become citizens their loyalties would be split between the United States and the emperor of Japan. They explicitly linked race and citizenship by arguing that people of Japanese descent were biologically predisposed to betray the United States if necessary.

"While American-born Japanese who have renounced Japanese citizenship may desire to be loyal Americans, not many could oppose the interests of Japan if there were trouble with that nation," the committee wrote as an organization in a January 1936 column printed by the *Grizzly Bear*.

In making citizenship conditional on adherence to subjective American values, nativists overlapped with reactionaries who identified with a similar movement known as Americanism. There was a key difference, though: many Americanists' ideological considerations surpassed their ethnic priorities. Americanists readily exploited existing ethnic tropes to stoke public anxiety, most often by alleging Jewish machinations behind purported Communist plots to topple democracy. But some, like Louise Ward Watkins, welcomed intercultural exchange so long as foreign entities shared the Americanists' pro-capitalist "civilized" ideals.

Watkins did not share the anti-Japanese prejudices of nativists with whom she might have otherwise aligned herself. Throughout the 1930s, Watkins—who was extremely fond of Japanese culture—participated in cross-cultural exchanges with Japanese American community members and related organizations. She even joined and became president of the Japanese American Society. Watkins welcomed opportunities to hear from Japanese diplomats and other dignitaries from the East Asian empire. Sometimes, this even meant inviting speakers to the Friday Morning Club to defend Japan's ongoing occupation of Chinese territory, as she'd done in 1932, shortly after Japan occupied Shanghai.

Perhaps in appreciation of the Japanese government's stated justifications that its increasingly noisy saber rattling was first and foremost an anti-Communist endeavor, Watkins staunchly if perhaps obliquely supported Japan's policy toward China. As that occupation simmered near all-out war that risked US intervention, Watkins promoted an isolationist but heavily armed defensive posture for the United States. In advocating for the United States to stay out of any war that would pit it against anti-Communist forces (regardless of how superficial those aims often proved to be), Watkins effectively added an international component to the militaristic, armed preparations she was trying to inculcate in members of the Friday Morning Club and American Women, Inc.

## The Nexis of Crime

Watkins was about to have a new example to point to in her warnings of approaching revolution. By spring 1935 much of the United States had moved on from the panic over rising crime that peaked with the previous year's clamor for streamlined law enforcement. Americans instead fretted about the worsening plight of Dust Bowl refugees and other migrants and debated the Roosevelt administration's plans for a second, more ambitious set of New Deal reforms poised to reshape the US government's role in society.

At the end of March the Western States Anti-Crime Conference finally began. Despite the public's shifting national focus, more than one thousand police, sheriffs and deputies, district attorneys, and other law enforcement professionals from eleven western states descended upon Sacramento for the event. The conference still included much of the advertised discussion of improving cooperation between law enforcement agencies across state lines, removing jurisdictional barriers, realizing the potential for technology like two-way radios to revolutionize policing, and promoting fingerprint registration drives. Attendees still believed that a crime wave plagued the West and that only interstate solutions could stop it.

Even as the broader attention to crime that spiked the previous year now seemed to be waning nationwide, rhetoric from the conference's speakers stoked an atmosphere of urgent crisis caused by the crime wave and contributing factors like migration. Officials like Governor Merriam and Chief Davis could use this sense of emergency to persuade the public that only extensive, immediate, perhaps even audacious police and government responses could help. They could capitalize on this sense of emergency to pressure legislators to take action against crime while presenting ideas honed at the conference into policy proposals for specific actions the legislators could take against crime.

Newspapers extensively covered procedural aspects of the conference but also described its more political undertones. Multiple speakers, including Chief Davis, veered from addressing technical aspects of policing to stir up audience emotions. Davis, for example, said that "hundreds of thousands" of US schoolchildren were ceremonially stomping and spitting on the US flag, then replacing it with the "Red flag of communism."

More outrageously, Davis also claimed that the Soviet Union was secretly recruiting young, white college women to seduce African American university students to exploit racial discontent. Tugging at racist fears of miscegenation, Davis alleged that these disguised Soviet agents weaponized their sexuality and lured young men throughout California and beyond to move in with them. He claimed that the women would bring their prey to meetings of Communist cells that would then radicalize the young men and prod them to agitate for civil rights. Rather than ascribe any legitimacy to any demands for racial justice (to say nothing of accepting the reality of interracial romance),

Davis only saw collaboration and subversion from anyone who might make such demands.

The conference ended with organizers planning to keep up the event's momentum through regional "crime prevention" events held in cities throughout California. These events gave further floor space to speakers who'd participated in the Sacramento event while allowing the California Peace Officers' Association to build public support for the legislation and other initiatives it supported. It also allowed members like Chief Davis to further stir public fears of potential criminal threats, such as labor activism and the new wave of migration, which was feared as Roosevelt's New Deal spending shifted.

Deputy Chief Homer Cross was selected to direct the first such event in Los Angeles, scheduled for April and just two weeks after the Sacramento event. Cross, a veteran of the World War, wrote to the heads of local patriotic and civic groups to invite them to participate. He told these organizations that the CPOA believed there was a "crying need" to promote American ideals to constrain subversive elements intent on using violence to overthrow the government. Every one of the association's members, he wrote, was dedicated to making the public aware of these dangerous forces and, as a key aspect of crime prevention, how to fight them.

"It is [the CPOA members'] purpose to portray those un-American forces which appear to be making great progress in the execution of their plans to bring about chaotic social conditions inimical to the welfare of the people of this commonwealth," wrote Cross, who served on the California Peace Officers' Association's crime prevention committee, in the forward of the manual on subversive activity that it released on January 20, 1935, the same day that CPOA leaders met at Elysian Park to establish plans for the Western States Anti-Crime Conference.

Cross repeated the statement in a written invitation to the Los Angeles event sent to Leon Lewis, then the head of the Americanism chapter of the Disabled American Veterans and the same man who in 1933 had urged Davis not to ignore Nazis and their allies in the LAPD's antisubversive efforts. Cross's invitation that April alarmed Lewis, who warned that the California Peace Officers' Association might be "abused" by anti-Semitic movements that "often masquerade under the smokescreen of anti-Communism."

The association, Lewis wrote, also risked amplifying stereotypes of Jews as Communists. He cautioned that a manual on subversive activities produced by the association might bias new police recruits' training, while its encouragement for police to cooperate with any organization fighting Communism might mean overlooking dangerous tendencies of white supremacist and Nazi sympathizers "and in fact any racketeer or pseudo-patriotic (but actually anti-Semitic) group or organization."

Meanwhile, California Republican Party members were meeting just a few blocks away from the anticrime conference the same week. While attendees of the law enforcement conference heard about what Davis called the "nexis" of Communism and crime, the state's GOP establishment—many of whom also participated in the anticrime conference—amplified attacks on President Roosevelt. On the same day that Davis delivered his speech about young women making revolutionaries out of Black men and disguised Communist schoolteachers indoctrinating children, former President Herbert Hoover was at the Republican event railing against FDR.

"Before us is the sink into which first one great nation after another abroad is falling," Hoover declared. "The freedom of men to think, to act, to achieve, is now being hampered."

Hoover lamented the emergence in Washington, DC, of what he called an "enormous bureaucracy" that, he claimed, established giant government-run monopolies to compete with private enterprise. "Small businessmen have been disabled and crushed," Hoover said. "Class conflicts have been created and embittered. The government has gone into business in competition with its citizens. Citizens have been coerced, threatened, and penalized for offenses unknown to all our concepts of liberty."

Some saw Hoover's speech as indicating that he would seek a rematch against the man who knocked him out of the White House, but he quickly quelled such talk. Still, like Davis's warnings about the indigent "invasion" had for Merriam's campaign, the Republican event and its proximity to the anticrime conference previewed the tack the party would take against Roosevelt in the coming year. It also underscored how closely coordinated law enforcement and right-wing politics were while highlighting how readily the GOP flirted with outright authoritarianism.

One of the primary initiatives that emerged from the conference was a plan Davis and his fellow conference organizers had been working on for months: a centralized California state police force in California. The CPOA and the California Taxpayers' Association lobbied state legislators to pass a law to authorize such a force. They argued that it would standardize law enforcement throughout California. Among other things, a statewide police force might save taxpayers money by making law enforcement in the state more efficient. They also argued that sheriffs were more easily susceptible to political influence as elected officials. Crime prevention required consistent, objective enforcement of the law that was not at risk of changing every election cycle or because of a particularly influential individual or movement's pressure on politicians.

Most of the state's county sheriffs opposed the idea. They feared that such a force would shift the local power they held to high-ranking police from California's biggest cities. Moreover, the draft legislation exempted Los Angeles. Jurisdictions elsewhere would cede power to the state force while Los Angeles remained accountable only to itself. They also saw a risk of one kind of political influence replacing another if such a statewide force gave outsized power to urban law enforcement officials. Existing jurisdictional, legal, and constitutional constraints helped keep police accountable, they argued. How could police trained in Los Angeles or San Francisco and commanded by officers in Sacramento be trusted to fairly enforce the law for Californians who lived in vastly different places, like Needles, Tulare, or Yreka?

An unlikely alliance coalesced against the legislation. Sheriffs who didn't want to lose their regional fiefdoms joined civil libertarians (with whom sheriffs frequently clashed otherwise) who dreaded the potential consequences of centralizing armed police power under authority closely linked to the governor. United by their shared antipathy, these strange bedfellows defeated the legislation.

Press takeaways of the conference were largely receptive to the ideas discussed and thus legitimized the locked-down, besieged mentality the event and its organizers cultivated. The conference reinforced the idea that California was under constant attack from foreign, unfamiliar threats and that patriotic, law-abiding citizens needed to be vigilant. James Davis, Frank Shaw, and the Los Angeles Chamber of Commerce would return repeatedly to that theme of a state under siege as they spent the rest of the year developing their most audacious scheme yet.

# 7 | SUNSET

FEW PRESIDENTS HAVE LEGACIES as physically tangible as Franklin Delano Roosevelt's. Americans today may not know the particulars of the New Deal or the rancorous politics from which they emerged, but it would be a safe bet to suggest that many, perhaps most, contemporary Americans recognize physical remnants of the program in their day-to-day lives.

Encouraged by their electoral success in the midterms, the Roosevelt administration and its Democratic allies in Congress prepared an even more dramatic set of initiatives to revamp the American economy. While cops and anti-Communists in the West converged on Sacramento for the anticrime conference, the White House readied sweeping expansions to the reforms it implemented when Roosevelt first took office. Just in time to lead into his first reelection campaign, this Second New Deal would launch two new programs set to massively shift American life: Social Security and the Works Progress Administration.

These new programs would also dramatically expand federal bureaucracy while shifting the existing bureaucracy's focus to preparations for the planned expansion. Preparations began with the White House commissioning a series of highly specific studies examining economic, demographic, and social conditions of the United States. The goal was to understand how Americans lived and worked halfway through the 1930s and how the first wave of New Deal programs affected their lives and jobs. Reports resulting from these studies detailed how local, state, and federal policies impacted life in the country and what conditions the programs the White House was developing might address. Transiency and migration were among the subjects these studies examined.

With the Roosevelt administration trumpeting the Second New Deal, it ran out the clock on earlier programs, like federal aid to transients, by the middle of 1935. When the Federal Emergency Relief Act was implemented during Roosevelt's frenetic first one hundred days as president, Congress included a sunset provision. If legislators chose not to renew the law by 1935, the federal government would be forced to shut down the programs the act funded. Congress didn't renew the law, and the White House didn't lobby it to do so, leaving the Federal Transient Service among those programs that would lapse. The White House knew that shutting down the FTS would destabilize the country's transient population, but it gambled that this was a sacrifice worth making in order to launch the costly flagships of the Second New Deal.

With the FTS due to shut down, responsibility for providing relief to transients would shift from the federal government to states. Suddenly states had to figure out how to manage relief cases that had been handled by the FTS for two years. Debates over how to address the unexpected burden divided Californians and residents of many other states.

Suddenly the country's forty-eight states and more than three thousand counties would be tasked with creating many aid systems to manage this transitory segment's needs. A web of fractured, imbalanced, and inconsistent bureaucracy existed, as cities, counties, and states blamed one another for shirking their responsibilities to provide aid. As anti-indigent relief measures emerged, most of the opposition to them didn't come from people concerned about transients' and migrants' essential humanity. Rather, critics of these measures feared that the FTS and FERA shutdowns might cause relief claims to surge as officials passed transients from jurisdiction to jurisdiction, tossing the burden to provide relief across borders.

Dust, drought, and the Depression didn't ease just because of policy shifts. California still expected thousands of relief seekers every year. Now, with federal relief unavailable and residency requirements stricter, even migrants who hadn't originally intended to become transients might have to leave communities where they'd initially settled and relocate elsewhere for work or other means to support themselves and their families. In so doing, these migrants would reinforce perceptions of themselves as drifting, rootless populations with uncertain prospects. That rootlessness would only make securing relief more difficult in whatever the next community might be.

The Federal Transient Service's sudden liquidation made Dust Bowl refugees and other economically displaced people easy targets for local politicians and media. Few were enthusiastic about governments—local, state, or federal—paying for *any* aid, let alone for helping recent arrivals. County and state jurisdictions in many localities already struggled to meet existing relief needs before the FERA sunset; those in charge of these jurisdictions feared their already overburdened local aid schemes would collapse under what they saw as added pressure from migrant relief.

It didn't matter that Dust Bowl refugees weren't the only Americans migrating during the 1930s. Despite perceptions that the bulk of migration in this era originated from hard-hit states in the central United States and southern Great Plains, later research suggests that drought and displacement disrupted lives throughout the country. Tens of thousands of migrants *did* flee places like Oklahoma and Arkansas during the Great Depression, but over the same period, similar numbers were also migrating between other US states, neither leaving the Dust Bowl nor headed to the West Coast and thus complicating the picture of masses of people trudging toward the Pacific. Meanwhile, as those who once promoted the state's bounty scorned newcomers, many Californians also left the Golden State for other locales, becoming migrants themselves.

Wherever they came from, as migrants drifted through the country, uncertainty over how California would manage the many headed its way surged anew. The renewed anxiety gave Davis and his allies an ideal excuse for seeking new antitransient police powers. They could justify such powers by claiming that the migrant "influx" to California had reached emergency levels.

After the FTS shutdown, the same people who used the All-Year Club to advertise Southern California as an idyllic, bountiful destination accessible and productive in any season fretted that the wrong kind of people heard the message. Four years earlier Los Angeles's titans of business and media had led the deportation drive that sent hundreds of thousands of Mexican immigrants and Americans of Mexican descent to Mexico, ostensibly to make room to employ US citizens (*White* US citizens, of course). Now they claimed that the tide of migrants cresting the Sierra Nevada and Cascade ranges—many of whom replaced the labor of deported foreigners at far lower wages—threatened California.

Many of these new arrivals came from Oklahoma. Many did not. But they were collectively dismissed as Okies, no matter where they'd originated. The term otherized the migrants. Established Californians portrayed refugees swept by the era's assorted misfortunes into their state as criminal invaders bent on leaching California's abundance. In Los Angeles, Chief Davis, the chamber of commerce, and their allies realized the uncertainty caused by the FTS shutdown could be easily exploited. With state and local relief agencies scrambling to fill the void left by the federal government's sudden departure, they again argued that migrants might overtax public institutions. The risk, they insisted, was those left out of state-driven relief schemes would prey on local citizenry to survive.

Davis could now frame interstate migration as an immediate, existential threat that justified emergency powers to stop. Business leaders bought in because they expected the state and county to lean more heavily on them for tax revenue to fill funding gaps left by the federal government's withdrawal. Local governments couldn't simply respond to the federal shutdown by cutting relief themselves. As distasteful as Los Angeles reactionaries may have found public relief, they knew that directly targeting aid-seekers while the Depression persisted would be a public relations disaster. Instead, they could present themselves as advancing local interests by focusing on supposed dangers from afar. They could argue that a state struggling to manage relief for people who already lived within its borders shouldn't have to provide aid to residents of other states. If those states couldn't manage their own finances and aid their own people, why should that be California's responsibility?

The state's funding crisis persisted throughout the summer of 1935. By that fall, once the shutdown of FERA-funded programs was complete, the Los Angeles Chamber of Commerce dubbed transiency and funding for transient relief an outright emergency. This was a crisis, the chamber argued, that needed an immediate solution.

But first, in May, the California State Assembly took up the issue of transient relief in the state when it voted on a proposed Indigent Exclusion Act. One of the act's sponsors was Democrat William Moseley Jones. Jones had endorsed Upton Sinclair's EPIC movement in the 1934 election, but that spring he teamed up with Los Angeles Republican Kent Redwine on the new anti-indigent legislation.

Harry Chandler's *Los Angeles Times* leapt to the hometown legislators' corner (Moseley Jones technically represented Montebello, just east of Los Angeles), declaring that the problem of transient indigents had grown "so menacing" that their bill was an imperative. Citing a host of California and US Supreme Court decisions that the *Times* asserted gave California the right to exclude newcomers who might become public charges, the paper began to lay the groundwork to justify increasingly severe efforts to restrict immigration to California. The paper argued that indigent migrants could be excluded simply by expanding the purview of the state's existing agricultural inspection stations, thus associating transients with agricultural pests even as it likened them to already-excluded diseased and criminal migrants. "The ending of this menace admits of no delay, and the legislature should pass the Jones-Redwine bill promptly," the *Times*'s editorial page concluded.

The *Times* would have to wait nonetheless. The California State Assembly delivered on the request and passed the legislation, but the State Senate rejected it.

Jones's advocacy for the measure split the already-fracturing EPIC movement. Still, his support of the bill meant its opponents could not as easily dismiss it as right-wing, probusiness reactionaryism. On the other hand, his cosponsorship also meant that other supporters of criminalizing indigents could not as easily portray opponents of the legislation as succoring Communists.

## Going to War

With statewide action barring migrants from entering California no longer an option, Davis turned again to Deputy Chief Homer Cross for help. Together, they developed a plan for Los Angeles to act independently to keep transients out of the Golden State. Cross was a perfect complement to Davis. He was a loyal, if quiet, deputy who would readily take Davis's orders and not expect the chief to share the attention.

Cross and Davis approached the Los Angeles Chamber of Commerce to set up a new Committee on Indigent Alien Transients. This committee would operate as the privately run chamber's quasi-public response to the transient "emergency," but it would do so with Cross as the committee's chair, joined by representatives of other state and local government agencies.

The new committee defined such an "indigent alien transient" in deliberately vague terms. Anyone "entering the state of California without visible means of support and where residence is foreign to the state of California" would meet that definition and therefore be subject to the committee's emergency "solutions." The lack of specificity afforded the committee significant latitude in suppressing the indigent migration emergency it claimed existed. Tying indigence to the mere *appearance* of poverty assumed in one's lack of "visible means of support" enabled the committee to retain more options to block transient migration than had they provided more quantifiable definitions. Whether police or otherwise, authorities at California's borders could subjectively decide whom to allow into the state and whom to block, then point at the committee's fungible language to support any assessment they made.

The committee thus provided a veneer of legitimacy to expressions of California exceptionalism. Terms like *foreign* and *alien* reinforced suggestions that rather than being one of forty-eight constituents of the entity known as the United States of America, California was something more akin to a quasi nation-state. Defining residents of other states as *foreign* gave further weight to rhetoric about "invaders" and "barbarian hordes," about "influx," "contagion," and "pathogen."

The Committee on Indigent Alien Transients included Cross and four other members: assistant Los Angeles city attorney Newton Kendall, Los Angeles County Department of Charities deputy superintendent Lawrence C. Schreiber, John O'Conor of the California State Relief Administration, and M. D. Benesh, a statistician in the Los Angeles County Sheriff's Department. Each was a relatively low-visibility envoy from state, local, and county agencies involved with indigent relief and law enforcement.

The relative anonymity of the committee members and the cross-jurisdictional perspective they represented allowed Davis, and the chamber of commerce's board of directors, distance from the measures the committee put forth and a credible argument that its members were experts on the subject. Davis could credibly claim to be responding to the emergency that this ostensibly independent body declared instead of appearing to dictate its existence. The distance gave him the cover he would need to crack down on Los Angeles's poorest residents along with the knowledge that Los Angeles's most powerful public and private institutions were behind him.

Confident in that support, Davis joined Deputy Chief Cross and the Los Angeles Chamber of Commerce in appealing to Los Angeles's police commission and city council to officially recognize the emergency conditions the Committee on Alien Transients had identified. That November, police commissioners endorsed Davis's plans to blockade California's borders come winter, when another tide of migrants traveling from colder climes was expected to reach the Golden State.

Among the institutions welcoming the plan was the *Los Angeles Times*, which invoked the fall of Rome as the committee issued its emergency declaration. As the sociologist Paul S. Taylor (also spouse of photographer Dorothea Lange, whose landmark images are among the most enduring ever produced of Dust Bowl America) noted at the time, such comparisons were a "common refrain" in that era.

Comparisons to Roman civilization would become a common theme in rhetoric surrounding the emergency and would continue once Davis and the LAPD launched the plan they were crafting in response to the migrant crisis. Los Angeles was Rome. Southern California, *maybe* the entirety of California, was the empire. Dust Bowl refugees were roaming barbarians. The police were the legionnaires at the empire's periphery, duty-bound to defend civilization itself.

Absent from the rhetoric for the moment was another fact: nearly all of California's leaders were themselves migrants. Los Angeles Mayor Frank Shaw was born in Canada and had spent portions of his life in Michigan, Colorado, and Missouri before reaching the Golden State. California Governor Frank Merriam might himself be dubbed an Okie. He began his career in the Sooner State and did not reach California until he was in his forties.

Then, of course, there was Davis. Columnists likening migrants to barbarians and invading hordes never seemed to bring up the chief's impoverished upbringing in Texas and Kentucky, nor his years of drifting as he sought lasting work. He certainly did not. If Davis's background was addressed at all, it was to illustrate how he found discipline and order, first in the army, then as a police officer, a career that also gave him a sense of purpose. Davis and his allies ignored the hypocrisy and used his history to paint a picture of a bootstrap-lifting, hardworking patriot dedicated to serving Los Angeles.

At the end of 1935, dangerous criminals clawed ever closer toward California. They approached the Golden State without hesitation, emboldened,

Davis and others suggested, by Communist conspirators to plunder the state's security and relative wealth. At least, that's what local chambers of commerce, major newspapers, police departments, and nativist societies claimed they saw as the year ended. They'd been saying that for years, in fact. Now it finally looked like someone was going to actually do something.

In December Chief Davis brought details of the proposed LAPD border patrol to the police commission. The commission, in turn, apprised Los Angeles's city council of the idea. Both the chief and the Los Angeles Chamber of Commerce wanted the city council to authorize a "prison camp where undesirable, indigent transients" could be placed if arrested for violating local or county ordinances. In 1927 when he was first chief, Davis had told the board of commissioners that the police department was holding people on suspicion of vagrancy to investigate them for other crimes. Similarly, he made it clear that the new war on "indigent alien transients" wasn't so much about managing the strain of relief infrastructures as it was about placing undesirable populations out of sight.

A migrant camp set up behind a Southern Pacific Railroad billboard. *Courtesy of the Library of Congress, Prints & Photographs Division, FSA/OWI Collection, LC-USF34-018515-E*

## A Different Emergency

While Davis and his allies honed the strategy for their war against Dust Bowl refugees, city, county, and state agencies, in addition to private charities and civic groups, scrambled to develop plans to fill the relief void left by the FTS shutdown. Some (though not all) of the social workers, charities, and staffers of these agencies were more sympathetic to migrants' circumstances. Instead of fearfully predicting havoc that migrants might wreak on California, these observers instead assessed what sort of havoc a transient existence might wreak on migrants.

"The conditions affecting transients in California were found to be so deplorable that it was felt the Commission and Administrator should immediately be cognizant of them," wrote California State Relief Administration director of special surveys and studies M. H. Lewis in the introduction of a report on transient conditions in the state as surveyed at the end of 1935 and the first two months of 1936.

Lewis implored state relief commissioners and the administrative staff he worked with to acknowledge that those horrible conditions constituted an emergency in their own right. That emergency required a response, but for reasons far different from those motivating the police department. In fact, the report from Lewis's organization—which wouldn't actually be published until nearly a year after Lewis's department started gathering data—claimed that the LAPD's yearslong war on vagrancy had exacerbated the deplorable conditions facing transients and migrants and that antivagrant policing should be counted among the "futile remedies" attempted for resolving California's transient aid crisis.

Whereas other cities relaxed their treatment of suspected vagrants during the Depression, Lewis explained, Los Angeles tightened enforcement. Often that had meant arresting anyone deemed suspicious whom police could charge with loitering in public parks or streets, with non-English speakers frequently singled out, even if they proved they had "plenty of money." Just as the Committee on Indigent Alien Transients tied enforcement of its antimigrant campaign to one's lack of "visible means of support," the LAPD long justified its arrests of suspected loiterers, Lewis noted, simply because "policemen thought they looked like vagrants" (to say nothing of the department's use of vagrancy laws to hold suspects ever since Davis first became chief).

While Deputy Chief Cross and the rest of the chamber of commerce's emergency council drew up plans for a blockade of California's state lines, Lewis's agency dispatched nine staffers throughout California. These investigators visited more than a dozen California cities to record the actual conditions transients faced. For six weeks, this team surveyed private charities and local public agencies providing aid to transients, visited jails, trawled "Hobo jungles" dotting creek beds and riverbanks, sat with transients at cafeterias, and took stock of attitudes at various other "non-constituted resources to which the transient might turn or which the community might provide."

None of the investigators' insights were available by the end of 1935, when the chamber's emergency council put the finishing touches on the border blockade. Instead, the findings wouldn't appear until nearly a year after the FTS shutdown when published in Lewis's August 1936 report. That was far too late, Lewis suggested in the report itself. The humanitarian crisis was growing much faster than any state and national officials could generate any responses, and those efforts underway to resolve the crisis were insufficient for the challenge.

"No doubt seeds have been sown that will bear fruit but the situation is so critical that each day's delay in the solution of the problem means untold suffering and misery for thousands of human beings," Lewis wrote.

Even though publication of the report was yet to come, the state relief commission gave Lewis permission to discuss the migration crisis with officials outside California. Such discussions might provide a fuller understanding of the transient crisis's dynamics beyond the state's borders, but they could provide nothing more. Lewis's colleagues could only talk about and catalog the misery they witnessed. Unable to act, investigators could only watch the crisis deepen by the day.

In California, police and border communities girded for the feared Okie onslaught. Meanwhile, actual Oklahomans were sorting out the aftermath of the Federal Transient Service's shutdown. Between 1935 and 1936, as many as fifteen thousand people passed through five transient camps in Oklahoma funded, in part, by the federal government. When the FTS closed, Oklahoma officials shifted relief spending from direct aid that wasn't tied to recipients' employment status to funding work relief programs via projects managed by the recently launched Works Progress Administration.

When the Second New Deal's 1935 implementation realigned how the federal government funded relief, budget priorities in states that depended on federal dollars to pay for their aid programs shifted dramatically and rapidly. By early February 1936, the same week that Davis would launch his blockade, all five transient camps in Oklahoma closed. Similar changes jolted tens of thousands of Americans from relief programs that had helped them survive the Depression.

"Families scattered, and discouraged men took to the highways, hoping for something to turn up," the *Daily Oklahoman* reported on February 4, 1936. "These transient camps were godsends to them. Many of them found new courage in the sheltered life of the closely-knit transient community and went forth to find jobs and start anew."

The same day that Oklahomans woke to newspaper articles about shattered, broken neighbors dispersed after the rare boon that the transient camps provided evaporated, residents of California's border communities woke to an alarming sight: armed police taking positions at nearby crossings and poised to stop anyone too poor from entering California, especially any of those Oklahomans scattered by the camps' closure but lucky enough to cross half a continent.

While state and local aid agencies in California, Oklahoma, and the forty-six other states were stagnating because of the shift in federal relief spending, the privately led Los Angeles Chamber of Commerce's emergency committee lacked the bureaucratic constraints of governmental agencies. Neither the chamber nor the Los Angeles Police Department were waiting for any other permission. They were ready to act. Two Gun Davis had his target in sight. In just a few short weeks, he would take his shot.

# PART III

# SPARK

Are these people riff-raff? Are they the almost unmitigated "moochers" that some declare? Are they an "invading horde of idle," as the newspapers call them? After having seen hundreds of them all the way from Yuma to Marysville, I cannot subscribe to this view. These people are victims of dust storms, of drought which preceded the dust, of protracted depression which preceded the drought.

—Paul S. Taylor, 1936

# 8 | THE GATE SLAMS SHUT

"TONIGHT'S STORY IS A TRUE STORY of one migratory indigent whose criminal career under a proper fingerprint and border patrol program might have been nipped in the bud." James Davis's words crackled across the airwaves. Ominous music swelled, then gave way to the urgent voice of Los Angeles Police Department Sergeant and radio dispatcher Jesse Rosenquist.

"Calling all cars! Calling all cars!"

On the evening of February 12, 1936, audiences on both coasts heard a specially produced, one-off live episode of Don Lee Broadcasting's *Calling All Cars* police drama. Hints of Davis's Texas drawl remained decades after he'd fled little Whitewright, but audiences, especially those tuned into Los Angeles's KNX, heard the authority in the police chief's voice addressing radio listeners in his adopted home, California, as if it were their duty to listen to him.

Davis helped create *Calling All Cars* in 1933 shortly after his reascent to the chief's office in 1933. The show was a pioneer in police dramas that reenacted stories based on real police investigations. Its source cases were typically ones that the LAPD had handled, and Davis typically hosted the show, though it occasionally featured guest hosts from other police departments whose cases were featured. Rosenquist was an actual dispatcher whose voice was used to heighten the immersion of each episode's opening.

Radio broadcasting had massively elevated public figures' platforms after its widespread commercial adoption in the 1920s and, by the '30s, was often used both to motivate audiences toward civic unity (e.g., Franklin Roosevelt's fireside chats) and to incite discontent and division (e.g., Father Charles Coughlin's popular anti-Semitic tirades). Radio had revolutionary potential, and Davis knew he could apply it to promote his vision of twentieth-century policing.

As he and Deputy Chief Cross put the finishing touches on the border patrol's deployment, Davis asked Don Lee Broadcasting and Rio Grande Oil, which sponsored *Calling All Cars*, to shuffle its programming, put together a special episode about migrant crime, and replace the already-produced show scheduled to air the second week of February with this one. Both agreed to the change, which was part of a public relations blitz Davis and the chamber of commerce launched to generate support for the blockade and, if necessary, to blunt pushback from city, county, and state officials.

The replacement *Calling All Cars* episode recounted the pursuit and arrest of Eddie Griffith who, Davis explains, was wanted for murdering an off-duty Seattle police officer before fleeing the state of Washington. Still carrying the murder weapon, Griffith hops a southbound train packed with migrant fruit-pickers. Disguising himself as one of the migrants, Griffith remains on board the train all the way to Los Angeles.

Griffith immediately launches a crime spree through the City of Angels. He steals cars, holds up mom-and-pop businesses, and assaults anyone who gets in his way. The remorseless killer enlists young low-level street toughs to help him pull off his crimes and charms young women with his ill-gotten gains. Two LAPD detectives close in on Griffith only for him to flee with two of the women he's lured. They reach a city in California's Central Valley, where Griffith's crime spree resumes until, finally, the detectives catch up with him.

It wouldn't have been an episode of *Calling All Cars* without unceasing crime solvers catching the villain, but this night's show was meant as a warning to law-abiding Californians. Griffith was Davis's ideal model for the kind of threat he insisted California faced if it kept its borders open to migrants: a one-time petty crook whose descent into depravity personified the chief's nightmare scenarios.

That was precisely the kind of danger that was disguised among the hobos and migrant laborers whom Californians had become so accustomed to seeing over the past six years of Depression, Davis warned. Sure, they might look innocent, downtrodden, desperate even, but should the city's guardians relax even a little, another Eddie Griffith might get through. Sinister people just like him were simply waiting for their chance to corrupt the city's daughters, enlist its troubled sons, and sack the Golden State.

But there was no Eddie Griffith. The character in Davis's radio morality play was an amalgam of various killers: parts of names, one criminal's age, another convict's hometown. Pieces of multiple stories showed up as details in "Griffith's" life. The episode's title, "Young Dillinger," was an unmistakable reference to the notorious gangster who'd died in a 1934 shootout with federal agents in Chicago even though this program was about a completely different criminal.

Before launching into his introduction of the replacement episode, Davis thanked Don Lee and Rio Grande for their "foresight and civic-mindedness" in airing it. That night's show had a dual purpose, Davis explained. He wanted his audience to know "what the migratory criminal problem really means to police agencies," and he implored those concerned about "peace and security" to understand that it was their "duty" to cooperate with police attempting to protect lives and property.

Though not real, Griffith embodied the evils against which the blockade was designed to protect. The hypothetical Griffith had not always been a killer; instead, Davis stressed, he'd started his sinister journey as a "typical migratory criminal." Corrupted by his transient existence, he'd murdered a cop, brought the gun he'd used for the crime into the Golden State, and immediately terrorized its residents.

"Although he was but twenty-three years of age, he came into California without any money, without any visible means of support, and, obviously, with no intention of working or giving to this state any service whatsoever in return for what it may give him," Davis warned.

The message was not subtle. Any one of the hundreds of people approaching the LAPD checkpoints at Hornbrook and Stronghold, Truckee and Needles, Blythe and Winterhaven could be another Griffith. They could be murderers planning rampages or thieves expecting to loot California of its largesse, but pretending to be migrant laborers and seasonal fruit-pickers.

The state needed the blockade. It needed the LAPD. It needed Davis's protection. Without them, it would get Griffiths and Dillingers.

## Outsiders

On the morning of February 3, 1936, squad upon squad of hand-picked officers hit the road, bound for frontiers hundreds of miles to the east and north of Los Angeles. Guided by meticulously outlined orders detailed in a memo from

Men board a freight car in Bakersfield, California. *National Youth Administration, courtesy of the Library of Congress, Prints & Photographs Division, LC-USZ62-97686*

Cross, the self-anointed vanguard began its mission to protect the Golden State from America's most wretched.

From Room 72 of Los Angeles's City Hall, police captain Clemence Horrall—a future police chief—managed a newly created command center for the blockade, known as "headquarters division." This nerve center coordinated the deployment's three large regional subunits: the Northern Division, comprising three counties bordering Oregon and a sliver of northern Nevada; the Central California Division, comprising four of eight counties adjacent to north-central Nevada; and the Southern Division, made up of the three large counties west of Arizona and the Las Vegas area of Nevada. Each was commanded by a lieutenant who reported to Horrall. These divisions were further split county-by-county with a separate police sergeant in each leading seven-officer squads assigned to sixteen highway and railroad points of entry into California.

Cross and Davis's orders outlined the deployment's administrative structure with exacting detail, but each squad—each individual officer participating in the blockade even—retained broad discretion in day-to-day conduct. Results were what mattered most, and officers were allowed to use whatever means they deemed necessary to achieve them.

"Individual initiative is encouraged to determine the proper modus operandi," the special orders instructed. In other words, it was up to officers to figure out how to enforce the blockade and stem the migrant tide, even if that meant that standard police practice must give way to them.

So amorphously had Davis and Cross outlined how officers should determine who to stop that the vagueness would be an asset when the blockade inevitably wound up in court. Without specifics to point to as circumventions of regulatory, legal, or constitutional constraints, opposing lawyers would struggle to find footholds against the blockade.

However, they were meticulous in what squad leaders were to do once people *were* stopped: shake them down for any weapons, take their fingerprints (with additional sets airmailed to the FBI and submitted to the local sheriff), contact headquarters division to determine if they're wanted anywhere else, and either take them into custody for evading railway fares if they have arrived by train, or, if they hitchhiked or walked across the border "without reasonable amount of funds," cite them for a penal code violation that would define them as "vagrants wandering from place to place without visible means of support."

Ten California counties, each hundreds of miles away from Los Angeles, would soon witness LAPD officers taking up positions within their boundaries. Among these were three northern counties bordering Oregon where forty-six officers were headed. Fourteen went to Del Norte County and split into two squads, one that drove up US Highway 101 as it hugged the last miles of coastline to the settlement of Smith River, California. The other turned onto California 199 just outside of Crescent City and drove northeast through a sea of massive redwood trees to an off-season cabin resort just south of the Oregon border and about twenty-five miles inland.

When off duty, they fished in the salmon-packed streams nearby or sat by a fire. When working, watches of two officers each half-heartedly scouted California 199 for what few transients might try to slink through the redwoods' shadows to invade the Golden State. They didn't even bother to stop cars during the blockade's first week. Instead, they focused on people entering the state on foot. But it was February. What few human settlements were in the area were spread far apart from one another, scattered amid the tributaries of the Smith

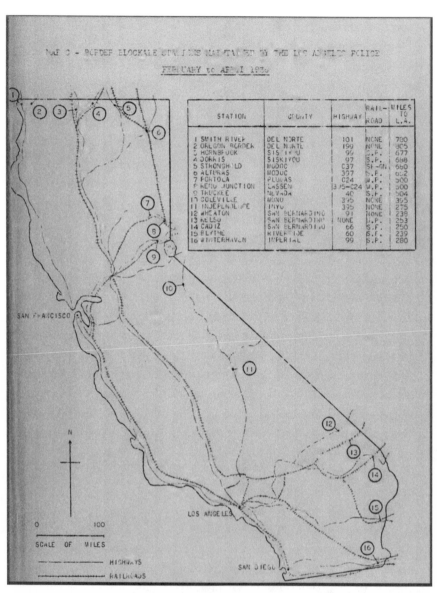

A map of the Los Angeles Police Department border blockade locations as presented in an August 1936 California State Relief Administration report. *Courtesy of the State of California*

River, the undulating hills of the Pacific Coast Range, and the evergreen canopy that shadowed it all. There weren't going to be many pedestrians.

Bored and far from home, when things got quiet, the officers practiced shooting, again and again and again. They knew how highly Chief Davis valued marksmanship, and they knew they could earn a few bucks extra if they shot well once they were back at the range in Los Angeles. Hell, they were already getting paid extra to come up here. Why not practice and maybe make a little bit more?

The officers in Del Norte told a state relief administration surveyor who visited them in February that they didn't want to spend off time in Crescent City or interact with locals. The Southern Californian lawmen knew as well as anyone that nobody who lived up here wanted them around. After initially signaling to Deputy Chief Cross that he'd deputize the border patrol, Del Norte County Sheriff Austin Huffman hesitated, then bowed out on the advice of his insurers. Huffman's rejection didn't deter the Los Angeles officers.

"[They] said they had a right to arrest anyone they wished, and quoted the common law that anyone may arrest a person whom he believes to be committing a crime," the state official later reported. "They were not clear as to what crimes any entering transient might be committing on the highway, but thought they might pick up a criminal. They believed the mere fact that 'they were stationed on the highways would keep criminals out of the State.'"

Two more squads drove to Siskiyou County, where they were more welcome than were their colleagues stationed in Del Norte County. One squad manned a highway checkpoint in the town of Dorris. Another was stationed in Hornbrook, which was located along the Southern Pacific Railroad and ideal for searching California-bound trains. Siskiyou's county seat, Yreka, also housed the northern area division headquarters.

Siskiyou County Sheriff W. G. Chandler agreed to deputize the officers, but Siskiyou's district attorney was hardly so amenable. "I thought there was something in the constitution referring to life, liberty, and the pursuit of happiness," the DA, coincidentally also named James Davis, said. Nevertheless, his protest was overruled by the county's board of supervisors, which approved Sheriff Chandler's cooperation with the *other* James Davis.

The debate may have been unnecessary. Bad weather in Siskiyou County left officers frequently idle. They spent much of the blockade's early days lingering by the fireplaces of the two-room cabins where each was lodged. When working, they focused on the train lines and ignored what few cars and trucks plied the highway, they told state investigators.

Those first days, the work was slow, but not completely. They told a state official that one day they'd taken a Washington State man with a criminal record into custody as a burglary suspect simply because he didn't have a job but had new shoes in a bundle he was carrying.

"The officers boasted that they knew how to make men tell the truth and that if they suspected a man of having a record, in 80 percent of the cases they were right," the state official reported, adding a detail about how they determined whether a person had a record that coincided with Chief Davis's own opinions about criminality. "They considered anyone to have had a record if they succeeded in making the person admit having been arrested on any charge, or ever having spent a night in jail."

The last northern area destination was Modoc County. There, Sergeant R. L. Bergman split the two squads he commanded between two checkpoints, one based out of Alturas to patrol the stretch of highway leading northwest from the town to the border crossing south of Klamath Falls, Oregon, and one tasked with checking trains just south of the border near the tiny community of Stronghold. With locals' advice, Bergman and his superiors had decided it would be a waste of resources to set up a third checkpoint at a crossing northeast of Alturas near the community of New Pine Creek, where the road was snowed in.

## A Citizen's Duty

Mrs. Frances Sweeney looked at the deep, dark purple ink staining her fingertips and stepped out of Sheriff Sharp's office. Once outside, she walked south, passed the colonnade of the Modoc County Courthouse, and turned right once she reached Carlos Street. Before she crossed Main, Sweeney glanced proudly at her smudged hands, then continued walking westward until she reached the Spanish revival building that housed the *Alturas Plaindealer*'s offices.

Gertrude and Bard French were busily recovering from putting out that week's edition of the paper, but they politely welcomed their unexpected visitor. A member of the local Townsend Club and an officer in the American Legion auxiliary, Sweeney excitedly displayed the souvenir of civic diligence on her digits. She had taken the advice printed in the paper just that morning for dutiful citizens to allow Sharp to take their fingerprints. Sweeney thought herself such a dutiful citizen, and she told Gertrude that with crime such a problem in California she knew she couldn't stand aside without doing her part to help stop it. Good citizens accepted the premise that they had their own roles to play in the war against crime.

French was pleased to hear about what Sweeney had done but then thought little more of it until she was finishing the next edition of the paper. After all, it had been a whirlwind of a week. Not only had she been named one of the newest board members at the chamber of commerce that week, she'd also just welcomed Sergeant Bergman and the rest of his officers into town. Only then did she recall what Sweeney said during her stopover.

"If they can prove you are a crook by your fingerprints they should also prove you aren't one by your fingerprints," Sweeney had said.

French had an idea. Maybe she could use Sweeney's visit to fill a little extra space in the Street Gleaning gossip column. The column usually padded the paper with stupid jokes about locals. This time French could use Sweeney's example to underscore both how pleased she was that her editorial had inspired her neighbor's civic-mindedness and how much excitement she knew Alturas was about to experience.

A dozen Los Angeles police officers had just arrived in town to help defend the California border. Thanks to Homer Cross, that very nice officer who'd come to town a few weeks earlier to start getting county officials and the press ready for the visit, French already had an interview with their commander scheduled. Now she could write up a little something about Sweeney's fingerprints and show the rest of the county, and everyone else in California, that her beloved community would do whatever it could to help protect the Golden State.

## The Work That Has to Be Done

John Sharp wasn't quite as excited about the blockade as French was. The sheriff might have been fine with the fingerprinting campaign as a useful tool to help with future investigations, but he wasn't at all pleased with the idea of police officers from Southern California harassing the people of his county. He certainly wasn't happy when he heard James Davis claim that sheriffs in every single border county in the state had signed on to the plan and agreed to deputize Davis's office. Sharp had done no such thing.

Whether James Davis was the head of California's largest police department didn't matter. He was acting like a bully and lying about what he was doing. He wasn't protecting California. Those folks down south could put as many pictures of farms and produce as they wanted on their tourist brochures about the Golden State, but that didn't mean they really understood the places that still resembled those pictures. Sharp was elected to protect Modoc County, not Los Angeles.

Davis's officers had been under Sharp's foot for a week when the sheriff finally wrote Davis a letter about why he was so upset. So far, none of the papers seemed to get what he was saying that entire time—not Gertrude French, not Claude McCracken, certainly not the *Los Angeles Times* or the *San Francisco Examiner*.

"I wish to make my position clear to you so that there will be no mis-understanding," Sharp wrote. "I do not believe that it is legal to stop itinerants from entering the state on the highways. My reason for refusing to deputize your men was because I do not want to place myself or this County in a position that would cause a lawsuit or trouble."

That was Sharp's "personal attitude," he told Davis. His "official attitude" on the matter seemed even more passionately felt.

"I have been deluged with complaints from citizens and taxpayers of this county in regard to your men taking the liberty to keep this class of people out of the county, due to the fact that this class of people are very necessary for the work, *chiefly ranch work* that has to be done."

True to his advice a decade earlier that the better businessman a sheriff is, the better a sheriff he will be, Sharp made it clear to Chief Davis just how intimately he understood Modoc County's demographics and business climate. He grew up in a ranching family and, as a rancher himself, knew that migratory labor was crucial to his county's economy. The sheriff explained that ranchers needed to import many laborers just to stay in business.

The letter seethed with exasperation toward Davis. He seemed to have had little patience for the public relations battle that Davis dragged him into. While the message was neither condescending nor impolite, the sheriff clearly chose his words with extreme care.

Sharp explained the nuances of Modoc County's geography to Davis and pointed out how its residents regularly traveled to nearby Oregon cities and loathed the idea of being stopped every time they crossed the border. Locals just weren't as complacent as the Los Angeles residents Chief Davis was used to.

"In fact, Chief you will find that the people here are quite different from the people in large cities in regard to police work," Sharp wrote. "They will not tolerate much restriction."

The sheriff wanted Davis's men out. He liked the ones he met—"They are a fine bunch," he wrote—and he even said he was upset about what he called "absolutely false" stories circulating of patrol officers in Modoc County mistreating locals. Nevertheless, they needed to leave, and, ideally, as inconspicuously as possible. Sharp resented the publicity he was already getting, and he didn't want it to persist or amplify.

It was, Sharp told Davis, a "very unfortunate" position for everyone involved, and he closed the letter acknowledging the crisis that had instigated the entire deployment. "Trusting you still see my position and hoping that in some other way I may help you to better the dire situation existing in your city," he wrote.

It's not clear whether Sharp attended Governor Merriam's Western States Anti-Crime Conference in Sacramento the previous year, or how involved he became in the ensuing debate over the proposed statewide police force, but his complaints about the L.A. officers' presence in Modoc County resembled the arguments his fellow sheriffs had made against that idea. They had depicted it as a dangerous power grab by California's big cities with potentially disastrous consequences for everyone else in the state. These counties featured significantly different social, economic, and demographic—not to mention, criminal—dynamics than in dense coastal and Central Valley cities. Sharp's letter stressed to Davis that he believed that his counterpart in Los Angeles similarly lacked awareness of the places where he'd sent his occupying police officers.

Davis didn't seem to care all that much, and Sharp could tell. The border patrol's deployment was proof that Davis didn't waste much energy listening to those who opposed him. Even when legitimately challenged, he opted to act first and deal with the consequences later. That's exactly what happened once he received Sharp's letter.

Sharp tended to treat Davis similarly to how one might treat a cranky child. Instead of blowing up, the sheriff simply ignored most of Davis's bluster. He didn't have any reason to think transients from out of state were more criminally inclined than any other California residents or transients originating from California who lived in other states.

"Insofar as the border blockade is concerned, I think it might be well if California rounded up all of her indigents in other states and brought them home before she tries to prevent unfortunates from other states from coming to California," Sharp told the *Sacramento Bee*. "I am a native of this state, but I am forced to admit that a fair percentage of all of the nation's unfortunates—particularly those found west of the Mississippi River—are natives of California and it's no more fair that we go and reclaim our own before we start trying to bar anyone else."

Sharp had taken a vastly different path into his law enforcement career than Davis had, but he had been doing the job almost as long. He resented Davis's refusal to pull the border patrol out of the county. So, that March, Sharp wrote a rare press release; in it, the sheriff raised the stakes with Davis. Not only did Davis need to cease claiming Modoc County as part of the area his officers patrolled, but also, Sharp announced, any tourist who might want to come to California would be allowed to enter by way of Modoc County. Visitors, the sheriff ensured, should feel safe in the knowledge that he would make sure "that their rights as citizens of the United States are not violated."

---

The sheriff's latest response to Chief Davis irked Gertrude French. He said he didn't want the press putting so much attention on Modoc County, and yet there he was writing press releases and making sarcastic statements to newspaper reporters.

Now the county was receiving plenty of coverage, that's for sure. It had been a long time since the rest of the country even acknowledged Modoc County in the press. The last, maybe only, time that newspapers all over the country mentioned the county was probably during the Modoc War. The only more recent instance might have been when French and Colonel William Thompson refreshed awareness of the region, memorialized the war, and unveiled the Native Daughters of the Golden West's monument to the US soldiers who gave their lives defending California. Now, it again fell upon French to demonstrate Alturas's—and Modoc County's—patriotism and civic-mindedness and to show the rest of the country that her community wanted to help protect the state from barbarism as much as any.

Five days before the border blockade began, the Alturas Chamber of Commerce's board of directors had elected French as one of its newest members. Fittingly, the arguments about the blockade and transiency that she printed in the *Plaindealer* largely echoed those made the previous fall by the chamber's counterpart in Los Angeles when it declared emergency conditions and set plans for the blockade in motion.

"If these itinerants are where they belong in their own states, they are eligible for government work," read an unbylined *Plaindealer* piece. "In other states they are objects of charity. Not only Los Angeles but Modoc county and all the other counties on the border will reach the point soon where they have no more to give them. Taxpayers all over the state are beginning to feel that charity is getting to be a burden which will eventually mean their own failure to carry on their business."

Sergeant Bergman had been clear with French when they talked at the Niles Hotel: his squads weren't in Modoc County to stop law-abiding travelers looking for opportunity; they were there because, he claimed, half of all the transients who came to California from other states were wanted criminals. If law-abiding Alturans like Frances Sweeney could be bothered to get their fingerprints taken, was it really a bother to at least get prints from everyone entering the state from who knows where in order to make sure they weren't wanted somewhere else, and if they were, to know exactly where that somewhere was and what they'd done? Bergman insisted that his officers wouldn't bother anyone who had "good reason" to cross the border or who "belonged" here.

The *Plaindealer* took it a step further than Bergman. Anyone too poor to meet California's residency requirements, let alone anyone stowing away on a train without a ticket, was breaking the law just coming into the state.

"Yet potentially all are law breakers by paying 'no fares,'" the *Plaindealer* wrote. "Los Angeles has given an answer to a query nearly every one has asked for some time now 'Why don't some one do something.' Well, Los Angeles, the main sufferer from penniless itinerants and criminals is doing something, or will if they are not prevented."

Why couldn't the sheriff recognize that Bergman and his squads were only trying to protect California and Modoc County? His father had helped "settle" the county, and he was a "native son." French wouldn't have been surprised if Claude McCracken had something to do with it. He was probably already looking for some way to twist his articles about the Los Angeles Police Department's presence at the county's border crossings into something negative. He was the Associated Press's local correspondent, so the stories that showed up in many other cities' papers about the blockade would have been written by McCracken. French would probably need to take care to review what ended up in some papers that used AP copy. It wouldn't do to have told Bergman that she represented the local press only to discover that her rivals' reports were what newspapers elsewhere in the country picked up, especially if Bergman or Davis or anyone else found anything in those stories that they didn't like.

While the blockade was in effect in Modoc County, much of the *Plaindealer*'s writing about the operation exhibited a practiced "we're waiting for more information" tone. It suggested readers not rush to judgment about the deployment. In an unbylined piece printed a day after the border patrol began, the paper suggested that other news reports had exaggerated Sharp's position and that while the sheriff refused to deputize Los Angeles's officers he still cooperated with them as much as he felt he could without getting Modoc County entangled in legal wrangling surrounding the deployment. Despite its insistence that it and the public wasn't sufficiently informed to render a judgment on the blockade, the paper nevertheless accepted Chief Davis and the Los Angeles Police Department's claims and justifications for the operation without skepticism:

> Were Modoc County located as is Los Angeles where it is a warm, winter climate and hundreds of people on the move were flocking in here where they could sleep outside but demand free food from charitable institutions: If of every three that came in, only one went away again and the crime wave arose out of all proportions to the general population even of that great city, would you not feel that to protect ourselves we should be entitled to stop the flow at the fountain head, if we paid the bill. There is now and has been for some time a population that is continually on the go by train, going nowhere and nothing to do and a whole lifetime to do it in. They purchase no tickets but hop aboard a train anywhere and any time, and go somewhere to be fed at the expense of state or county or citizens.

French could not conceive of any good reason why Sharp hadn't quickly deputized Bergman and his colleagues. They just needed to get on with their duties. French knew Sharp as a reasonable person and a savvy businessman. He was also independent-minded, so why would he have been swayed by McCracken or anyone else any more than by her or Chief Davis?

However Sharp came to his decision, it meant that the nation now looked toward Modoc County to see what he might do next. Thinking about how important it was that she take extra care to demonstrate that people in the county were dutiful when the state's safety was on the line, French took one last look at the galleys. She spied the bit she'd written about Sweeney's fingerprinting, cut it out, then swapped it with another chunk of text that was right next to her own story about the border patrol's arrival.

There—what a perfect place to underscore what civic duty looked like.

# 9 | IT CAN HAPPEN HERE

JOHN LANGAN WOKE BEFORE DAWN. Three days of stubble darkened his face. His khakis were crumpled. Dust covered his boots. He normally kept his dark brown hair slicked and combed close to his head, but on the morning of February 10, 1936, he didn't bother. He had to get out the door and back to Morris Sides's car. More than 200 miles lay between Cleator, Arizona, and the California border. Another 220 or so stretched from Blythe to Langan's home in East Hollywood. If he wanted to get home at a decent time, he and Sides needed to get on the road before the sun came up.

Langan and Sides got in the car, started the engine, and carefully navigated the clattering vehicle along the perilous twists and turns of Crown King Road and onto a paved highway, before finally heading out of Arizona. By about 5:00 AM, their car—covered in dust after a weekend at the mica mine north of Phoenix where Langan and Sides went to discuss a joint investment in the operation—reached the Colorado River and the approaches of the California-Arizona Bridge.

That's when Langan saw the police standing in front of an agricultural inspection station at one end of the bridge, waiting. He cursed. These weren't just any police officers. They weren't patrolmen from Blythe. They weren't Riverside County sheriff's deputies (not real ones, anyhow). Langan could be sure of that.

These were Los Angeles Police Department officers. They were half a day's drive from the city that paid their salaries. Langan could see them looking his way, peering across the Colorado, legionnaires at the edge of an empire scouting the horizon for vandals on the way to pillage their homeland.

That's clearly how they wished to be perceived, anyhow. For a week now, stories about Two Gun Davis's "bum blockade" had filled the papers. Just before they'd headed up to the mine that Friday, Langan and Sides might have even chuckled about the cartoon on the front page of the *Arizona Republic* depicting a "New Tourist Post Card" of California scenes, with images of a "new Los Angeles Chamber of Commerce map" showing the entirety of California and an inmate in jail stripes sketched breaking rocks under the watchful eye of a police officer as Los Angeles's new "Winter Sport."

Langan knew that these weren't actually vigilant sentinels guarding civilization. They sounded more like bored beat cops from the city who wanted to make some extra dough and maybe, if they were lucky, rough up a few hobos on the clock. Langan fumed as he and Sides approached the officers' checkpoint.

Sides told him to just give it up, not make trouble, and, he hoped, get the stop over with so they could get back on their way. A lot of road lay ahead, a lot of desert.

No. Langan wasn't going to just let the cops stop an American minding his own business in the middle of the country just because he *looked* like a bum to them. He had rights! The Constitution gave him rights. No. He wasn't going to cooperate.

Langan's simple decision to assert his rights likely meant more than he expected. It wouldn't just mean an uncomfortable day and—at best—a few hours in custody before he could sort everything out and get back to his family. By standing up against James Davis's border patrollers, Langan, a Hollywood dialogue director who'd long worked in theater and film, would cast himself a role in a drama that would topple—albeit not for another two years—Los Angeles's entire political power structure and destroy his family. (By the end of the year, he would add directing multiple plays for the Works Progress Administration–run Federal Theatre Project to his repertoire, with his first production a wildly popular adaptation of *It Can't Happen Here*, Sinclair Lewis's 1935 novel about a US senator turned fascist dictator.)

After stopping Langan, one of the officers began questioning him like he was a wanted criminal. The cop acted like Langan was one of the perps on that show on KNX where Chief Davis liked to stroke his own massive ego, *Calling All Cars*.

*What's your name? Where are you from? Do you have a job? Any money?*

*John Langan. I don't have to tell you anything else. What authority do you have? You can't just stop anyone because they look suspicious.*

The officer wasn't amused. He arrested Langan, took his fingerprints, and told him that he had a choice: either start answering questions or get the hell out of California. No, it didn't matter where he went. He just needed to get out.

Unlike other arrests by the border patrol, Langan's detention made some sense. Despite the likelihood that Davis made up or altered many of the statistics about violent drifters and criminal migrants to fit his aims, a bank robbery suspect also named John Langan had been on the run since the fall after an accomplice's body was found in a car in St. Louis. Police checking *this* John Langan's name against their criminal catalogs no doubt would have taken a second look at the file after reading about that case.

However, that theory doesn't really work out if one realizes that the border patrollers would have to have known in the first place that the passenger in Sides's car was indeed named John Langan before stopping him. Meanwhile, Davis had ordered the patrollers to use their discretion when making stops. Langan was dirty and disheveled from the weekend spent at the mine, and Sides's car was filthy after driving there and back, partially on dirt roads.

## No Feeling of Hope or Responsibility

While wintry conditions quieted the border patrol in Northern California during the blockade's first days, Los Angeles police officers were busy along the state's southeastern border, near Arizona and near the southernmost tip of Nevada. This included Blythe, the desert community in eastern Riverside County next to which Langan was stopped.

Blythe had always been a frontier town. It grew in importance after its incorporation as a city in 1916. When the Arizona-Blythe Bridge (also known as the California-Arizona Bridge)—the same bridge near which police had detained Langan—was completed in 1928 as one of the first automobile crossings over the Colorado River, it dramatically shortened the driving distance between Los Angeles and Phoenix, positioning Blythe as an early transportation hub connecting California with Arizona and the rest of the country.

By the 1930s Blythe also became a labor and logistics hub for massive water and hydroelectric projects under construction along the Colorado. These projects would help irrigate and power Los Angeles and its environs for decades, and, coupled with a century of growth and water-intensive land use, have since drastically altered the river's water supply and led to a water crisis that now imperils much of the southwestern United States. By the time of the blockade, Blythe was both a key transit point for people migrating westward into California and a destination for thousands of California residents working on the nearby power and water projects.

It was also, suggested Rose Marie Packard in a March 1936 letter published by the *Nation*, a place whose vibrance had dimmed over the course of the 1930s. Packard and her husband, John C. Packard—who would take up John Langan's case in a lawsuit against Chief Davis—visited Blythe that February (likely while investigating Langan's case). It was their first time in Blythe since 1932, Packard wrote, when there had been an active Socialist political organization and local merchants whom Packard called "tolerant, approachable people." Now, she said, independent merchants were all but gone and a colder welcome awaited. "Liberal groups had disintegrated," Packard said. "The chain stores have moved in and the local Chamber of Commerce is now the dominant organization."

Packard and her husband were cofounders of the American Civil Liberties Union's Southern California chapter. Their organization was one of the blockade's earliest and most vocal opponents and would become more so once John took up Langan's case. While their politics may have colored Rose Marie Packard's perspective, her account of watching border patrollers turn away an Oklahoma family with ten dollars left to their name, an old Ford piled with possessions, and two hundred miles of desert before the next town was not unlike countless others that witnesses reported over the next two months from any of the deployment's sixteen border checkpoints. On the same trip, the Packards visited nearby Yuma, Arizona. At a "hobo jungle" in Yuma they toured on a local sheriff's recommendation, the couple heard similar stories from inhabitants who, to Rose Marie, seemed to have checked out from society.

"The inhabitants were very bitter, had no feeling of hope or responsibility toward society," she wrote. "They could plainly see there was little chance of justice for them."

If figures from the Los Angeles officers at the checkpoint in Blythe were valid, more than two hundred people would have been able to share a similar sense of embitterment and injustice after only a few days of the blockade. When a state investigator checked on the operation a week later, though, officers could only produce forty-four sets of fingerprints. The police claimed that they hadn't had proper equipment to take prints at the beginning, so the actual numbers were far lower than what had been reported. In any event, that was still dozens of people stopped and treated as criminals simply because officers suspected they couldn't afford to be in California.

Moreover, the officers would soon have ample visible evidence of their work, at least for one day. Since Blythe was much closer to Los Angeles than other border patrol checkpoints, it was relatively easy for Hollywood studios to send production crews to film newsreels. Even two minutes of footage from one of these newsreels recorded the first week in February suggests that their claims of hundreds of stops may well have been accurate.

That film, produced by William Randolph Hearst's Metrotone News, depicts the Blythe crossing packed with migrants on foot, in cars, and aboard trains (film of train searches came from other checkpoints, as there was no railway in Blythe) and with the hardworking police pushing them out of the Golden State, making sure they stay out. Famed for connecting California to the rest of the country, the bridge now represented California's break with the nation.

"Los Angeles police adopt the motto 'They shall not pass,' and back to the borders go wanderers barred from the promised land in what is said to be the first state blockade of its kind ever attempted," announced Edwin Hill, the newsreel's narrator. Beginning February 10, filmgoers sitting in air-conditioned cinemas throughout the country could see officers unloading dirt-smeared families from the back of vans into the desert heat, lining everyone up to be fingerprinted and marching frowning men over the Colorado River, watching closely to make sure they kept on their way into Arizona.

That was exactly the kind of publicity Chief Davis and the Los Angeles Chamber of Commerce hoped the blockade would spark. They wanted word to get out that if someone was broke and wanted to come to California to soak up sun and charity, that person might end up like one of those wretched, worried faces at the end of the Metrotone newsreel.

Still, the film also shared critiques of the blockade, though not support for the migrants' plight. Partway into the reel the scene shifts to a shot of Arizona Governor Benjamin Baker Moeur speaking directly to the camera about the blockade, demanding that his state not become a "dumping ground for transients." The narrator almost bemusedly observes that the question of where families ejected by the ban will go from here is "something of a riddle" and later closes the narration with something of a both-sides approach while the video shows close-cropped, full-face shots of stern-faced men—presumably transients—staring ahead as if wondering, *What's next?*

"Criminals," the narrator asks, "or just human beings in search of happiness? They make a perplexing problem."

These newsreels and other publicity took few pains to acknowledge how imbalanced enforcement really was. After the FTS shutdown, the California State Relief Administration sent surveyors around California to study how transients in the Golden State were faring. Between December 1935 and the end of February 1936, these surveyors exhaustively catalogued the conditions transients experienced and obstacles they faced, including the blockade. These observations appeared in M. H. Lewis's report later in 1936 that, among many other details, recounted many discrepancies in how officers decided which visitors to question and which to wave past, sometimes based solely on travelers' appearances.

One of the study's investigators came to Blythe in early February. Los Angeles border patrol officers stationed there told the surveyor about the newsreel crews who'd just been there.

"The officers at this point were interested in securing publicity so that undesirables might stay away from California," the California State Relief Commission's study reported. "They said that they were being careful not to offend anyone who might be rich or have political influence."

The investigator visited Blythe a day after Langan's arrest. According to the later report, the squad in Blythe was comfortable making arrests so far from Los Angeles given their deputization by the Riverside County sheriff's department. According to the surveyor, the police walked from car to car, not detaining those they thought "looked like wealthy tourists" longer than needed to check for prohibited weapons, while suggesting to people who did not—people whom Langan might have resembled after his long drive from the dust and dirt of the mine in Cleator—that they turn around, as California didn't have any jobs for them. People who came by other means than private cars all got the same spiel.

"They talked to all of the bus passengers, advising them to write east to their friends, telling them not to try to hitch-hike into the state or even come in their own automobiles unless they had plenty of money," the state report said.

---

Transients stopped at the border by Los Angeles Police Department border patrol, Imperial County, 1936. *Courtesy of Los Angeles Times Photograph Collection, Special Collections, Charles E. Young Research Library, UCLA*

Langan's arrest was just part of the drama that took place in and around Blythe during the period the Los Angeles border patrol was in operation. Some of this drama was heavily publicized. Other aspects were more private. Most eventually faded from the public eye. Many were dismissed as simply the cost of preserving the shine on the Golden State.

In Southern California, attitudes toward the border patrol were generally much more favorable than those expressed in the north. Columnists and editorial writers largely lauded the blockade, particularly in Southern California. In Los Angeles's San Fernando Valley, for example, *Van Nuys News* editor Walter Mendenhall described the operation as a courageous act of self-defense, with Davis and his department bravely preventing an otherwise unstoppable criminal "influx."

"Los Angeles is facing a desperate situation if we permit every freight train to bring us a new shipment of unemployed, penniless vagrants, to consume the relief sorely needed by our own destitute, and to create a crime menace almost beyond conceivable control," Mendenhall wrote. Credulously accepting Davis's claims about the numbers and backgrounds of those arrested by the blockade on its first day, Mendenhall praised the chief for taking "initiative" to keep fugitive "vermin" off the streets. Mendenhall was far from alone in his credulity, though he'd clearly very thoroughly digested Davis's and the Chamber of Commerce's preferred rhetoric.

Some editors clearly gravitated to the hyperbolic, with poetic, sometimes overwrought metaphors and historical comparisons. For example, one widely circulated United Press wire report compared the presence of Los Angeles "shock troops" at the Arizona border to the sixth-century BCE Roman hero Horatius who, legend avers, saved Rome from an invading Etruscan army by refusing orders to retreat from a key bridge, thus preventing the army from crossing.

Randall Henderson, an editor in the desert community of Calexico who advocated improved education to better address employment problems in the long run, recognized the Horatius story's relevance to the broader messaging supporting the blockade. The invocation of heroic soldiers defending the heart of civilization from foreign threats provided the operation with a mythic veneer. Other coverage that described Davis's handpicked squads as the chief's Foreign Legion—which a young patrolman Davis once considered joining—simultaneously invoked the original Roman legionnaires and struck adventurous comparisons to the contemporary French Foreign Legion.

California became Ancient Rome's civilized, if besieged, successor. "Bums," "vagrants," and "hobos" became stand-ins for barbarians, Goths, and Huns salivating over the riches they might plunder. Despite his reference to Horatius on the front page of the *Calexico Chronicle*, Henderson wrote an editorial, positioned a few pages within the paper, in which he attempted to carefully balance arguments the blockade's opponents and proponents made.

"No one objects to 'regimenting' the criminals by locking them up in prison, or the insane by putting them in asylums," Henderson wrote. "And on the other hand, our American ideal of Freedom demands that we impose the least possible amount of regimentation on honest intelligent American citizens."

Henderson seemed to freely accept Davis's claims that "60 percent of the transients who mooch their way into the state have criminal records" and accepted the premise that those with criminal records were "undesirable" in California. But, hinting at a critique angry leaders of other states would make,

Henderson pondered if they would be any less undesirable in any other state. Still, he gave Davis the benefit of the doubt and credited him for doing what he could with difficult circumstances, even if in so doing he'd inadvertently underscored how arbitrary the blockade's existence really was.

"It is only a makeshift scheme—and no one knows it better than Davis," Henderson wrote. "But perhaps it will give Americans a jolt which will start them thinking about a more permanent answer to the problem."

Others were less forgiving. Two days after news of the blockade broke, American Civil Liberties Union Northern California Chapter Director Ernest Besig visited US Attorney H. H. McPike's San Francisco office, urging McPike to investigate Davis and the LAPD.

Besig followed up his visit to McPike's office with a letter to him. The border patrol and similar crackdowns, Besig wrote, were "repugnant to the United States constitution." Besig told McPike that the prosecutor needed to use the power he wielded on behalf of the nation to find out why armed police from outside McPike's jurisdiction of Northern California were in it, denying fellow Americans' due process with impunity. "It is one of the privileges and immunities of United States citizenship to go from State to State without interference," Besig wrote.

Besig wanted McPike to convene a federal grand jury to examine whether Davis and others unnamed had conspired to exclude poor people from California without legal authority. He even called the chief a fundamental, subversive threat to democracy.

"We submit that acts in question constitute an offense . . . and that the denial of the right to enter this State by the use of armed police officers, in contravention of the Constitution, may well be held to a conspiracy to overthrow the United States," Besig wrote.

Chief Davis and others argued that even though individual transients and vagrants might be very fine, moral people, vagrancy overall dearly cost the community. The numbers were what mattered—the data.

But what numbers? Which data? The chief claimed that more than half of 1,400 transients fingerprinted by LAPD officers in January 1936 (before the blockade's launch) had criminal records and that nearly 73 percent of those were what Davis termed the "street beggar class," of whom nearly half "were sent back to other states seeking those criminals."

The blockade's proponents see-sawed between stressing the need to take decisive action against the menace transients posed and arguments that the patrol was hardly a big deal, that its deployment fundamentally changed nothing about how the state policed vagrancy. The latter arguments pointed to earlier antivagrant laws on California's books as evidence that restricting indigent travel and limiting vagrancy out of concern for public safety had ample statutory precedent. Put more straightforwardly, police were simply enforcing laws that had already long been on the books.

## A Multi-Purpose Tool

The sound of gunshots in the distance was all but drowned out by the clubwomen's applause. Davis had just finished presenting a report on his two-week-old border patrol to an auditorium packed with Friday Morning Club members. A few days after John Langan's encounter with the patrol in Blythe, the women roared their approval of the arrest figures Davis reported.

"Perhaps the greatest enthusiasm toward any public endeavor shown by the Friday Morning Club this year," wrote *Los Angeles Times* society-page writer Crete Cage.

The officers he deployed to California's borders were keeping them safe, keeping the entire state safe. Each shot they heard ringing from the police target range outside was a comfort. The women, most of whom practiced at the range weekly, knew it was the sound of Davis's best and bravest ensuring that they were prepared to take on any danger in this uncertain time. It was February 14, and in return for that protection, the women gave Davis the best valentine he could get this year: unanimous passage of a resolution from the club supporting the blockade. Its text stressed the very message Davis repeatedly pitched, that transiency and crime were intertwined. It also stressed that women were especially in danger from these perceived evils:

> WHEREAS—large numbers of persons without visible means of support are daily coming into Los Angeles and Southern California by means of freight trains, and of hitch-hiking, AND
>
> WHEREAS—records of recent arrests show that a large percentage of persons arrested in Los Angeles for begging, railroad-fare evasions and vagrancy, have criminal records, AND
>
> WHEREAS—the existence of such type of persons in this community is not alone a menace to the citizens and taxpayers thereof, particularly to women, but results in large losses from stolen and

damaged property, and also in large costs to the community in prevention of crime, and in the care of such persons in public institutions when arrested and committed, AND

WHEREAS—such persons are not eligible for relief in this community until they have resided here for one year, but must return to their original place of residence to obtain relief,—

BE IT RESOLVED—that the action of the Los Angeles Police Commission, and of the Chief of Police, JAMES E. DAVIS, in instituting the present border patrol, whereby large numbers of such persons seeking to come to this community from other parts of the country are turned back at the borders of California, BE APPROVED, and that Chief of Police Davis be commended upon the present manner in which he is handling this difficult situation, AND

BE IT FURTHER RESOLVED—that copies of this Resolution be transmitted to the Mayor, FRANK L. SHAW, the Los Angeles City Council, the Los Angeles Police Commission, Chief of Police Davis, and to the Metropolitan Press.

The blockade deepened existing divisions in California. It consolidated support behind Davis, Shaw, and Los Angeles's business powerbrokers, but it also galvanized labor, New Deal supporters, and civil libertarians. Even some county sheriffs and rural Californians opposed the blockade.

"No one can tell an American citizen he can't travel on the highways or enter a town," Plumas County District Attorney Michael C. Kerr said after eight members of the LAPD patrol came to Quincy, the county seat. Kerr was joined in his refusal to support the blockade by Plumas County Sheriff Arch Braden, then in the middle of nine terms as the top lawman in this northeastern California county.

Supporters of the blockade all but ignored such responses, even when they came from people like Braden, thus putting the lie to Cross and Davis's claims the operation had every involved border county's sheriff's permission. Instead, supporters shifted attention and repeated talking points about the criminal "floods" the blockade dammed.

"The double purpose is to check the flood of criminals and divert the stream of penniless transients into California," Los Angeles Chamber of Commerce assistant secretary F. L. S. Harman said. That Harman and not a government representative was the first source quoted in many versions of an Associated Press wire story about the blockade that ran in newspapers nationwide after the blockade's first day speaks volumes about his organization's role in the operation. The chamber held sway and de facto authority equal to that of Mayor Shaw or Chief Davis.

The chamber *had* been the central driver behind both the blockade and Los Angeles's many earlier attempts to police poverty. Moreover, Harman's statement contradicted the widely circulated defense that the blockade's only purpose was to stop criminal ingress. If diverting "the stream of penniless transients" was an equally central purpose of the deployment, as Harman said, then it really wasn't just about dangerous criminals. Few would have believed otherwise, but the stark, unapologetic inconsistencies illustrate, if nothing else, that nobody involved with setting up the blockade seemed to care very much about mounting a consistent defense. Rather, they simply seemed to care that it was happening at all.

A third purpose—perhaps more worrying to some—was left more or less unspoken, but another incident in Blythe at the end of February rendered it tangible. Aside from the busy crossing into Arizona, Blythe was a bustling hub for work on the Metropolitan Water District's massive project building the Colorado River Aqueduct. This 242-mile-long project employed a total of thirty-five thousand people over eight years of construction.

One of those workers was Josiah Hamilton Dillard, or "Joe." Born in Oklahoma, Dillard slowly made his way west, stopping for jobs as a ranch hand in Yuma, Arizona—where, when he was just eighteen, he married a Californian named Lottie Ranson—and the Central Valley city of Bakersfield, where he did construction work.

The couple and their two children, Joe, born in 1931, and Jack, born in 1932, finally settled in to live in Lottie's hometown of Oceanside, a coastal community north of San Diego. Then Joe was hired as a laborer for the aqueduct project at a worksite outside of Blythe. Living just west of there in the tiny community of Rice, Joe soon bonded with his coworkers.

One Saturday in late February 1936, two nights before his and Lottie's sixth anniversary, Joe went drinking with his fellow workers and ended up at a dance hall. It was early on Sunday morning by the time William J. Atkinson, Blythe's deputy police chief, approached the crowd, Joe included, spilling from the dance hall.

Atkinson told the group to quiet down. They ignored Atkinson. A former chief of police in the Riverside County town of Beaumont, Atkinson, who'd been investigated for two deadly shootings earlier in his police career, was annoyed by the impertinence. He repeated his request—still no cooperation.

This time Atkinson stepped toward the "unruly" laborers. Instead of ignoring him again, some of the workers started to surround Atkinson. Their numbers grew as more people emerged from the dance hall. Atkinson sized the group up and decided to place the loudest of them under arrest.

It was Joe, who, Atkinson said, refused to cooperate. Atkinson tried again. One of Joe's friends tried to free him from Atkinson's grasp. That was the moment Atkinson decided to draw his service gun, he later recounted.

The sight of the weapon incited a fiercer melee. Atkinson struggled to hold on to the gun with one hand while using his other to keep Joe in his grasp. Suddenly, he felt a searing pain. Someone had slashed him with a knife from behind right as someone else yanked his weapon from his hand. Atkinson immediately reached across his chest, pulled a second pistol from a shoulder holster, and fired six times.

Joe collapsed instantly. The others screamed as their friend's bleeding body crumpled to the ground. More flocked from the crowd and fell in on Atkinson. Punch after enraged punch pummeled the officer.

Tires screeched and doors slammed as a car skidded to a stop next to the crowd, and four men jumped out. Throwing off the leather jackets they'd been wearing to ward off the chill of a night spent next to a Mojave Desert highway, the men plunged into the fracas. Sergeant Varas B. Eubanks took the lead. Three other Los Angeles officers followed close behind as they cut a path to Atkinson. While California Highway Patrol officers and Riverside County sheriff's deputies arrived to clear the crowd, the border patrollers freed Atkinson from Joe Dillard's vengeful friends.

Complete details of what had first drawn Atkinson to the dance hall in Blythe or why the crowd gathered there had been so "unruly" in the first place are not forthcoming. Tensions between the aqueduct's contractors and its laborers had been high all month, ever since a deadly fire at another aqueduct site's worker dormitories. What is known is that the incident left one man dead, a woman widowed, two children without a father, and the Los Angeles Police Department's border patrol taking another violent step away from their mission of stopping indigent migrants.

By inserting themselves into the fight that killed Dillard and might have killed Atkinson had they not intervened, the Los Angeles cops dispelled any lingering illusions that officers assigned to James Davis's Foreign Legion would stick to simply stopping transients at the border, regardless of how many times he insisted that their mission was only that.

This was a bigger fight, and these officers knew full well that they were empowered by Davis to protect California from all who might undermine the state. They would fight alongside anyone trying to ensure law and order, just as they knew they had Atkinson's and his officers' support when they arrested people like John Langan. The mission couldn't be simpler: defend order, subdue radicals, and protect fellow police above all else.

Joe Dillard's death was one tragic example of the kind of mission creep that the ACLU had warned about in the operation's first days. Another sign that the LAPD officers would not limit themselves to enforcing California's anti-indigent laws was Chief Davis's announcement that the police department planned to install shortwave radio linkups between headquarters and each border outpost. The justification Davis supplied to the *Los Angeles Times* for the linkups had nothing directly to do with keeping out incoming migrants and everything to do with helping him create the kind of statewide police that he had been advocating for more than a year, albeit a makeshift version thereof. It was more about keeping wanted criminals *in* California even as they continued to stay vigilant to keep those set to invade the state from doing so.

The new radio links would let the LAPD or other law enforcement agencies in California instantly notify border patrollers about wanted criminals who might try to flee the state. They "would greatly increase the difficulty of fleeing the state and link border patrol directly with police activities of the city," the *Times* explained. Davis now had a statewide extension of his law enforcement capability even though his idea for a state police force had failed the previous year. Thanks to technology and the support of newspapers like the *Times*, perhaps he had something even better now.

Chief Davis also had another asset: Earl Kynette. Without Kynette's intercession, John Langan may have sustained the legal challenges against Davis and the blockade that emerged from his arrest.

Kynette was a notorious LAPD lieutenant. He was smarmy, depraved. And John Packard, Langan's lawyer, knew that Kynette would stop at nothing to destroy Langan. His pressure on Langan went well beyond typical policing to near-sadistic intimidation that completely overturned Langan's life. After Langan filed his lawsuit, Kynette repeatedly dropped in on him and his family at their apartment. The officer was friendly at first. He invited Langan out for drinks and gently asked him to drop the case. After Langan ignored the ruse, Kynette invited Langan to his own house.

There, he dropped the amicable ruse. Kynette brought out some records and played them for Langan. They were dictaphone recordings—clearly very secret ones—of powerful local figures discussing various lurid matters and subjects that would have sparked earthshaking scandals if made public. Kynette also showed Langan candid photographs of influential Angelenos in compromising situations. Langan got the message immediately: if Kynette could document elites' scandalous behavior so easily, he surely had the means to destroy someone of lesser stature like Langan should he not cooperate.

When Langan still did not acquiesce to Kynette's demands, the police officer increased the stakes. He returned to Langan's apartment, this time with Langan's wife, Lorna (a British citizen who went by the stage name of Joan Manners) and the couple's three-year-old daughter, also named Joan, as his targets. Kynette threatened to kidnap the child and exploit Lorna's immigration status if Langan didn't relent.

Lorna raced to the apartment bathroom and tried to scream for help after Kynette threatened her daughter. An irate Kynette raced after Lorna, pulled her from the window, and demanded that Langan help him restrain and silence her. Fearful of the lengths Kynette would go to, Langan complied and, at the police lieutenant's command, taped her mouth shut.

Kynette shouted at Lorna that if she didn't remain silent he would throw her into a mental institution. Whether consciously or not, the threat evoked the 1928 case and ensuing scandal that helped end James Davis's first stint as police chief, when officers responding to a child disappearance case had the child's mother, Christine Collins, forcefully committed. Despite the political fallout that case had generated, Lorna risked deportation if Kynette delivered on his threat to institutionalize her. Realizing now how relentless Kynette could be, her husband backed down.

The damage was already done. Not only did Langan's retreat keep Davis and the border blockade out of further federal court scrutiny, but the entire episode would also do irreparable damage to his relationship with Joan. Lorna would leave John the following year. The couple's split would be rancorous and spark a brutal custody battle over Joan. Langan and Manners would spend the better part of a decade bitterly wrangling in court and newspaper headlines over their child's future. The dispute would become a regular press fixture throughout the country, usually with little mention of Langan's experience during the border blockade or Kynette's harassment of the family. At one point the custody battle would become so venomous that Lorna would picket outside a movie studio where Langan worked—earning her a contempt of court charge and possible deportation—and claim in news coverage and legal proceedings that he was never the girl's biological father in the first place.

The couple was still together in March 1936. When the morning for Langan's appearance before a federal court finally arrived, US District Court Judge Albert Lee Stephens was waiting.

Packard drove to Langan's apartment in East Hollywood so he and his client could travel to court directly. Lorna Langan answered. John wasn't there. He'd left earlier to meet some police officer.

A suddenly concerned Packard asked Lorna what the name of the officer was who John went to meet.

"Earl Kynette."

*Kynette.* Now Packard *knew* something really was wrong.

Langan had just reopened his case. Now he was gone. In fact, he'd vanished two days earlier, John Packard, his attorney, told Stephens.

Packard asked on Langan's behalf that his lawsuit against the LAPD be dismissed. It wasn't what the longtime ACLU lawyer had advised his client to do, but he had to accede to his wishes. Packard told the court that Langan wanted to give up "for the best interests of everyone," or so a note Langan sent Packard had read.

This was a strange situation. Reluctantly, Stephens dismissed the case. Almost as immediately, he asked US Attorney Pierson Hall to look into the matter.

"I am not convinced that the plaintiff desired to call off this action, despite the letter he wrote," Stephens said.

Packard knew the note didn't tell the whole story, but he was hamstrung. He'd recently been hearing strange noises whenever he picked up his phone. He and his cocounsel, James Carter, were certain their phones were tapped. When Langan told Packard why he wasn't going to come to court after all, his lawyer put the pieces together immediately. Kynette was up to something.

# 10 | BACKLASH

WHEN WILLIAM JOHNSON FOUND OUT his sister was sick at the end of 1935, the fifty-two-year-old Hollywood resident immediately started looking for some way to get to Olympia, Washington, to spend the holidays with her. By December 17 Johnson had scrounged up the $27.40 he needed for a train ticket from the Los Angeles suburb of Glendale to Olympia. (Adjusted for inflation, his one-way ticket cost the equivalent of more than $500 in today's terms.)

It was such an expensive trip that Johnson couldn't afford a return train ticket when he decided to return home in early February 1936. Instead, he decided to hitchhike. He made it as far as Ashland, a small Oregon community just north of the California border. Crossing the border would require traversing the Siskiyous, a mountain range running east-to-west along the border. When Johnson woke up to the prospect of a frigid Siskiyous crossing, he decided hitchhiking wouldn't be prudent. He'd survived a bout of tuberculosis a few years earlier and worried that standing alongside a mountain highway waiting in the February cold for a ride was too risky for his fragile lungs. He might be there for hours. It might even take days to get a ride. Johnson decided to find a different way over the Siskiyous.

Johnson couldn't afford a bus, let alone another train fare. Finally, he decided to just hop a cargo train over the mountains. That could also be cold, but it was a sure thing, and the body heat of fellow train-hoppers inside the shelter of a boxcar was at least likely to keep things warmer than trying to thumb a ride.

The train journey began as smoothly as Johnson could have hoped. But then the train stopped almost as soon as it had crossed the California line. A few of Johnson's fellow stowaways were just about to see if there was anything doing in tiny little Hornbrook when someone shined a flashlight into the boxcar he'd settled into.

"Everybody out!"

The border patrollers took Johnson and the other detainees to a drafty abandoned hotel that they'd converted into a makeshift jail precisely for suspected indigent migrants just like Johnson.

The police officers who stopped Johnson didn't care when he protested that he was a Californian and was just trying to get home. They sent him back into Oregon just like the others they'd pulled off the train.

This time Johnson went to Medford, about fifteen miles north of Ashland and the largest city in southern Oregon. There he found an Oregon state trooper on duty. He told the trooper how the LAPD had treated him like a "professional hobo" and provided a statement describing how he'd ended up crossing the state line in a boxcar and what happened to him once he was pulled off the train. There was little the trooper could do besides take Johnson's report and suggest he take his case to US Attorney Carl C. Donaugh.

Stories of experiences similar to Johnson's appeared in newswires daily. Papers throughout California and the United States published them on their front pages, though just as many stories, if not more, about menacing criminals snared by the blockade also appeared. Still, an undercurrent of anger and frustration with the blockade seemed to be spreading. Much of it came from civil libertarians like Ernest Besig and progressives like Parley Christensen, to say nothing of people caught in the blockade, like John Langan, but Sheriff Sharp was a perfect representative of those who were frustrated by both the operation and the handling of it by James Davis's police department.

Public officials otherwise likely to have supported the blockade's aims also found themselves upset about its implementation, especially where they thought it might pull them into a courtroom. Even Los Angeles city attorney Ray Cheseboro was at first hesitant to sign off on the blockade. When Los Angeles's city councilors addressed the blockade at their February 13, 1936, meeting, Cheseboro refrained from taking a position. Instead, he told councilors that he would have to report back with a full assessment of the legal implications for the city.

If Davis, Cross, Shaw, or anyone else had made Cheseboro aware of the blockade before newspaper readers did, he didn't let on to the city council. Davis had either recklessly proceeded with the deployment without verifying that it was even legal (or whether it exposed the city to potentially costly court challenges), or Cheseboro had feigned ignorance of the blockade to remove some of the obstacles its launch might otherwise face.

It very likely was the former. Once the blockade began, Chief Davis and Deputy Chief Cross told reporters that the operation began with Cheseboro's support, but that doesn't mean they had it. Cheseboro was caught off guard when news of the deployment first reached him, or, at least, that's what he told the public. Given that Davis and Cross had lied about getting numerous sheriffs' support for the blockade, it's conceivable they had done so with Cheseboro too. Nevertheless, he would soon lend his public legal blessing to the operation.

Officials from the state government weren't as persuadable. California deputy attorney general Jess Hession warned right after the blockade began that it probably wouldn't survive a court challenge. Hession stressed that one's poverty alone was insufficient grounds for negating constitutionally protected rights to migrate from state to state, California's 1933 anti-indigent law notwithstanding.

Hession's boss was more publicly circumspect. Attorney General Ulysses S. Webb was a political giant in early twentieth-century California. A Republican from Quincy—the Plumas County town whose district attorney and sheriff each rejected participating in the blockade—Webb first became attorney general in 1902 and would remain in that position until 1939, making him California's longest-serving top prosecutor. Philosophically, Webb was a nativist who staunchly supported migration restrictions. A die-hard member of the Native Sons of the Golden West, Webb helped develop and enforce racist residency laws and other restrictions targeting Asian migrants to California and the United States. Despite his long history as a xenophobe, Webb warned friends at the Los Angeles Chamber of Commerce who'd written him for his private legal opinion that it was unlikely to survive a court challenge.

Webb told longtime Los Angeles Chamber of Commerce managing secretary Arthur Arnoll that although the blockade's aims of keeping indigent people who might become a public charge out of the state was "worthy of unqualified approval" if done in a lawful way, no organized government at any level should "attempt the achievement of a laudable purpose by unlawful means" and that a police department from one city attempting to conduct its duties in another jurisdiction was clearly unlawful in Webb's view.

"The police of the city of Los Angeles have no jurisdiction beyond the city's territorial limits, and the police department of the city of Los Angeles is not authorized to interfere with or discharge the duties devolving upon police authorities of another government, municipal or county," Webb cautioned, adding that this principal of jurisdictional independence had been well established. "If the invasion by one of such governments of the domain of another and the effort there to discharge the duties of the local officers of such other government were permitted, it can readily be apprehended that the evils which might result in given instances would far outweigh any good that might be accomplished in other instances."

The attorney general reminded Arnoll that in late 1931 they'd both attended a meeting with Frank Merriam to discuss potential statewide responses to, in Webb's wording, "the evils" posed by "the invasion" Arnoll and his allies hoped to check. Those proposed solutions, Webb said, had all been lawful but had ultimately petered out because they weren't cost-effective. Stressing that a shared sense of purpose with the chamber remained, Webb nonetheless reiterated the dangerous precedent the blockade might set.

"In this as in other matters we should steadily keep in mind that we are one of the sisterhood of States, and while asserting our own rights we should recognize fully the rights of other States. As other States must do unto California, so must California do unto them, for such is the mandate of the Federal Constitution," Webb closed.

Despite the attorney general's attempt to quietly warn Arnoll this time around, his letter soon reached reporters' hands. Blockade critics jumped on the leak. If even one of California's most powerful nativists couldn't endorse the blockade, was it really as well supported as Davis claimed?

## Decrying the "Ridiculous Spectacle"

Just as they'd acted before securing favorable legal guidance, Davis and Cross brazenly committed Los Angeles's police force to patrol the Golden State's borders—at local taxpayers' expense—without approval from the city's elected representatives. The chief and deputy chief were working closely with Mayor Shaw and his brother, of course, and a majority of city councilors supported the blockade once they knew about it, but the council's support wasn't unanimous, and councilors who did oppose the operation opposed it vehemently.

Parley P. Christensen, a progressive Democrat who represented downtown Los Angeles, was the blockade's most vocal city council critic. Christensen had been one of the success stories of the End Poverty in California (EPIC) movement, despite Upton Sinclair's loss. Though Sinclair withdrew from politics after the grueling election, his unexpected competitiveness against Governor Merriam had mobilized some EPIC candidates to victory in down-ballot races, including the one Christensen won for the Los Angeles city council's ninth district.

Christensen described Chief Davis as "our strutting Mussolini" after learning about the blockade and called the operation a "most obvious violation of a fundamental right of Americans, who derive their citizenship, not from California or Kansas, but from the U.S.A." Stressing the blockade's similarities to Fascist Italy's invasion of Ethiopia the previous fall, Christensen demanded that Chief Davis appear before the body in person to defend the blockade, and he put forward a resolution calling for his recall.

"I don't know how other Councilmen feel about the ridiculous spectacle of Chief Davis's Foreign Legion, or storm troops, as his preceptor Hitler would call them, but as for me, I am disgusted and ashamed," Christensen said. "We are the laughingstock of all friends of freedom and liberty."

One major Los Angeles figure who did know about the blockade before its launch was Harry Chandler. Chandler's *Los Angeles Times* willingly worked with Chief Davis and the chamber of commerce to stoke the community's fear of transients for months. The paper had always been a mouthpiece for the city's business interests and a chief promoter of the idea of Los Angeles as the "white spot." Now it lauded the Los Angeles Committee on Indigent Alien Transients.

Thomas Scollan, a California state senator who represented Sacramento, immediately excoriated the blockade's launch, calling it "damnable, absurd, and asinine." The *Times* retorted almost immediately with an editorial headlined LET's HAVE MORE OUTRAGES and lauding Davis for eschewing the kind of chatter most public figures waited for before taking any significant action.

"His unheralded plan—already in effect—to use Los Angeles policemen to keep out of the State the bums, crooks, won't-works and indigent who regularly make this city their winter haven got off to a running start by virtue of its sheer, calm audacity," the editorial read.

Insisting there were "no finer" than "this city's 'finest,'" the *Times* denounced critiques from people like Hession and Scollan who suggested that the blockade was clearly illegal. "Maybe so," wrote the *Times*, "but it is the kind of outrage that ought to have been perpetrated in California several years ago."

The editorial implied that stemming migration years before 1936—perhaps after the 1931 meeting between Walter Gifford and local and national leaders, when the idea of using officers to bar migrants from entering the state was discussed—would have transformed the state. Instead, the piece argued, indigent migrants from other states had bled California taxpayers dry to the tune of millions of dollars. It purported that California's $70 million budget deficit in 1936 was directly caused by these migrants. Again, migrants, the *Times* suggested, were the root of California's political instability and crime. They were an alien force brought to the Golden State by malevolent actors to wreck its prosperity. If something had been done about it earlier, the paper argued, the state "would have been spared the depredations of our present army of imported criminals. If it had, California would not now be the paradise for radicals and trouble-makers that it is."

Dismissing other state and local figures who questioned the blockade with little hesitation, the *Times* gave Chief Davis's brash new strategy public relations cover as soon as the operation began. It also called Hession's legal analysis into question, chastising the assistant attorney general for questioning various counties' deputization of LAPD officers when, the editorial lectured, "it is a pretty well-established principle of law that any community has a legal right to bar out of its confines any person likely to become a public charge and this, under the Davis plan, is all that several counties are doing."

Other defenses of the blockade more cynically implied that public outrage over the blockade was less about concern for Dust Bowl migrants than it was concocted to win political points. Some, like the *Los Angeles Times*, looked toward history to illustrate why some of the shock expressed about the blockade may have been feigned. As features in the *Times* and other papers illustrated with special features on sixteenth-century English "poor laws" and similar subjects, one just had to look to Queen Elizabeth I's reign to see that regulating poverty was far from an unprecedented or outrageous concept.

In Modoc County, meanwhile, Claude McCracken was not going to let Gertrude French's front-page welcome of Bergman and his fellow officers go completely unnoticed. Claude critiqued the blockade directly in the *Modoc*

*Mail*, a mimeographed, stapled-together newspaper Claude launched in 1936, even as he more neutrally reported on the operation for national newswires. Though he remained enmeshed in Modoc County politics, Claude understood that the blockade's fate rested more on national politics, as he described in a March 25, 1936, letter printed by the *Sacramento Bee*. He predicted that in the upcoming presidential election, Republicans would attack Roosevelt and the Democratic Party as flouting the US Constitution, with Frank Merriam dutifully making such an attack.

"That is a day I long to see, because the alleged violation of the constitution, which the GOP will pile at the door of the administration are asserted invasions of property rights," McCracken wrote. "Of course Chief of Police James E. Davis of Los Angeles has flagrantly invaded human rights with his establishment of the border patrol. He has violated the clauses of the constitution which deal with human rights, and has been told so by Attorney General Webb. But small stuff, such as the invasion of human rights, does not interest such eminent donkey hunters as Governor Merriam."

Claude's opposition underscored yet another divide in the ever-more-venomous rivalry between him and Gertrude (aside from attacking Governor Merriam, whom she had long admired). She was a Native Daughter who cared about heritage, tradition, and history, all of which seemed to her increasingly under assault. Claude, on the other hand, was an itinerant newspaperman who'd bounced around throughout the country, never staying long enough to really be from anywhere. How could anyone take seriously his opinion of the blockade if he didn't have a stake in California, or anywhere? How firm could his stand be if he didn't have footing anywhere?

## Angry Neighbors

Reactions to the blockade from outside the state were less reserved. For residents of places like Klamath Falls, Oregon; Yuma, Arizona; and Reno, Nevada, let alone California border towns like Alturas, Blythe, and Quincy, the sudden appearance at their doorsteps of heavily armed police from a city hundreds of miles away significantly disrupted normal life.

Travelers leaving Oregon, Nevada, and Arizona had already long complained about invasive searches at the Golden State's plant quarantine stations. These were ostensibly meant to prevent agricultural pests imported alongside

A satirical sign placed at the California-Nevada state line by residents of Reno, Nevada, in February 1936. *Courtesy of Los Angeles Times Photograph Collection, Special Collections, Charles E. Young Research Library, UCLA*

outside produce. As one letter writer from just across the Columbia River in Vancouver, Washington, wrote to Portland's daily *Oregonian*, these quarantines already made travelers feel like they were in a "chain gang." Now Oregonians, Arizonans, and Nevadans used to regularly traversing the state for daily business had to also consider their appearance, their income, and their confidence communicating with armed police officers before going about their business.

Meanwhile, government officials in these states seethed over the sudden militarization of their domestic borders. These officials quickly decried the blockade, though their reasons varied and were typically pragmatic rather than idealistic. Disruptive as the blockade may have been to their constituents' daily lives, they weren't particularly concerned about freedom of movement or human rights. They were aggravated by the prospect that those turned back by the blockade might intensify pressure on their own relief infrastructure.

While most of the dramatic scenes and confrontations that took place during the blockade seemed to occur along the desert frontier between California and Arizona, disruptions to everyday activities were arguably more tangible to residents of northern California and southern Oregon, who were accustomed to traveling back and forth over the state line as they pleased. Any border is an imaginary construction, but a particularly abstract boundary blurs the transition from Oregon to California, where people living immediately adjacent to the state line seem to share more with those just across the line than with others in their respective states. That shared identity continues to evolve.

Over the decades following the blockade, many people from Oregon and California communities far removed from each state's economic and political centers have come to identify with a mythologized State of Jefferson. Mythology notwithstanding, in the mid-1930s in this region, life, work, and commerce smoothly flowed between the border's two sides.

Until the police arrived.

On paper, Davis's blockade wasn't supposed to alter the rhythms of life along the Oregon-California border. Oregonians didn't worry the Foreign Legion; Okies did. In fact, both Oregon and the state of Washington also attracted displaced Dust Bowl refugees and other migrants and saw population growth during this period. Despite the relatively small number of migrants from their state detained by LAPD border patrollers, Oregonians did not welcome the blockade; the state's residents and politicians loudly attacked it, but idealism didn't drive their opposition.

Once the blockade began, Oregon governor Charles H. Martin warned that many problems similar to the potential showdown along the California-Arizona border or William Johnson's ill-fated attempt to cross the Siskiyous were in store. Martin was not sympathetic to Johnson's plight. He was not a bleeding-heart politician appalled by the conditions Dust Bowl refugees experienced in their travels. He did not have any enthusiasm for his or any state government to provide transient relief. A stalwart Democrat, Governor Martin vocally criticized the bulk of Roosevelt's New Deal programs and regularly disagreed with his fellow party members' management of the Depression's ongoing impacts.

Whether driven from their homes by genocide, war, environmental disaster, or economic collapse, migrants rarely find open arms welcoming them to new lands. This was as true in Martin's Oregon as it was in California—or anywhere else—before Davis deployed his blockade. Just the month before the LAPD blockade started, for example, Martin ordered Elmer Goudy, the administrator of Oregon's state relief committee, to close a transient camp in Roseburg, a southern Oregon city about 125 miles north of the California border. Martin saw no daylight between the terms *transient* and the more pejorative *tramp*, as the Portland-based *Oregon Daily Journal* memorably quoted.

"'Transient Camp?' Martin asked Goudy. 'Tramp camp would be a better name. Those men should be kept moving out of our state the same as criminals.'"

Nothing changed about Martin's dismal opinion of migrants after the blockade began. He loathed the prospect of using state resources to provide relief to them, whatever term one used.

Martin's problem with Los Angeles's deployment to Oregon's borders was not that it was antidemocratic or risked violating migrants' rights; he feared the precedent the deployment would set and the cascading impacts it might trigger. If California sent unwanted migrants back into its neighboring states, what would happen when its neighbors tired of migration themselves and tried to deport the people just sent back across their borders? What would happen if *those* states' neighbors also set up blockades? Where would migrants be sent next? Who would be responsible for them then?

"[Oregon] has enough misery without having to care for these unwelcome visitors," Martin told newspapers. Martin resented the mess he'd inherit if Davis's police force sent transients back into Oregon. The governor pointed to increasingly dire news from Europe to inform his reaction. Nations throughout that continent were slamming their doors in the face of Jews fleeing Germany's ascendant Nazi regime and Joseph Stalin's purges in the Soviet Union.

Martin warned that a cascade of border blockades would have similar consequences. If California's borders remained closed to transients, officials in other states would soon close *their* borders. Before long, a stateless tide of Dust Bowl refugees would erode the United States' shaky recovery from the Depression. Fearing a situation similar to the European refugee crisis, Martin asked Governor Merriam to intervene.

Oregon's largest paper, Portland's *Morning Oregonian*, echoed Merriam's concerns in a February 7 editorial.

"Certainly if California piles up the transients on her borders, and Washington does the same, Oregon cannot but do likewise, and then such action would swell across the mountains like a wave," the editorial argued. Like the

*Los Angeles Times*, the *Morning Oregonian* looked to Elizabethan England for historical context of so-called poor laws. Unlike the Southern California paper, the *Oregonian* scrutinized the history more closely. It described England's seventeenth-century Settlement Act as "perhaps the most notorious poor law ever enacted." The paper argued that by restricting peasants' ability to seek work in other parts of the country the act severely constrained the English labor force and hypothesized whether the LAPD might also find inspiration in earlier, more severe punishments for begging and loitering enacted in England.

"Such laws came into existence because England had its little Californias which did not want to accept the good with the bad," asserted the *Morning Oregonian*. "They were a logical climax, and yet even they failed."

The *Oregonian* wasn't really against the motive of the Los Angeles police blockade, as the newspaper lectured on the "many exceptions" that exist to constitutional provisions for "our endowment to inalienable rights." Like the *Los Angeles Times* during the previous year's run-up to the blockade, Portland's daily newspaper asserted that there existed "no sound objection" to states' exercise of police power to keep out paupers, the sick and infirm, criminals, and others likely to become public charges. Just as Oregon's own vagrancy laws made criminals out of residents who didn't seek work when otherwise physically able to do so, the editorial argued that Davis's border patrollers likely would argue in court that they were merely advising any approaching destitute migrant that they risked violating similar California laws—and jail time—should they proceed across the border.

"And if he persisted in entering and was jailed, what jury of solid, tax-paying California peers would grant him damages?" the *Oregonian* asked. "As the 'vag' will tell you—sure, there's justice, but try and get it."

These facts were true—antivagrancy laws were nothing new. Davis sent his legions to California's borders to enforce laws already on the books in the Golden State. Other states also rejected transients and migrants, and, yes, some critics seemed to oppose the blockade because doing so gave them chances to carve out political wedges. But all of these realities were selectively invoked to support arguments for or against the blockade. Chief Davis himself regularly contradicted himself in his public defenses of the campaign.

Martin's fears were shared by many local governments in Oregon. Even before the border blockade, many Oregon cities and counties openly opposed transients. Just as had happened with the closure of Oklahoma's transient

camps just before the blockade and so many other shifts to relief infrastructure throughout the country in late 1935 and early 1936, localities throughout
Oregon responded to the FERA shutdown and the FTS closure by slashing
aid. In mid-January, for example, officials in Multnomah County—home to
the state's largest city, Portland—recommended closing a local transient camp
and kicking nonresident relief seekers out of the county.

Some of the loudest voices opposing the blockade weren't even directly
impacted by it. Portland, for example, is hundreds of miles north of the border.
Still, its city council quickly seized on the opportunity to score points criticiz-
ing its counterparts in the south. In February Portland City Commissioner
Ralph C. Clyde introduced a resolution condemning the patrol as a "blight
on our civilization."

The politically progressive Clyde was contemplating entering Portland's
upcoming mayoral election, and challenging the blockade offered him an
opportunity to establish his campaign platform. He provided proposed text for
similar resolutions to other Oregon cities, such as Ashland, as well as municipalities in other states, such as Phoenix, Arizona. Portland's city commission
passed the motion, though it did so over the objections of Democratic mayor
Joseph K. Carson and an *Oregonian* editorial board that wrote that while it
didn't agree with the patrol, Portland could do little about it; Clyde and the
commission should therefore focus more on matters in Oregon.

Indeed, the resolution was purely symbolic. Meanwhile, despite the commission's condemnation of the blockade, efforts throughout the Portland area
to clear local transient encampments persisted after its passage. While Portland's city council was a separate entity from the county commission that had
shut down local relief facilities just a few weeks prior, its members shared a
similar constituency with similar political pressures, including local hostility
toward relief seekers.

Nevertheless, the presidency wasn't the only office up for election in 1936;
local elections were also ahead in Portland. Going on record against the police
deployment in California gave Portland city council and mayoral candidates—
Clyde included—a low-stakes opportunity to present themselves as standing
up for fellow Americans and Oregonians without necessarily taking action or
committing to policies that might impact local taxpayers and voters.

Closer to the border, municipal governments approached the blockade
from a more pragmatic standpoint. City councils all along the state line decried

the deployment, but they were motivated by concerns similar to Governor Martin's. In Klamath County, just over the state line from Modoc County, relief administrators worried that transients ejected into Oregon from California would overwhelm local aid efforts, especially since those sent there probably would have already spent everything they had trying to reach the Golden State. By then, it was even more likely that they would lack the necessary resources to make it much farther than Klamath Falls.

Other southern Oregon jurisdictions felt similar concern, and many officials were outraged. Medford, the city where William Johnson was urged to complain about the blockade to state and federal officials, was less than thirty miles from California. Its mayor, George Porter, decried the deployment as soon as it began.

"We are not going to let this section be a dumping ground for California, or any other state," Porter declared, noting that he'd asked Medford's city council to counter Los Angeles's attempt to push rejected transients back into Oregon. Officials in Jackson County—which contained Medford—and other jurisdictions in the state immediately began working on similar measures they could take to block deportations of transient populations they potentially would have to then manage. Porter wasn't frustrated solely by Los Angeles's actions; he was also upset that he and his neighboring border communities had to manage responses to the blockade's impacts independently. "It is a state problem," he told the United Press, adding that a state or even national response to the blockade was urgently needed.

The sudden "hot potato" transient issue was exactly the kind of problem that Governor Martin foresaw when first informed of the blockade.

With the Sierra Nevada mountains and sparse desert comprising much of the border between California and Nevada, migrant traffic between the two states was somewhat lighter than it was between California and its other two neighbors. Still, large numbers of homeless transients purportedly resided in "jungles" (makeshift encampments in creek beds and other undeveloped spaces) near Las Vegas, from which they could easily enter California by way of Needles. Another major migration route between Nevada and California passed through the town of Truckee near Lake Tahoe, as it had for more than a century. In 1936 the check point at Truckee remained closed for some time because of snowy conditions.

Nevertheless, Nevada Governor Richard Kirman also asked Frank Merriam to intervene against the LAPD to prevent the Southern California expeditionary force from "throwing indigents back." The Silver State's attorney general, Arthur Gray Mashburn, joined Kirman's protest. "[Nevada] will not stand idly by and have a flood of indigents turned back from the California border," Mashburn told the United Press, invoking the same negative flood imagery Californians used.

Arizonans may have felt the most antipathy toward the blockade, especially outside of Blythe and in Yuma, just across from the border patrol checkpoint in Winterhaven, California. More Dust Bowl migrants entered California from Arizona than anywhere else, in part because Route 66—the famed Mother Road—and other popular migration routes passed through the Grand Canyon State and in part because seasonal conditions rendered travel over the Rocky and Cascade mountain ranges particularly uninviting each winter. Arizona was the final hurdle before the Golden State for many migrants. For Californians fearing a migrant "invasion," it was the last buffer against incoming "hordes."

Arizonans saw the situation differently. To them, Californians were to blame for beckoning travelers and opportunity-seekers in the first place. Like so many other states after the sunsetting of the Federal Emergency Relief Act, the Grand Canyon State's relief budget was overstretched and ill-prepared to absorb new cases all at once. Adding to the problem was the fact that Arizona's own unique climatological conditions translated to growing seasons that differed from California's for many valuable crops, meaning that many migrants could shift between the two states to find work from season to season.

Once the blockade started, a front-page headline in the *Tucson Citizen* described city officials' fears: TRANSIENT BACKWASH. Arizona's highway patrol superintendent said patrolmen would watch the border, ready to "step into the picture" to keep that state's highways from being congested by returned transients, while the state's attorney general told the *Citizen* that people just like those Davis's officers turned back were the ones who "formerly traveled in covered wagons" and built California.

Arizona leaders watched the armed deployments along their western frontier and sought to respond in kind. The bridge between Winterhaven, California, and Yuma, Arizona, became a flashpoint. Los Angeles police lined up on one side, ready to send migrants into Arizona; on the other, Yuma sheriff deputies faced off against their Californian counterparts, ready to send all who tried to stay in Arizona back across.

Even the risk of a military escalation loomed. One Arizona city's mayor asked Governor Benjamin B. Moeur to activate the National Guard and deploy its troops to border crossings, where he hoped soldiers would counter the LAPD officers' attempts to send transients back across the Colorado. Whatever happened, migrants, as they so often were, would find themselves stuck in the middle.

---

The outrage wasn't solely felt outside of Los Angeles.

Fifteen days after the blockade began, Los Angeles Limited Train No. 7 had just left Chicago bound for California when Roy Raymond Colby decided to write a letter to the Los Angeles City Council. Colby, a lawyer and a Los Angeles resident, noted that there were hundreds of passengers on the train—including, he scrawled in pencil at the beginning, the entire Chicago Cubs baseball team—many of whom were fretting about the stories they'd read in newspapers about the blockade of California's borders.

How would Colby or anyone know who among the riders had some disqualifying factor that might keep them out of Los Angeles based on Davis's criteria? Maybe one of them had once been accused of a crime. Perhaps someone on board had even been convicted once but later pardoned. Maybe a few passengers didn't have round-trip train tickets or had borrowed money for the trip. Colby provided example after hypothetical example of all the ways passengers might be ensnared by the blockade.

"Just where are you going to draw the line?" Colby asked, wondering if Davis himself would adjudicate every case without bothering to have trials, despite constitutional guarantees. "What section in the Constitution of the United States, or in the Constitutions of California, Arizona, Nevada, or Oregon, gives [Davis] authority to not only stop immigration, but also to arrest, imprison, and kidnap people and transport them forcibly and against their wills over the lines into other states?" Colby asked, adding later in the letter that any police officer, government official, or elected representative who deliberately violated the constitution was unfit to be a citizen, let alone hold office. "Such a person is a crook," Colby said, "just as much a crook as those we have in our jails, or those that we are stopping at our borders."

# 11 | AFTERSHOCK

JOHN SHARP ONLY HAD TO LOOK at Orville Sycafoose, Leon Slate, and Charles La Rue to realize how little patience he had left for Chief Davis's antics. The blood on one man's face said it all. Not one to anger easily, the sheriff was livid. He couldn't abide by anyone running roughshod over the peace and safety of his county, not even fellow law enforcers. It would have been bad enough if the police who'd pulled the men off a train at Stronghold were drunk and had beaten them, as the men had sworn to District Attorney Wylie. But what angered Sharp more was that the Los Angeles cops were still acting like they had authority in his jurisdiction.

Sycafoose, Slate, and La Rue had been working together at a lumber mill in Klamath Falls, Oregon. After they were offered work at another mill in Westwood, a small town about eighty miles south of Alturas in California's Lassen County, they decided to travel there aboard a Great Northern freight train. All three were California residents—Sycafoose and Slate were from Westwood itself; La Rue was from Weed, a town in Siskiyou County—and they had documents confirming their job offers.

That didn't matter to the LAPD patrol officers stationed at Tulelake, a tiny community by a reed-filled lake of the same name just south of the Oregon border. On the night of March 9, 1936, three officers working at a railroad siding in Stronghold, a few miles further south of Tulelake, stopped the train, climbed on board, and eventually found the trio of millers. The cops tried to arrest the men immediately. When they protested that they were California residents and, besides, had proof that they had legitimate jobs at the other end of the train line, the officers yanked the workers off the train, punching and slamming the flashlight into one of the men's lips. They then put the men in back of their car and drove them to a jail cell in Tulelake before releasing them the next day.

The men found a ride into Alturas, where they reported what had happened to Sharp, who in turn told them to swear an affidavit with District Attorney A. K. Wylie. Sharp had already stressed to Chief Davis the dynamics of Modoc County life and the frequent travel taken by workers on the ranches, forests, cattle ranges, lumber mills, and other worksites both in Northern California and across the state line in Oregon. Now Davis's men had completely ignored that warning, even after Sharp told Davis to leave people in his county alone.

"These men are respectable working men," Sharp stressed after the arrests.

Sharp—and Modoc County—had been in the national spotlight's glare for more than a month. Sharp had never been enthusiastic for that kind of attention. Now he'd spent weeks at the center of a political power struggle in which he'd had absolutely no interest in participating.

This struggle was getting angrier—and now bloodier—on California's periphery when it really should have been happening in Los Angeles, or at least in Sacramento. It was dividing Modoc County residents, impeding the local economy, and putting in jeopardy the people who worked for the county's ranchers and businesses. Sharp might not have started the fight, but that didn't mean he could avoid it.

Sergeant Bergman needed to leave the county along with the fourteen officers he'd brought. If they didn't do so immediately, Sharp was prepared to arrest them, an ultimatum he made clear to Bergman and Chief Davis.

Instead of cooperating with his counterpart in Modoc County, Davis denied the allegations against his men. That denial might not have been likely to sway Sheriff Sharp, but Davis probably didn't expect that it would. What he *did* know was that Sharp wasn't the only person of any influence in Modoc County. Just as was the case in Los Angeles, Davis's antitransient crusade and his broader anticrime agenda depended on a sympathetic press in border counties. If newspapers like the Alturas *Plaindealer* lined up in support of his officers, Davis might be able to sway local opinion in Modoc County and, perhaps eventually, chip away at political support for people like Sharp who didn't defer to the chief's dictates.

Even though at the beginning of the operation Gertrude French had, through the *Plaindealer*'s unsigned articles, urged readers to wait to come to a decision about the blockade and to weigh all facts equally, over the course of the LAPD's presence in Modoc County, her paper's coverage treated it ever more forgivingly than it did Sharp's resistance and other local opposition. After the arrests at Stronghold, French willingly accepted Davis's defense of his officers while implying that political motives informed Sharp's challenge, as did resistance from other local figures, like Sharp's brother, Jake, and District Attorney A. K. Wylie, both Democrats and known friends of Claude McCracken.

"If I were sheriff instead of bandying meaningless words with the L.A. police chief, I would go out and spend a great deal of time finding out what is going on and what the police is really doing where there would be an advantage to my county, and what the advantage will be to the State in the long run," argued the *Plaindealer*'s Rambling 'Round column that March. "If the men's story is true, it is contrary to the practice and aims of the blockade, and Chief Davis orders, that we know. If the men tried to resist the officers it is probable they got just what Sheriff Sharp and his deputies deal out when necessary."

French may have been motivated to take Davis's side for no deeper reason than that it placed her and the *Plaindealer* on the opposite side of the issue from Claude McCracken. One piece French published after the incident at Stronghold implied that Wylie's friendship with McCracken and other past actions of his disqualified him from treating the border patrol fairly. French once again seemed to assert that her longtime foil was corrupting other public figures, disrupting Modoc County life, and sowing divisions in her beloved community.

## The Tide Ebbs

Davis's posturing against Sharp notwithstanding, his operation was already losing steam when the sheriff ordered border patrollers out of his jurisdiction. By April, only a few weeks after pulling squads from Modoc County, he suspended the entire operation. Despite increasing bad press and widening public outrage about the blockade, Davis framed the deployment as a success, and it would be treated as such by many, though not all, local leaders. The following January, the Los Angeles County Grand Jury would also praise the operation in its annual year-end report.

Continuing to dismiss his critics, Chief Davis claimed that he'd achieved exactly what he'd set out to accomplish with the blockade: the migrant tide was easing; crime was dropping; California was safe. None of these were accurate claims.

In actuality, the complications besetting the deployment from its outset had only mounted. John Langan's lawsuit was still winding through the court; his sudden disappearance and withdrawal of the case would happen at the end of March. U. S. Webb's letter to the chamber of commerce's Arthur Arnoll questioning the operation's legality had become public, and John Sharp was not the only border county sheriff publicly frustrated with the LAPD's impertinent presence in their jurisdictions.

Davis brushed all of these challenges off, but he couldn't ignore a more prosaic challenge: the blockade was expensive. Somebody had to pay to house, feed, clothe, and arm each of the 136 LAPD officers deployed hundreds of miles away from Los Angeles. Since the officers deployed on a volunteer basis on top of their regular duties, Chief Davis needed to detail how he planned to cover the expense of sending volunteer officers so far from city limits, and he simply wasn't doing a good job of justifying the operation's cost for his city's taxpayers.

For one thing, Davis paid for the blockade using the same controversial and amorphously defined special projects fund that financed Red Hynes's strike-breaking and Earl Kynette's spying. For another, police department records would eventually show that crime in Los Angeles actually rose during the period the blockade was active. The legionnaires may have questioned, fingerprinted, and arrested or deported many of the thousands of migrants they stopped. They likely scared untold more from even trying to enter the state (or so Davis may have hoped). However many people the blockade kept out of California, Davis's own statisticians documented *more* crime reports made to police than over the same period in 1935. Then, lawlessness had ostensibly become so widespread that calls for a war on crime, a statewide police force, the drafting of anti-indigent legislation, and increased interstate law enforcement rang loudly. That's why the California Peace Officers' Association had claimed its Western States Anti-Crime Conference had been so necessary. A year after that conference, if Communist plots really were responsible for crime in California, as Davis so passionately insisted, and if crime remained on the rise, then the chief's attempt to use law enforcement to crush Red subversion was clearly failing.

## Colorado Follows Davis's Lead

Sheriff Sharp may have won a publicity battle—some Californians even suggested he run for governor—but advocates for poor and displaced migrants faced a long war. Davis's obsession with vagrancy persisted. So did the nation's.

Other states, and some cities and counties, launched (or resumed) blockades of their own. The first major imitator was Colorado, where on April 18, 1936, Governor Edwin Johnson declared martial law along the state's 360-mile southern border. Johnson, who was preparing for an ultimately successful bid for one of Colorado's US Senate seats later that year, borrowed language from the L.A. operation and claimed that "aliens and indigent" persons were planning to "invade" the state. To counter that alleged threat, Johnson deployed fifty national guardsmen to six checkpoints along the state line with New Mexico. The troops would be backed by Colorado highway patrol officers and other state authorities.

Though Colorado was more than five hundred miles from any international border, Johnson claimed that the soldiers he deployed would prevent Mexicans from entering the state. He said his border patrollers would differentiate between Mexican citizens trying to come into Colorado and US citizens of Mexican descent by counting how much money each person had.

"Our main object is to head off destitute people from other states who will come here, perhaps work in the beet fields for a few weeks, and go on relief," Johnson told the Associated Press. "If we catch a few aliens among them, so much the better, but the big thing is to keep out those who will become public charges."

Johnson's ten-day-long deployment of National Guard troops to Colorado's borders was transparently politically motivated. Aside from the state's distance from the Mexican border, the fact that troops only blocked crossings from the New Mexico state line left the blockade incredibly porous. Moreover, argued Elisa Martia Alvarez Minoff in a 2013 doctoral dissertation, Colorado and other states' various border patrols were unnecessary thanks to the Hoover Administration's repatriation campaign and other existing anti-immigrant policies.

"These states did not need to deter immigrants, because President Herbert Hoover had already, through a major deportation drive and a tightening of immigration regulations, significantly reduced the number of immigrant aliens living in those and neighboring states," Minoff wrote.

The state of Florida, meanwhile, had instituted blockades of its interstate borders to keep out transients from the North who arrived each winter. Florida Governor Dave Sholtz had actually launched these blockades two years prior to James Davis's operation, but they gained renewed attention after the California blockade began. Various other small-scale, copycat transient bans followed. There was even one in Nome, Alaska.

## Davis Returns to the Antimigrant Well

With the truth about rising crime during the period of the blockade still to surface, Davis continued to crow about the deployment after its cessation. For the most part, the press willingly obliged. Instead of examining stubbornly rising crime numbers or determining whether the blockade had actually been effective, newspapers instead used crime as a tool to indict dysfunction they perceived in California's political bureaucracy. Gertrude and Bard French's *Alturas Plaindealer* joined the publications reporting California's rising crime rates even as it elided any mention of the foreign police forces that had so recently riven the community.

Meanwhile, Republicans were trying (and largely failing) to find a presidential nominee who could take on Roosevelt in the rapidly approaching elections, as the state's GOP splintered into competing camps squabbling over the party's future. That November, Republicans would lose their fight against Roosevelt, and badly.

Before the election, though, James Davis was looking ahead to another winter and the possibility of another wave of seasonal migrants to California. His refusal to acknowledge the blockade's challenges meant that the police department's efforts against transients and other indigent people could continue, especially given that the public's antimigrant sentiment had not changed. Rather than retreat in the aftermath of the blockade's failure, Davis retooled the police department's enforcement of antivagrancy laws.

Despite his repeated attempts to use police as a tool to suppress migration and vagrancy in Los Angeles, Chief Davis ultimately recognized that it would be impossible to completely seal Los Angeles off from outsiders. By their very nature, migrants and transients weren't one city's problem. Instead, Davis believed that Southern California would never be able to stem the influx of migrants and relief-seekers without law enforcement jurisdictions and local governments throughout the region cooperating on the issue.

Davis never retreated from his assertion that indigent migrants posed a grave danger to Los Angeles. By October 1936, as harvests ended in cooler parts of the country, the number of migrants to California grew again. Despite the chief's insistence on the earlier blockade's success, Davis knew that this time around he wouldn't be able to recruit enough support to again send officers to the state lines. He could, however, lock down Los Angeles itself.

City leaders readily authorized this new plan. Again working closely with Deputy Chief Cross, Davis ordered officers to set up checkpoints at Los Angeles's city limits and pick up where the first antimigrant operation had left off. This time, officers surveilled highways entering Los Angeles, looking for ostensibly telltale signs of vagrants and transients bound for the city. Just as they had at border crossings from Arizona, Nevada, and Oregon, Davis's legionnaires stopped and searched trains for stowaways before they could enter the City of Angels. Davis enlisted Sheriff Eugene Biscailuz to assist the localized blockade. With Los Angeles police deployed throughout the city and focused on their own jurisdiction this time, Biscailuz's deputies extended their reach through the county's sprawling unincorporated areas.

Geographically, this was a more limited operation, but the officers participating had a more expansive charge than the original patrol had had, at least on the surface. This was a full-scale crackdown that all but made being poor, or appearing to be poor, a crime in Los Angeles. Davis's officers weren't solely tasked with keeping indigent migrants out of the city. During the original blockade, patrol officers had also rousted vagrants already within Los Angeles and ejected anyone who could not provide a legitimate reason why they should be allowed to remain.

This time, antivagrant squads patrolled Los Angeles streets and scoured city blocks looking for anyone looking like a vagrant. Davis coupled these increased patrols with more stringent punishments for those violating loitering ordinances and similar laws. This punishment often even included compulsory labor, such as street cleaning for people caught sleeping on a sidewalk.

What Davis lost in geography of his blockade he gained in press sympathy. That December, for example, a writer named Harry Nelson produced a lengthy sympathetic feature for the Ledger Syndicate about Los Angeles and Florida's competition to develop effective blockades. Nelson's feature appeared in newspaper Sunday magazines throughout the United States. Not only did he, with little sourcing, make Davis's case for the blockade, but also Nelson bought the police department's argument that its necessity wasn't just due to the 10 percent of migrants with previous criminal records. Police must also keep out people who might *become* criminals. Migrants with little recourse upon arriving to California were too liable to be exploited and corrupted.

"Being alone in a strange city and not knowing where his next meal is to come from, he is likely to resort to thievery as a means of 'getting by,'" wrote Nelson. "Such a person is too proud to ask for relief, or to beg, or to write friends for aid. He doesn't want to admit being a fraud."

With voters that November expressing overwhelming favor for Roosevelt—and, by extension, the New Deal—officials and politicians in Los Angeles and surrounding communities again turned to focusing on what they continued to describe as a migrant crisis. Once again, Davis made Homer Cross his public point person for the antivagrancy campaign. Cross, in turn, gathered police, sheriffs, and county supervisors from throughout Los Angeles County and nine other Southern California counties that together comprise Southern California, in the hope of together developing a regional plan for stopping transient migration.

The officials Cross convened devised plans for yet another new blockade. This regional plan was again geographically limited, but larger than that October's Los Angeles County operation. The newly proposed plan would ignore the trouble-prone crossings that February along the California-Oregon border and instead only focus on crossings from within their region, all of which bordered either Arizona or southern Nevada. Most domestic migrants entered California by way of these crossings anyhow. More detailed than the original blockade, this operation would use fifty-man shifts to stake out highways, railroads, and pedestrian crossings into California.

This time, Davis didn't have to bother with Sheriff Sharp or anyone else who wanted to raise a fuss. Momentum toward the new blockade initially seemed promising. Officials throughout the participating counties aligned behind the plan. Even Governor Merriam endorsed it.

Questions remained, of course. How could it avoid messes like John Langan's arrest? Could it circumvent a publicity nightmare if cops picked up someone who still should be allowed into the state? The solution, as one newspaper reported, seemed like a straightforward one: only experienced officers "capable of distinguishing between desirable and undesirable arrivals" would be deployed to the new checkpoints. No one made clear, however, how those officers' experience would be assessed.

Officials from throughout the nine-county region started lining up behind the new plan through the course of that November and into December. Boards of supervisors approved the idea; Governor Merriam remained on board; Biscailuz again stressed that the Los Angeles County Sheriff's Department would participate. Every cog of local law enforcement and political machinery was turning against incoming migrants.

Then the carefully tuned apparatus slipped. Just before Christmas, Sheriff Biscailuz reversed his position, asking Los Angeles County supervisors for official permission to withdraw his deputies from assisting the blockade. Biscailuz gave the board a surprising reason for wanting to withdraw. Instead of telling the board that he wanted to avoid overextending the department's resources or to avoid jurisdictional conflicts, or instead of offering some other technicality, the sheriff called Chief Davis's credibility into question.

County investigators couldn't find any evidence of a transient influx in Los Angeles County, Biscailuz told the board. Their report undermined the central claim of Davis's entire antimigrant agenda, that indigent transients were entering California in numbers that so strained the state that their continued presence represented an urgent crisis whose resolution required authorities to invoke emergency powers. Public reactions to the plan suggested that many county residents believed Davis and Mayor Shaw were pressuring the rest of the county to participate. Wary of both exposing the county to legal challenges and draining county resources for a futile operation, the board permitted Biscailuz to withdraw.

## Meanwhile, in Modoc County

While Southern California weighed whether to launch another border blockade, Modoc County was still coming to terms with its role in the original blockade. Voters there would not decide for two years on another term for John Sharp as sheriff, but the question of his political popularity came to the fore in the months to come. The sheriff's resistance to Los Angeles's police deployment had earned him and Modoc County significant fame, especially for a place that felt so remote from any other part of California, let alone the rest of the country. That fame could be interpreted as a positive or negative influence on Sharp's electoral chances as he looked ahead to the 1938 election.

Thanks to the blockade, whispers about the campaign were already circling, even as the county prepared for the current presidential election. Once again, the whispers and rumors could be traced to the simmering feud between Claude McCracken, Gertrude French, and French's family. Inevitably, the animosity between the two publishers poisoned what might have been a passionate but civil debate about the role of law enforcement in Modoc County.

Claude and Gertrude's rivalry had been worsening all year, and Sheriff Sharp's response to the border patrol hadn't aided matters. The barbs Claude and Gertrude traded seemed more damaging. The Democrats' resounding victory at the polls—let alone McCracken's return to publishing—already felt to Gertrude like a defeat. Now their rivalry threatened to rip apart the community she loved so dearly, and, if she wasn't careful, such an outcome could be overshadowed by a far deeper, far more personal loss.

Gertrude and Bard French's control of publishing in the county kept McCracken from finding a printer locally. Undeterred, he crossed the Oregon border to have the *Modoc Mail* newspaper printed in Lakeview, a small community frequented by Alturans for professional services like dentistry and legal representation.

*Newspaper* might be a generous term. McCracken wrote most of the content filling the three columns of mimeographed text. Each week (Claude had shifted the *Mail*'s publication from daily to weekly to save money) after McCracken picked up the freshly duplicated sheets from Lakeview, he collated and stapled the publication himself, though later he would find a business partner to help him with the task. McCracken substituted passion for the polish his publication lacked.

Irked by their upstart competitor, perhaps because McCracken solicited sponsorship from the same bars, shops, and other Alturas businesses that advertised in the *Plaindealer*, Gertrude and Bard tried at first to ignore the *Mail*. But soon attacks in the *Plaindealer* made it clear that articles in the *Modoc Mail* had not escaped the publishers' attention.

One of the items that so troubled them was Claude's allegation about Gertrude's cousin, Jim Payne. Claude wrote that Sheriff Sharp's stand against Chief Davis and his border blockade had incensed Payne so much that Payne threatened Sharp's political future. At least, that's what McCracken claimed he'd learned in the report he ran in the *Modoc Mail*.

The problem with the claim was that McCracken made it amid the charged atmosphere of his feud with Gertrude and her family. At that point, any allegation McCracken leveled against them, and vice versa, raised significant credibility questions. McCracken always insisted that he was the more professional newsman and that he only sought to elevate Modoc County's journalism standards, but that insistence didn't prove his sincerity. The *Mail* did print claims attributed only to vague "rumors." Moreover, it would later emerge that McCracken had used Payne's alleged attempt to block Sharp's reelection to illustrate what he thought was Gertrude's and her relatives' exaggerated sense of self-importance in local affairs. Even if Payne *had* threatened Sharp, McCracken likely would have relished the news for the chance to score points against Gertrude rather than for its newsworthiness.

Few copies of the *Mail* survive, and no extant copies showing the particular Payne news item could be located by the time of this book's publication. So it's unclear precisely what McCracken claimed Payne said, let alone the source to which he attributed the rumor. The claim did not appear in other newspapers. Naturally, the *Plaindealer* wouldn't have repeated such a rumor about Gertrude's own relative, but it also hadn't been credible enough for outside papers like the *Surprise Valley Record* to run it, assuming it had reached them. No documentation of the supposed threat exists, except for later court records. The trial from which those records derived was still to come, however, and for the time being, Sharp never publicly acknowledged any such threat or any awareness of the allegation, even if it hadn't been true.

Gertrude wasn't just troubled by her dislike of Claude. Their feud also clearly impacted her son, Harry. Every new barb flung by Claude seemed to upset Harry further, sending him into vengeful rages quelled only when Gertrude urged him to show restraint. Even then, Harry followed his fits with long bouts of sullen apathy that invariably affected his work worse than had his anger. These episodes had the potential to significantly influence his entire family. America was under siege. California was under siege. Alturas was under siege. Gertrude felt like even she was under siege.

Some of the blockade's extended consequences occurred immediately; some would take years to appear. For now, as the end of 1936 approached, Los Angeles power brokers, including Davis, seemed willing to move on to other priorities, even as they continued to scorn and criminalize relief-seekers, transients, and other down-on-their-luck newcomers to California. The coming year would bring new battles, including antigambling campaigns, natural disasters, and local political scandals, all of which would distract Davis, Biscailuz, and the rest of Los Angeles from waging campaigns against transiency and vagrancy. Meanwhile, the wounds in Modoc County worsened by the blockade were about to rip apart.

# 12 | OFF GOES THE LID

HARRY FRENCH AND HIS WIFE, Vayle, spent the evening of March 23, 1937, as guests of friends who were hosting an impromptu dinner party for out-of-town visitors. After dinner, the party indulged in a game of the recently published board game Monopoly.

The chance to play the surprisingly popular game was novelty enough for Harry to mention it when he stopped in to see his parents at the *Plaindealer* newsroom the next morning. Gertrude was just finishing that week's paper, and, as she had when Frances Sweeney stopped by to show off her fingerprint stains, noticed some extra space where she could squeeze a bit of room for a news item about the social engagement. That might have been the last bit of pleasant news about her family Gertrude would print.

A few blocks away from the *Plaindealer*'s headquarters, Claude McCracken was getting ready to prepare the newest edition of his own paper, the *Modoc Mail*. That afternoon, he kissed his wife goodbye before she left for her overnight nursing shift at Modoc General Hospital, chatted briefly with their housekeeper Evelyn Olen, then started gathering up the week's articles as he waited for Donna Conwell to arrive.

Ever since starting the *Mail*, Claude had been putting whatever money he could into the paper whenever he couldn't sell enough ads to keep it afloat, but by August he couldn't afford to keep doing that. Then, in December, Conwell offered to buy a stake in the paper. He could resume publication with her as its business manager. The investment revived the paper and reinvigorated Claude.

They were finally starting to hit their stride. Sure, the silly spat with Gertrude and Bard kept going. Claude couldn't help himself from including some cracks here and there in the paper, but it was just some fun. Small towns all over America were used to seeing this kind of needling, especially when there was more than one paper. Gertrude had been unwelcoming toward Claude since he came to town. If the issue was competition, why hadn't she been as upset a few weeks ago when Gop Sloss moved to town and brought the *Record* with him from Cedarville? In any event, the *Modoc Mail* was back, and there was work to do. As soon as Conwell showed up they got to work.

They finally set the work aside when Olen let them know dinner was ready. Claude gathered up the newspaper materials and smoothed out the checked tablecloth. While Olen finished putting the food on the table, Claude tuned his radio to a show airing that night that he had wanted to hear. They lingered at the table listening to the show even after their meal was done. With Frances gone for the night, Claude felt little urgency about having Olen clean up the kitchen, and he and Conwell still had plenty of time to finish arranging the paper.

Outside, a chilly late March afternoon gave way to cold and rain. Not many people were strolling outside with the wet conditions and temperatures hovering around freezing. Nobody was likely to stop in unannounced, and Conwell was the only guest Claude had expected. Maybe they could just sit there a bit and really think of a good retort to the *Plaindealer*'s latest ridiculous broadside about Claude. Surely there was a joke to be made about that game Harry had played the other night. Why was Gertrude's son attending a dinner party and playing at being a real estate magnate so noteworthy that it merited a mention on the front page?

As they laughed at some dumb joke they knew immediately was too mean to print, a cold breeze blew into the kitchen. That was strange. Right as Claude got up to investigate, Harry French burst into the kitchen. He was drenched, slightly disheveled, and . . .

*Was that a gun?*

Indeed, French's fingers were tightly wrapped around the stock of a little .22 caliber target pistol. Conwell thought at first it was a toy. Before she could say anything, French grunted at the gathering—"Hello" maybe, or just gibberish; Conwell wasn't certain when she later recounted the evening's events— lifted the pistol, and thrust it toward Claude. *Bang!*

Conwell screamed and lunged at French. As she tried to knock French's arm away, she saw the muscles in his fingers tense a second time. *Bang!*

His finger tensed once more. And again. And one more time right after that. *Bang! Bang! Bang!*

Claude gasped and scrambled toward the kitchen counter. Conwell tried to push French, but he'd already scrambled out of the kitchen and into the street.

Conwell turned around and saw Claude propped against the kitchen sink and grasping at his chest. Evelyn was already calling the sheriff when Claude finally found his breath and started speaking to Conwell. *Get my typewriter*, the lifelong newspaper man told his new business partner. *Start typing what I say.*

"Tonight about 6:30," Claude struggled for breath, then continued, "Harry French shot Claude L. McCracken, editor of the Modoc Mail, with an automatic pistol. Condition of McCracken serious.—McCracken"

Claude gasped again and looked at Conwell with insistent, serious eyes. *Go. Wire that to the AP in San Francisco. They'll know what to do with it*, he told Conwell. Then Claude collapsed.

Olen and Conwell tried to stop Claude's bleeding and make him comfortable until an ambulance arrived. The ambulance crew loaded him up on a stretcher and whisked him to the county hospital.

————————

Frances McCracken had been working for a few hours when a report came in that an ambulance was on its way with a gunshot victim. As soon as she heard the report, Frances notified Dr. John Stile, then started prepping an operating room in case he needed to perform an emergency surgery. There was little doubt he would. Frances didn't know how bad the victim's injuries were or who he was, but she knew he had been shot five times. Surgery was all but certain, and as the head nurse in the hospital's emergency department it was her job to make sure everything was ready for that or any eventuality.

Finally the ambulance approached. Frances waited at the door as its driver parked, ran to the back of the ambulance, and flung its doors open. The driver gently lowered the stretcher, then wheeled it slowly toward the hospital. Then Frances recognized the man on the stretcher.

Horror washed through Frances's body. Her head went light. Her limbs tingled. The man clinging to life in front of her was Claude—her husband.

Frances's balance faltered as adrenaline rushed through her veins. Other hospital staff took over and rushed Claude's gurney to the operating room Frances had just finished preparing. Frances caught her breath, regained her footing, inhaled again, then went inside after them. Her husband might have been the one bleeding on the stretcher, but she still had a job to do. As soon as her heartbeat slowed enough for her to feel steady, she washed up, breathed deeply once more, stepped into the operating room, and got to work alongside Dr. Stile.

Despite the surgeon's efforts, and Frances's, Claude simply didn't have much of a chance. His wounds were just too severe. Bullets had hit his heart, lungs, and liver and torn up his intestines. One had gone through his arm into his body.

Claude died within a few hours. His last words had been the ones he told Conwell to send to the newswire. Frances said goodbye, comforted, at least, in the knowledge that in the end they'd both done their duties in their last moments together.

"As her husband was a faithful true reporter to the leaf, Mrs. Frances McCracken was a true nurse," reported the *Nevada State Journal*.

Maybe someone in San Francisco was already getting the story out on the AP newswire. Just a year after the feud over the Los Angeles border deployment, bad news again brought Modoc County back to the nation's attention.

---

Harry French's day had started rather typically. He'd gotten a haircut around ten that morning. George Kelley, one of Sheriff Sharp's deputies, was at the barbershop himself that morning.

Later in the day, Harry French went for a drink at the Tavern, a semiprivate clubhouse where he often socialized. While he drank, French noticed a stack of the most recent issues of the *Modoc Mail*. He picked up a paper, took a look, and, incensed, pushed away from the bar.

French left the bar and went to A. A. Hafter's second-hand shop. There, French asked Hafter if he could borrow a pistol so he could settle a bet with a friend about who was the better shot. Hafter didn't think it a strange request, and he knew French was a good guy, so he leant him a .22 caliber target pistol.

French thanked Hafter, got in his car despite his inebriated condition, and drove to Claude's home. Two teenage neighbors were talking in front of a nearby house when they saw French drive up, get out of the car, and approach the McCrackens'. French stumbled in the muddy yard, got up, took a few more steps, then stumbled again. Standing up once more, he halfheartedly wiped mud off his pants and walked toward the residence, this time with more determination.

The teens looked at one another briefly, then returned to their conversation as Harry walked around the house to an exterior door on the kitchen. A light was on inside, and the boys could see Claude conversing with two women inside. They thought it had been strange that Harry hadn't gone to the front door—especially considering the feud between his family and McCracken—so they followed to see what he was doing. They peeked in the window just in time to see a sudden struggle, hear five quick gunshots, and watch Donna Conwell push Harry from the kitchen door as Claude staggered into another room. French stumbled past the boys, got back in the car, and drove off.

A few minutes later, French arrived at the home of Charley Chapman, a friend of French's since childhood. French told Chapman what had just happened, then demanded that Chapman shoot him. Chapman refused to shoot his friend but instead told him he needed to call the sheriff. Breaking into tears, French agreed.

Chapman, who still didn't completely believe French had done what he said, nonetheless asked French why he'd done it. It was clear his friend was in distress, and he thought talking to him while they waited for a deputy might calm him down.

"The son of a bitch insulted my folks," French snarled, right as Sheriff Sharp's deputy, George Kelley, showed up.

Kelley brought French to the jail and booked him on suspicion of murder. He was muddy and sweating, maybe slurring ever so slightly, but seemed to have his wits about him.

The murder stunned Modoc County. The discord between the two newspapers was not at all surprising, but the violent depths to which the dispute had plunged was shocking.

## The Price of "Filial Solicitude"

Harry went on trial that June. Nobody could argue that he had not shot Claude. Harry's lawyers, two of whom were his uncles, instead persuaded him to plead that he'd been rendered temporarily insane. Neither McCracken's behavior over the past two years nor his mother's attentions had helped matters for Harry.

Jurors didn't buy it and sentenced him to death at San Quentin. Justices in higher courts didn't seem to have any more patience for arguments from French's lawyers when they appealed the verdict, in part on grounds that the jury hadn't been allowed to fully consider evidence about the feud between his family and McCracken.

"Counsel for appellant rest their defense on the psychopathic condition of the defendant which it is claimed had its origin in the attachment and deep-seated affection for his mother from early infancy," wrote Associate Justice Emmett Seawell (coincidentally, a former president of the Native Sons of the Golden West) in the California Supreme Court's decision dismissing French's appeal. "They argue that an increasing devotion to his mother's well-being developed in him a sense of filial solicitude so overmastering that her cares became his cares and he became grieved to an inordinate and exaggerated degree whenever his mother manifested the slightest unhappiness."

Setting aside whether murder could ever be justified by one's filial solicitude, there's no surprise that Harry was devoted to Gertrude, just as she had been devoted to R. C. Dorris, Colonel William Thompson, and the greater lineage, both of blood and of tradition, to which she felt so devoted. One feature of the feud with Claude, as it escalated so explosively over its final months, was how those bonds were targeted over and over again. These were sacred bonds, ones that Claude had challenged since the moment he arrived in Modoc County and continued to challenge as he overstayed what little welcome he had.

Gertrude wound her individual and family identity tightly in their California heritage and the political leaders and organizations whom she saw as that heritage's staunchest advocates. She had hoped Harry did too. Perhaps he had gone to work in 1933 as a state senate clerk and later accepted a job as a tax collector for the state because he shared Gertrude's sense of duty to one's own land.

By the time Harry shot Claude, exchanges of scandalous, deeply personal accusations dominated the feud between his family and McCracken. Their dispute had started with simple political differences, but the political enmity deteriorated into a feud that blurred the lines between personal and political, as well as public and private. Fear and xenophobia nurtured by the likes of James Edgar Davis and Louise Ward Watkins hastened that deterioration. Instead of rationally assessing migration to California and seeking sound analysis of how to either welcome or exclude migrants from the state, Gertrude bought into Davis's alternate reality. With the blockade's standard-bearer manufacturing stories about Communist-instigated crime waves to justify the operation, inventing statistics about police efficacy to support it, and dispatching lieutenants to manufacture dirt about those who challenged the operation to rescue it, how surprising could it have been that the deployment's rippling unexpected consequences might muddy clear-eyed assessments of politics and local affairs in the communities it impacted?

## Gangland

James Davis's and Frank Shaw's repeated attempts to block indigent migrants from coming to California didn't seem to slow in the new year. Once 1937 rolled around, their efforts to police Los Angeles's image and suppress dissent shifted to a more publicly palatable crusade: fighting gangsterism.

Almost as soon as the year began, Davis joined District Attorney Buron Fitts and Sheriff Biscailuz—neither were people with whom he easily cooperated—to publicly announce a war on gangsters in Los Angeles. After the border blockade wrapped up, Davis spent the remainder of 1936 claiming that he'd made the city safer with it, along with his simultaneous vagrancy sweeps within Los Angeles. Despite the national scrutiny, neither had failed, not by any means. They succeeded, Davis insisted, and the proof that they had was that the operations ended. The city was safer, and the police deployed to the state's borders could go home.

However, numerous dramatic violent crimes in Los Angeles that year— many involving full-scale casinos operating on ships anchored just outside of US territorial waters from Los Angeles but easily accessible by water taxis— showed the city how little had actually changed.

Fortunately for Los Angeles's political leaders, spectacular, violent crimes also meant convenient opportunities for local politicians to deflect public scrutiny from other matters. Throughout the 1920s and into the 1930s, police chiefs, prosecutors, and politicians in the city regularly declared wars on gang violence to score political favor. Davis, Biscailuz, and Fitts had all done so in the past themselves. As sure as the sun rose over the Mojave Desert and set beyond Malibu, it seemed, city leaders' crackdowns and sweeps would give way to revelations of crooked cops, corrupt prosecutors, and bribed politicians who struck deals with the city's vice lords. Such deals then became object lessons around which civic leaders could build corruption-fighting platforms and introduce reform measures. In turn, aided by their seemingly intractable hold on the bureaucracies implementing such reforms, underworld figures simply adapted to reform, and sometimes even steered them toward their own interests.

Shaw's 1933 election and Davis's return to the chief's office had only perpetuated this cycle of vice, corruption, and reform. By the time Davis rejoined the call to finally dismantle Los Angeles's underworld in 1937, new questions about his and the mayor's relationship to vice were growing louder. *Still*, Shaw easily won reelection that spring.

## Pay What You Wish

Robert Walker Kenny had just finished parking when he heard the explosion. He hurried out of his car, noticed neighbors running up his street to investigate the sound, and raced up Serrano Avenue himself. When he reached Los Feliz Boulevard, Kenny turned west to follow the crowd chasing the source of the noise. The blast's origin was clear then, and Kenny, a judge in the Los Angeles County Superior Court, knew instantly that it hadn't been an accident. Someone had tried to blow up Clifford Clinton's house.

Clinton hadn't been home when the bomb went off, nor was anyone else. The damage to his house from the October 28, 1937, explosion could have been much worse, but Clinton was still lucky. The owner of Clifton's Cafeteria, a popular eatery in downtown Los Angeles that Clinton had opened in 1931 and where diners were invited to "pay what you wish," was becoming an ever-louder critic of Frank Shaw and his allies as the decade progressed. It wasn't news that one of those allies might want Clinton dead. What might turn out to be more shocking for Angelenos was who was behind the blast, which might have spared Clinton but not necessarily Los Angeles as they knew it.

A year and a half earlier John Anson Ford—the Los Angeles County supervisor who'd opposed Los Angeles's border blockade and unsuccessfully challenged Shaw in the 1937 mayoral election—had persuaded Clinton to investigate the county-run hospital's food-purchasing contracts. Clinton's ensuing investigation uncovered questionable contracts and other malfeasance reaching far beyond the hospital system. Casting himself as an anticorruption crusader, Clinton rode a wave of popular outrage and newfound attention all the way to a nomination for the county grand jury.

Other reform-minded Angelenos were also selected for the investigatory panel, but its majority remained firmly in the hands of Los Angeles's power brokers. They remained in control of which allegations the grand jury pursued, which recommendations they made, and what to ignore. The power brokers ignored evidence of vice Clinton found on his own, linking brothel operations and other wrongdoing to a host of local officials and institutions, including alleged kickbacks and protection rackets benefitting the district attorney and the Los Angeles Police Department.

Undeterred by the majority's attempt to quash his inquiries, Clinton turned over enough rocks to fill a minority report with plenty of dirt. The local political machine had used its sympathetic majority to prevent the grand jury from indicting its central cogs, but Clinton carried on. In concert with other anticorruption crusaders, that August Clinton launched the Citizens Independent Vice Investigating Committee, or CIVIC, to continue their investigations.

The attempt to bomb Clinton's house dangerously escalated the situation. Clinton wanted to know who tried to kill him. He turned to Harry Raymond, a former LAPD cop who'd spent only three months on the job as San Diego's police chief when he was fired for investigating vice there. Now a private investigator, Raymond's sleuthing had already turned up much of the evidence Clinton and CIVIC were gathering against Frank Shaw, his brother Joe, and James Davis.

Then, on the morning of January 14, 1938, another explosion shattered windows and shook homes throughout Boyle Heights, a neighborhood just east of downtown Los Angeles. Raymond had gone to his garage to start his car while waiting for his wife, who wanted to hitch a ride with him to the store but was talking to a neighbor. The car blew up as soon as Raymond started it. Though he wasn't killed and remained conscious for some time, he fell into a coma after arriving at the hospital.

Raymond clung to consciousness long enough to tell CIVIC's lawyer, A. Brigham Rose, that he believed not only that he knew who planted the bomb that might have killed him (or, that at that point, possibly still would) but also that he worked for powerful figures. He had evidence—carefully safeguarded by associates in four cities far from Los Angeles—that Raymond said would, as Rose recounted it, "blow the tower off City Hall."

Within weeks, credible evidence emerged about who planted the bomb and who allegedly sent the bomber. These and other revelations that followed would rock Los Angeles. The central suspect in the bombing was a cop, and not just some disposable beat cop. It was Captain Earl E. Kynette, the very same man whom Chief Davis promoted from lieutenant to thank him for silencing John Langan and saving Davis's border patrol—and perhaps his career—from serious legal scrutiny.

Kynette was later charged with attempted murder for the attack on Raymond, as were officers Roy Allen and Fred Browne. Multiple other officers were charged with lesser, related crimes, though not all were accused of direct involvement.

Few believed that Kynette and the other suspects acted independently, but their higher-ups pleaded ignorance when they were first contacted about the attacks. Both Joe Shaw and Chief Davis were in Mexico City, where an LAPD pistol team was competing in a shooting competition. Frank Shaw was in Washington, DC. Davis returned to Los Angeles immediately. The chief told the reporters who called him before he left Mexico that he knew of no attempts by any police officers to intimidate Clinton and Raymond, nor had he ordered Kynette or anyone else to pressure the mayor's critics. He said he was surprised that two policemen had been arrested and said it would be absurd to suggest any of his officers might have been connected with the attacks in any manner. "No member of the Los Angeles police department could possibly be guilty of a bombing offense," Davis told reporters.

The same man who insisted that any penniless migrant could easily be swept up into a life of crime could not publicly admit that those who worked under him or close to him could be corrupted themselves. To do so would mean admitting his own fallibility, let alone any more extensive or sinister implications about his or other officials' involvement. Davis savored the results Kynette had produced for him; he apparently hadn't anticipated how Kynette's current actions might threaten everything he so cherished.

The bombings were dramatic events in their own right. They also sparked a public relations inferno set to engulf Davis and the Shaws. Investigations into the bombing's aftermath—and their antecedents—not only shook these people's hold on power but also illuminated how far Chief Davis had been willing to go in 1936 to defend his antitransient blockade. Only through these investigations did a fuller accounting of Kynette's role in defending Davis against Langan's challenge came to light.

Had Angelenos kept track, much of the evidence of Kynette's own less than ideal behavior might have come to light. Kynette's frequent, sometimes sadistic pursuit of the LAPD's targets as the head of the city's intelligence squad had already often been featured in news articles, though not always in a negative light. His own background had its murky elements too.

Originally from Council Bluffs, Iowa, Kynette worked as a drugstore chemist and vaudeville actor who studied dentistry at the University of Southern California before joining the LAPD in 1925. Through the years, a string of troubled romances had led to a child born when Kynette and the girl's mother were just eighteen, an annulled marriage with an oil heiress who'd lied about her age after she and Kynette eloped, and another marriage that ended when Kynette's soon-to-be ex-wife claimed he preferred spending time with his dog over her.

Kynette's questionable private life was tame compared to his policing. State legislative hearings investigating the bomb attacks and vice in Los Angeles launched in late January 1938, in response to Harry Raymond's claims. Among other revelations produced at the state inquiry, ACLU attorney John Packard—who'd represented Langan in his ill-fated suit against the LAPD and Chief Davis—finally detailed the extent of Kynette's depraved campaign to blackmail and threaten Langan into dropping his complaint. Long after the border blockade ended, the public finally learned why the case ended so suddenly. Moreover, the new information about Kynette's visits to the Langan household and threats to deport Langan's wife added new perspective to an ultimately yearslong, deeply bitter, sordid, and tragically public divorce and custody battle being waged between the former spouses, mostly on newspaper front pages.

Other sordid revelations about the bombings, Los Angeles corruption, the border patrol, and even alleged collaboration between local law enforcement and various enemy spies and saboteurs would follow. The most notable of these would appear in *Liberty Magazine*, which Frank Shaw successfully sued for libel. In the years since, scholars have noted various liberties that piece took, including Los Angeles police historian Gerald Woods, who said it "contains much valuable information but is so distorted by errors of fact and interpretation to be useless to the general reader." Still, Woods continued, "The Langan incident suffered from the [*Liberty Magazine* series'] authors' florid style but is factually trustworthy."

Despite Shaw's later victory in the libel case, in 1938 he and the rest of his administration were in trouble. That June, Kynette was convicted of attempted murder and sentenced to prison at San Quentin. The verdict spooked Davis. Publicly, he washed his hands of Kynette, casting him as a malevolent outside actor, but privately he feared that blame for the bombings would eventually fall at his feet. Once again, he turned to Harry Chandler for help and went to see him at the *Times*'s headquarters. While Davis told Chandler about his worries, Chandler asked managing editor R. W. Trueblood to come up to his office to listen to the police chief's concerns with him.

Davis feared that he would be unable to escape fallout from Kynette's crime without the paper's help preparing a public response. The chief suggested that he might abolish Kynette's old intelligence squad to demonstrate that he

Los Angeles Police Chief James E. Davis testifying before the grand jury about the attempted murder of Harry Raymond, Los Angeles, 1938. *Courtesy of Los Angeles Daily News Negatives, Special Collections, Charles E. Young Research Library, UCLA*

was taking the public's concerns seriously, but the newsman cautioned Davis that such a drastic action would actually appear like the chief was admitting wrongdoing. The newsman suggested Davis take a subtler course of action. The *Times* could even shepherd it. Instead of abolishing the spy unit, Davis should reorganize it, promise future oversight, and make a public statement about those changes. The paper could then cover each of these actions, lending them some credibility.

"We went round and round with the final decision that the *Times* should print what it can calculated to be helpful to the chief without the appearance of inspired propaganda," Trueblood wrote in a memo at the time.

He and Chandler decided to arrange for a *Times* writer named Chapin Hall to see Davis first thing the following week to go over the column. The chief, meanwhile, would prepare his statement and his plans for the squad separately, though, Trueblood confided, he hoped for help from Hall for that as well.

These actions were insufficient. Shaw's critics launched a recall campaign against him and enlisted a superior court judge named Fletcher Bowron to run against the mayor in the new election. Bowron won, and the Shaw era ended. Shortly thereafter, Davis resigned under pressure from Bowron.

Bowron was mayor. Kynette was in jail. The Shaw brothers were out of city hall. Two Gun Davis was out of a job and, it turned out, finally taking some leisure time, thanks to an offer from the owner of a shipping company to let Davis sail as a crew member aboard a tuna trawler. The 1930s were almost over. Pages were turning, but tens, if not hundreds, of thousands of Americans were still struggling to survive. As ever, the glimmering golden fortress on the edge of the continent beckoned, its walls hiding the hatred and fear inside.

# 13 | "BASIC TO ANY GUARANTEE OF FREEDOM"

THE FUTURE BECKONED MINNIE Atkins westward, toward California, toward a new start. Atkins was remarried, pregnant, and headed west on Route 66. Her new husband, Charlie, was behind the wheel of his 1928 Pontiac sedan. So many had traveled this highway—the "Mother Road"—since that car was manufactured, searching, as Atkins was, to begin again.

It was September 3, 1939. A decade of despair and drought was nearing its end, mercifully.

The rest of the world seemed to be circling in on itself. Europe had just gone to war again, while millions had died in two years of fighting between Japan and China. No one knew if America would get involved in either conflict, or if it should. War was how the world got into this mess and how it seemed the world would get out of it.

That was the rest of the world, though, and far from Minnie Atkins's mind. The late summer sun lingered over the panhandle, its golden light stretching across the horizon and luring Minnie forward. Behind her was everything that hadn't worked. Behind her was the night.

That light, though—that light was right there, just beyond this dry, dusty prison that tore at her soul as viciously as it ripped the paint from Charlie's car. She felt like she could actually see that golden beacon.

Minnie, Charlie, and Minnie's four children—fifteen-year-old Leon, thirteen-year-old Mary, ten-year-old Iver, and Delores, just five—were two days out of Tulsa. Three hundred miles of Dust Bowl highway were behind the Atkins family. More than a thousand remained before they reached the Golden State.

It was a little after 6:00 PM. Amarillo, Texas, was only seven miles ahead. English Airfield was coming up soon. They were just about to pass it as a shiny, new 1939 Mercury Club Coupe drove toward them in the opposite lane of the highway, approaching from the west. Minnie wondered what type of people might be inside.

Then the world cracked open. Charlie's Pontiac slammed headlong into the Mercury.

Nothing had ever been, nor would ever be as horrifying as the sound that followed. In an eternal instant Minnie plunged from her reverie into a screeching, screaming, crunching, shattering, tearing, grinding, grunting, ripping, wailing, gasping, gurgling, sobbing sea of terror.

The impact launched Charlie and the children from the Pontiac and knocked its engine loose. The motor shot through the dash into Minnie and pinned her to her seat. The vehicle spun across the highway. It settled in a drainage ditch as its steering column—having been flung skyward at the moment of collision—crashed to the asphalt. Trapped by the engine, Minnie could not escape the battery acid spraying over her groin and searing her thighs.

The carnage and chaos horrified the crowds massing around the accident scene. They gawked at the cars' crushed hulks and the jumble of luggage, glass, twisted metal, and torn cloth they'd strewn all over the roadway. Nobody looking on remembered ever seeing a crash so grisly, though only Minnie, Charlie, two of the children, and one of the Mercury's four occupants suffered serious injuries. Remarkably, nobody died.

*Except*—sometime, amid it all, in spite of it all, because of it all, Minnie gave birth, prematurely. Her child was born that night.

Her child died that night.

The light on the horizon was now out. Despair remained. Night surrounded.

The darkness persisted the next morning. The pain remained. Minnie—an infection now spreading through her scalded thighs and up her body—remained. She would not leave the hospital for two months—*two months!*

Charlie was gone too.

Minnie didn't know this at first, but the police ran Charlie's name after the crash. They'd radioed him in. Authorities back in Tulsa had a warrant for his arrest. He had to go back to Oklahoma, to McAlester, to a place that wasn't here, with Minnie.

*Two months of pain.*

Minnie didn't just lose her baby. She was in no condition to care for her other children. For now they were at a local Salvation Army, though that was only a stopgap measure.

Their mother burned and broken in the hospital. Their stepfather on his way back to jail. Their father . . .

Their father was somewhere in California . . . somewhere that seemed impossibly distant now.

*Two months of loneliness*: their little baby brother, or little sister—it didn't matter—was gone.

*Two months*—how would the kids manage? The Salvation Army would do for now. But for how long? How long could a Salvation Army in Amarillo care for five children from Oklahoma whose mother was in a hospital, whose father was a broke farm laborer in California, and whose stepfather was a convict heading back to the McAlester prison?

---

In Tulare County, in California's agriculture-rich Central Valley, William Ensminger, Minnie's former husband, worked as a farm laborer. Minnie's brothers also lived in Tulare County. They told Ensminger about the crash and that they planned to travel from California with their own spouses to see family in Oklahoma. Ensminger asked to come along, and they took him as far as Amarillo, where he could swoop up his kids and Minnie and take them back to Tulare.

Ensminger's former brothers-in-law did as they promised. As they continued their trip, he stayed behind in Amarillo. He found Minnie and the kids and brought all of them along to finish the drive.

The trip was grueling, especially given Minnie's condition. It was all too much for Ensminger. Once they'd made it back to California, he abandoned his family again.

Now what could Minnie do? She couldn't work in her condition. Despite her condition, or, indeed, because of her combined lack of California residency and inability to work, she also couldn't seek any kind of relief to help her and her family.

Minnie's ordeal still was not over. Tulare County judge Gareth W. Houk decided to make an example of her and similar indigent cases in the county. First Houk charged Ensminger with violating California's anti-indigent statute. Then, on November 30, Houk ordered Atkins and sixteen other indigents—the two brothers of Atkins's who'd assisted her among them—to return to Oklahoma. She could be that state's burden, not California's. Houk also cited Atkins's brothers for violating Section 2615 of the Welfare and Institutions Code, but suspended their sentences as long as they agreed to stay out of California for two years.

Tragedies like Minnie Atkins's abounded throughout California during the Great Depression even as, by 1939, many in the state and the country finally felt like they might be emerging from the crisis.

## Edwards v. California

Then Fred Edwards was arrested. Edwards was an unordained Pentecostal minister who lived in Marysville, California. A one-time Gold Rush boomtown located north of Sacramento in the foothills of the Sierra Nevada, Marysville was also home to one of the Farm Security Administration's first and best-known camps for migrant agricultural workers.

In the summer of 1939 Edwards had made headlines after managers and even some residents at the Marysville FSA camp complained about Edwards's preaching there. The dispute simmered until Edwards agreed to leave the camp if residents of the facility arranged an election and voted to have him exiled. Few residents ended up participating in the poll, but Edwards decided to leave anyway.

The battle in Marysville exhausted Edwards. That December, he and his wife decided to spend the holidays away from California visiting the wife's sister's family in the tiny town of Spur, in northern Texas. Edwards left California—and the 1930s—a free man. Three thousand miles driven and a month into a new decade, Edwards was behind bars.

Edwards's brother-in-law, Frank Duncan, was living in Texas and unemployed. Duncan had applied for and received work relief through the Works Progress Administration when he lost his job, but Duncan eventually lost that assignment. When his sister and brother-in-law visited, they invited Duncan to accompany them back to California to look for an opportunity there.

Duncan applied for aid from the Farm Security Administration a week after he and Edwards arrived. J. E. Barton, an agent working as a deputy for the state controller's office, learned of their situation and soon charged Edwards with violating Section 2615 of California's Welfare and Institutions Code. Originally passed in 1933 and amended in 1937, the law made it a crime to help indigent migrants come to California. On February 9, a Yuba County sheriff's deputy took Edwards into custody. He stayed in jail overnight but was then released on $1,000 bail.

News of Edwards's arrest quickly spread even as Barton investigated other potential violations of Section 2615. The arrest could be used as a warning to other indigents—and other well-meaning Californians—that authorities meant to start enforcing the legislation.

Barton wasn't alone in sensing broader implications in Edwards's case. ACLU of Northern California director Ernest Besig and other lawyers connected to the organization had been scouring California court filings and relief agency filings about unconstitutional arrests and complaints about unfair treatment sent to the ACLU, in search of cases to challenge the state's anti-indigent laws. Soon San Francisco–based attorneys Philip Adams and Wayne Collins agreed to take Edwards's case. Seeing its potential as a vehicle against Section 2615, they took advantage of existing nuances of California's appellate process that allowed them to circumvent higher state courts and instead take their challenge of the constitutionality of Edwards's arrest and conviction directly to the US Supreme Court.

The ACLU's national board of directors was still cautious in the wake of John Langan's suit against Chief Davis and Langan's withdrawal from the case, Earl Kynette's intimidation notwithstanding. If ACLU lawyers from one of California's chapters wanted support from outside the state for a new challenge, they would need a compelling *and* legally airtight case to use as a springboard. The organization meticulously catalogued county-by-county reports of cases prosecuted under Section 2615. Though many of the incidents wouldn't meet the ACLU's standards for a case that would change the law, most underscored the despair the country's migrants continued to experience at decade's end. The Great Depression may have been officially over, but great depression persisted.

Despite the number of incidents failing to meet the standards, those that might satisfy the requirement for a compelling case abounded. Stories of misery, discomfort, and abuse in California's migrant labor camps and throughout migration routes were common. But many of the technical details surrounding them made a successful, lasting challenge unlikely. The Edwards case was different.

Interestingly, in his argument to the Supreme Court on behalf of Edwards, Samuel Slaff—the New York–based ACLU attorney who handled Edwards's case before the Supreme Court—argued that allowing states to bar migrants from entering a state would also give states permission to do the reverse: prevent residents from leaving. That, Slaff argued, would mean "chaining people to that part of the land where accident of birth has first placed them."

Vagrancy was and remains a broad, formless charge to which law enforcement frequently turns when it lacks other tools to advance and defend the state's interests. Since Elizabethan England, if not earlier, the powerful have exploited fears of needy, unwashed masses to help them remain in charge.

This was true one late October Sunday in 1941, when District of Columbia police arrested seventeen women in an early morning roundup. Though the raid was likely a crackdown on suspected prostitution, the police turned to that old trick of James Davis's that he'd been so proud of in his 1927 annual report: charging the women with vagrancy in order to keep them behind bars. They reasoned they could get the vagrancy charge to stick because the women had no legitimate way to prove that they could support themselves.

But the next morning, a local official ordered the women released. The police could not legally use negative facts, such as whether the women lacked the means to support themselves, to sufficiently justify keeping them in custody. By their very nature, negative facts were impossible to prove.

That morning, law enforcement practices based on one's means began to crumble. Elsewhere in Washington that day, lawyers arguing on Edwards's behalf launched an even bigger salvo against the nation's antipoor laws, as US Supreme Court justices heard debate over the constitutionality of Fred Edwards's 1940 arrest.

## A Pivotal Decision

Most Americans can cite a few pivotal dates from United States history: July 4, 1776; December 7, 1941; September 11, 2001. Few likely count November 24,

1941, among them. That day marked two seemingly separate but intertwined events.

Late that morning and far from Marysville, Modoc County, Los Angeles, or anywhere in California—indeed, thousands of miles from anywhere in the United States whatsoever—Japanese warships massed amid the Kuril Islands, just off Russia's Kamchatka Peninsula, set sail southeastward across the Pacific. They would reach their destination—Hawaii—on December 7. Once there, squadron after squadron of dive bombers took off from the fleet and attacked and heavily damaged the US naval forces stationed at Pearl Harbor.

Throughout 1941 the Roosevelt Administration had been preparing for the ever-likelier prospect of entering World War II. Meanwhile, *Edwards v. California* wound through the American legal system. After hearing the case that October, the Supreme Court reached its decision six weeks later. On the same November day that Japan's attack fleet embarked for Hawaii, all nine US Supreme Court justices ruled in favor of Edwards with three separate opinions upholding the right of all Americans to move about the country as they pleased.

When the court decided the Edwards case, twenty-seven states had statutes on their books barring destitute Americans from entering their boundaries. As a 1942 congressional report succinctly described, these statutes in effect "set up immigration barriers at state lines." More than half of the states in the entire country prohibited fellow American citizens from their territory based solely on these visitors' economic status—or their perceived economic status. The *Edwards* decision obliterated such restrictions.

Once the United States officially entered the war, the House of Representatives rebranded the select committee examining migration conditions that Congressman John Tolan led. The Tolan committee's new charge was investigating "National Defense Migration." With the United States officially at war, Tolan's committee viewed facilitating migration as essential to national defense. It portrayed the antimigrant restrictions enacted over the past decade as obstacles to war preparations. When the committee issued its report on migration problems—composed of dozens of individual volumes, each hundreds of pages long—it dedicated an entire volume to the *Edwards* case. In a summary of the circumstances surrounding the case and its litigation, the committee noted how both Edwards and the brother-in-law whose indigence made Edwards's aid a crime wound up gainfully employed.

Fred Edwards and his family in 1942. *Courtesy of the Miriam and Ira D. Wallach Division of Art, Prints and Photographs: Picture Collection, New York Public Library Digital Collections, 1942*

By early 1942 Edwards was working as a state inspector at a California fruit cannery, while Duncan had moved to the San Francisco Bay Area community of Pittsburg, where he was hired to work at a chemical factory. That work, the Tolan committee's report noted, directly contributed to the war effort. For the remainder of the war, at least, proponents of policies restricting domestic migration would have to avoid being seen as interfering with the war effort.

The congressional inquiries into domestic migration that Tolan led began well before the attacks at Pearl Harbor and the US entry into the war. Tolan and his fellow committee members toured the United States for more than a year, visiting multiple cities throughout the country to host multiday hearings on interstate migration, learning what the region's experience of migration had been and how the city's stakeholders understood migration and responses to it.

Tolan's committee began the Los Angeles segment of its hearings on September 28, 1940. More than four years after Chief Davis's border blockade, the city continued to grapple with the impact of domestic migration. Significant time had passed since the dramatic events that swept Mayor Shaw and Chief Davis from office, but attitudes about migrants still had not shifted significantly under Fletcher Bowron's regime.

"The city of Los Angeles is the hub of the migrant problem in Southern California, of course," said Bowron deputy Arlin Stockburger on behalf of the mayor, who was traveling in the South Pacific during the committee's stop in Los Angeles.

## "Relocation"

In some ways, Modoc County considered itself as far from the rest of the world as Los Angeles considered itself central to it. Modoc *was* and *is* far— from everywhere. It was far from Los Angeles, from Oklahoma, from the San Francisco Bay that had welcomed the gold miners, from Nicaragua, where John Sharp's father and other Walker filibusterers had participated in the ill-fated colonial expedition. It was far from the communities from which the original homesteaders traveled and it was far from the seats of power that had sent US soldiers to conquer its original inhabitants.

Modoc County was still far in 1936, when Sheriff John Sharp stood up to James Davis, and it remained distant a year later, when Harry French shot Claude McCracken and thrust his hometown into the national spotlight once more. The very fact that Modoc was so far away, and usually so far out of sight, was what made it an ideal place to send a portion of the hundreds of thousands of Americans whose lives would be completely upended by the beginning of the war, even as—thanks to the *Edwards* case—their fellow citizens experienced a massive expansion of their right to travel freely in the country.

On February 19, 1942, President Roosevelt issued Executive Order 9066, which severely limited the rights and freedoms of a large group of American citizens based solely on spurious, racist assumptions of dual loyalties and potentially sinister intent. Under the order, citizens of Japanese ancestry, regardless of when their family arrived in the United States, were rounded up throughout the country, pulled out of their homes with businesses shuttered, and put in ten "relocation" camps in seven states. Most would spend the duration of the war in these camps. Though the camps offered a semblance of normal life— internees worked, went to school, and, in some camps, even organized baseball leagues—those held in them were not permitted to leave, except in rare cases where they received special advance permission.

The White House framed the order as an emergency measure aimed at shoring up security throughout the western United States, but it also satisfied the decades-long campaign of the Native Sons and Native Daughters of the Golden West to cast Japanese Americans as dangerous interlopers. The war, members of the groups insisted, simply proved their long-alleged points about the infiltrators' nefarious plots.

The reality of the war in general, and the Japanese incarceration in particular, tested the stability of the seemingly solid legal foundations that the *Edwards* decision (or decisions) had just laid down. It also once again made Northeastern California, distant as it was from the conflict and the power centers waging it, a testing ground for the essence of American citizenship.

The US government promptly opened the Tulelake Relocation Center in Newell, California, just outside Stronghold, the place where Chief Davis's legionnaires had arrested Sycafoose, La Rue, and Slate in March 1936. There, a familiar face helped provide security at the camp: John C. Sharp.

After Sharp's showdown with James Davis, Modoc County voters had elected him for another four-year term in 1938, despite McCracken's allegation that Jim Payne had threatened to run against him as payback for opposing the blockade. Sharp would be up for reelection again in the fall of 1942. After the internment camp opened that February, though, the sheriff didn't hesitate to cooperate with the outside authorities operating in his jurisdiction.

Residents of Modoc County stood united behind Sharp and the internment camp's presence in the region. That November, they reelected Sharp for a sixth term. Similarly, Fletcher Bowron, the judge turned mayor who helped bring down Shaw and Davis, fully supported the removal of Japanese Americans and others of Japanese descent from Los Angeles.

Wartime conditions complicate comparisons between Japanese incarceration and the Depression-era anti-indigent laws, but only after the war would the full impact of the *Edwards* decision be fully realized. Even then, the concept that freedom to travel within the United States' borders was a fundamental liberty would not be settled until the civil rights era.

John Sharp's readiness to assist Japanese internment suggests that what motivated him to oppose the LAPD's blockade in 1936 had not necessarily been progressive civil libertarianism or a heroic opinion about militarized policing. He was more likely motivated by his era's ongoing tension between rural and urban America. Sharp intimately understood Modoc County's social and political dynamics. As the son of a "pioneer" who "settled" the Surprise Valley, built a home for his family, and sustained them through hard work, he probably would have recognized the kind of independent, self-sufficient imagery that contemporary conservative movements mythologize, though he may not have welcomed them either.

These are the same kind of myths seized upon by secessionist factions like the one that in 2016 occupied the Malheur Wildlife Refuge in southeastern Oregon, just a short distance, relatively speaking, from Modoc County. These contemporary movements perceive outsized influence from distant power centers and large, wealthy coastal cities, just like rural Californians in 1936 mistrusted decisions made in San Francisco, Sacramento, and especially Los Angeles, to say nothing of their thoughts about Washington, DC. Further, they believed that the people making these decisions that impacted their communities so dearly and constrained their hardworking residents so much were themselves too cozy in their urban bubbles to make much of an effort to understand the people whose lives their decisions affected.

Just as one wouldn't be correct to attribute a purely progressive motive to Sharp's opposition to the blockade, one should be wary of misconstruing Sharp in the other direction. Modoc County's sheriff wasn't a mouthpiece for rural resentment any more than he was a progressive crusader. He was a shrewd politician and a savvy businessman. Sharp ignored Davis's much higher visibility and the influence the chief's enormously powerful backers wielded and recognized their antimigrant drive's hypocrisy. Despite his roots in Modoc County, the sheriff didn't place a premium on California exceptionalism.

Not so Gertrude French. People like her considered themselves Native Daughters and Native Sons of the Golden West because they believed their ancestors had civilized a wild land on behalf of America and christened it as virgin soil from which their sons and daughters sprang, only for it to then be threatened first by "Indians" then by wave after wave of malicious, rapacious migrants: Chinese, Japanese, Blacks, Mexicans. Amid the twin disasters of financial collapse and environmental disaster, these groups were joined by the Okies, the Arkies, and all the other purportedly criminal transients whose lawlessness, disorder, and pestilence, if left unchecked, would undermine the Golden State, if not the entire country.

# Conclusion

# ATTACKING DEMOCRACY TO SAVE DEMOCRACY

> Regardless of its demagogic slogans and fancy proc-
> lamations, fascism is the voice and will of monopoly
> capitalism. Not only will fascism indulge in allur-
> ing slogans, but it will not hesitate to raise the most
> contemptible issues as a smoke-screen to disguise its
> grisly operations and to conceal its ghastly failures.
> —Carey McWilliams, 1935

AT THE END OF SUMMER 2019, before the world changed forever, flames metaphorical and literal swept over the United States. The ill winds fanning this inferno preceded the pandemic, stay-at-home orders, recession, isolation, extrajudicial killings by police, and tear-gas-filled summers. They spread before a defeated despot's last grasp at relevance, before desperate flurries of disin-formation flung against reality, and before his followers' deadly, anger-fueled attempt to subvert democracy.

We'll reflect for decades—perhaps even centuries—on the aftermath of 2020, but the conflagration had been smoldering for years. The previous summer, record-breaking temperatures throughout the western United States (which would be surpassed just two years on) were matched by President Donald J. Trump's incendiary rhetoric. First, there was his July 25, 2019, phone call to Ukrainian President Volodymyr Zelensky. Two months later, House Speaker Nancy Pelosi ignited a political inferno by announcing the congres-sional inquiry that would lead to Trump's first impeachment.

The same weekend Pelosi announced the impeachment inquiry, Los Angeles City Councilman Joe Buscaino demanded that California Governor Gavin Newsom declare homelessness in the Golden State a public health emergency. Buscaino was using homelessness and public fears of it as a political platform, and the ensuing two years would see him place the subject at the center of his campaign to become Los Angeles's next mayor.

Decades after the Great Depression, the Dust Bowl, and Los Angeles's shutdown of California's borders, American politicians, American law enforcement, American businesses, and American people still relentlessly besiege, police, and restrict the poorest and most rootless of their neighbors in the name of safety, livability, peace, and commerce. One's economic liquidity and housing status continue to be fair criteria for acceptance into American civic and political life, in addition to the ethnic, social, and demographic factors strongly influencing access to wealth and housing, despite both official and de facto prohibitions on such discrimination.

Today, one might hear a familiar tone in the great bluster with which James Edgar Davis spoke. Like contemporary public figures, Davis was loud and cocky, but his words were often as illusory as his purportedly exacting leadership style was simplistic. Los Angeles's two-time chief of police was an uncomplicated individual who desperately tried to make himself seem complicated.

The border blockade exemplified Chief Davis's direct manner and his approach atop one of the country's largest police departments. It also neatly encapsulated Davis's legacy and the direction of the police department for decades, even after Davis's ignominious departure from the chief's post. Successive LAPD chiefs, many far better known today than Davis, would adopt similar approaches.

As described by police historian and author Joe Domanick, one future chief, William H. Parker, served directly under Davis as a young lieutenant. Parker, perhaps even more than Davis, became emblematic of the LAPD's militaristic, antisubversive approach. The response of the LAPD, under Parker and future chiefs, to shifting racial and economic dynamics, riots, and antiwar activism as well as the LAPD's cooperation with anti-immigrant forces and its ongoing treatment of vagrancy and poverty matched the divisive and antidemocratic characteristics of earlier generations of police leaders.

Parker's leadership, in turn, informed how Daryl F. Gates, the LAPD's infamous chief from the late 1970s to early 1990s, led the department. Over the two decades between Two Gun Davis and Gates, the LAPD became argu-ably the most admired model for law enforcers nationwide. Another three decades after Gates's tenure, in our post–George Floyd world, it remains a model—perhaps not as enviable—of policing's true role in the United States.

Davis made subduing critics of the police and those in power look easy. First, he labeled critics and anyone amplifying their criticism as subversives or, at least, apologists. Second, he quelled purported subversive elements even more efficiently by associating them with enemy ideologies. Davis exploited public fears by linking his and Mayor Shaw's opponents to Communism. They became Reds, radicals, and even terrorists. Davis's most useful tool was one still successfully employed today: describe drastic, authoritarian, and some-times unconstitutional police activities as emergency measures necessary to defend democracy. To save the democratic village, one needed to destroy the democratic village.

In 1936 Earl Kynette's intercession in John Langan's case all but ensured that Davis's antimigrant border patrol avoided significant legal challenges. By keeping the operation away from the precedent-setting Supreme Court's scrutiny, Kynette enabled these and future attempts to police poverty and its perceived ills in the city, throughout California, and beyond the state lines. Although the blockade ended earlier than Davis and the Los Angeles Chamber of Commerce had wished, keeping it away from damning legal opinions meant officials could simply tweak their antitransient strategies. Even after Kynette's downfall, and the subsequent downfall of Mayor Shaw's administration and James Davis's police career, these attempts to police poverty persisted.

Of course, Davis and Kynette were not alone. Thousands of fellow law enforcers, politicians, scholars, business leaders, and journalists applauded his 1935 speech to the Sacramento anticrime conference. At that point, few in the audience likely predicted the coming border blockade. Some among them may have even ultimately opposed Davis's Foreign Legion. Yet in the days, weeks, and months afterward, policy makers and the media swallowed Davis's unfounded claims that he was an expert on Communism and subver-sion. Mainstream newspapers accepted his suggestions for how municipalities and other jurisdictions should address and suppress crime as if his ideas were scientifically calculated, methodically developed social intervention. To suggest otherwise, even to simply publicly express skepticism that a major city's police chief had all the answers, would have been an alien and potentially explosive position to take.

It was easy for people like James Davis to secure public order. All such a person really needed to do was cultivate fear. As was the case all around the world in 1935, Davis's vision of security required little more to champion than repeatedly evoking the proverbial *other* as a looming existential threat to civilized society. Nefarious invaders were infiltrating communities. Criminals from distant locales thirsted for hard-working citizens' land. Agitators dispatched by scheming outsiders undermined local businesses. Unfamiliar newcomers snatched up scarce jobs and in so doing stole bread off dinner tables. Imposters from distant lands defrauded social service providers and thus starved vulnerable local neighbors. Alien forces plotted against traditional ways of life behind the guise of idealism. As Davis and his ilk viewed it, all that could stop them was immediate, decisive, dramatic, and authoritative action.

Historical hindsight might treat Davis's border blockade as a curious blip. Perhaps they'd dismiss it as all bluster with little impact, but the deployment operationalized antimigrant attitudes that had long pervaded California's ruling institutions. The LAPD chief's policing philosophies made tangible a generation of reactionary politics in the Golden State and laid the groundwork for militarized policing that the LAPD would hone to the point that it became the preeminent model for law enforcement agencies for the ensuing century.

Davis presented police officers as guardians of the city, as professional arbiters of order. Not even Davis's scandal-ridden downfall could blemish the department's veneer to any lasting degree. His vision of the ideal police officer stuck, even if he did not.

Davis elevated order as the LAPD's highest value, but it was order as Davis and his allies framed it. Protecting it often paradoxically required chaos of their own making, tactics that did not exclude assaults on core constitutional values and, sometimes, outright violent corruption. The LAPD was by no means alone in developing law enforcement as a tool to maintain the status quo's grip on power, but the department—aided in no small part by its proximity to Hollywood—was pivotal to enshrining the mythologies of policing we most commonly share.

To minimize the blockade's significance by pointing to low numbers of those arrested and limited reports of blatant abuses, or by comparing it to the bomb attacks or other explicitly egregious abuses of power by the Shaw administration and Chief Davis, mars contemporary observations of the event in two ways.

First, such comparisons risk filtering history so as to leave us vulnerable to other future attempts to upend the US Constitution and endanger society. Individual and institutional memories of the blockade recede as we elevate other recollections. This is precisely what is taking place as I write nearly three quarters of a year after the January 6, 2021, attempt to overthrow the results of the 2020 presidential election. People like House minority leader Kevin McCarthy, who'd condemned the terrorist siege of the capital as it happened, later attempted to minimize that history and negate the day's significance to serve his party's political aims. A failed audacious attempt to subvert democracy is still an audacious attempt to subvert democracy.

Second, dismissing the LAPD border blockade (or similar events) as sideshows or aberrations that did little to impact history or as minor chapters in larger narratives erases the thousands of individual stories from people for whom the blockade was a pivotal experience. Would their stories survive as long as the official accounts, assuming they were even recorded in the first place? Would Kansas corn farmers who cowered beneath blaring inspection-station lights outside of Needles as sneering cops pressed their fingertips into ink and called them criminals want to write home about the experience? Would broken parents keep diaries of settling in Brookings, Oregon, to spare their kids from witnessing armed, uniformed men at the California border liken them to infectious diseases? How many veterans would want to talk to reporters, paid by Harry Chandler or William Randolph Hearst, to defend themselves against getting called Communists or tools of anti-American conspiracies when all they wanted was to rest their bodies, which had been broken while defending democracy and starved by waiting for veterans' bonuses? And even when people opted to document such experiences, how many were able to preserve their records through the decades the way governments and other institutions have?

Even this book gives voice to people like James Davis, John Langan, Gertrude Payne, and John Sharp, whose experiences of the blockade were considered important enough in their time to be accessible. It only glimpses at the people who spent nights in unheated hotel rooms that police transformed into jails, who were herded across the Colorado by cops as Hollywood cameramen recorded their shame, or who were pulled off a crowded train and beaten up by police officers who knew they'd face few, if any, consequences for their violence. Such stories would have had to be captured and preserved in the first place. It's a consequence of a world that elevates "authoritative" voices like police chiefs, publishers, and widely published scholars while minimizing the unknown and quotidian.

One of the records that surfaced distills the real stakes at play here. R. R. Colby, the Los Angeles lawyer who wrote city council to protest the blockade from aboard a train from Chicago to California, knew that even if the blockade ended before his train reached Los Angeles (it wouldn't), some of its consequences would be permanent. "But you will never undo the misery which you have already inflicted upon hundreds of good, innocent, unfortunate people, and you who are the leaders in such action should be punished," concluded Colby. It's too late for punishment now, but his observation is a warning for the future.

Still, our selective memory isn't only about access. Histories of Depression-era America often afford little more than a few pages to the blockade—if they include it at all—perhaps because it didn't succeed or linger. They discuss even less the reality that the blockade was part of a broader effort on the part of institutions such as the California Peace Officers' Association, the Los Angeles Chamber of Commerce, and the Los Angeles Police Department to militarize law enforcement, criminalize poverty, exclude entire populations they deemed undesirable, and suppress dissent under the cover of fighting crime and subversion. At our own peril, we justify such omissions by conflating their *unsuccessful* attempts to overthrow democracy with *insignificant* ones.

Moreover, the blockade did significantly impact the lives that *were* given voice in this book and elsewhere. Some of the impacts might seem tangential. Take the feud between Claude McCracken and Gertrude French. With Modoc County being so far from Los Angeles and so much personal drama interwoven with their dispute, it would be understandable to think that it bore no connection to the blockade. Even if the rumor that McCracken circulated about Jim Payne's alleged threat to unseat Sheriff Sharp as retaliation for Sharp's opposition to the border patrol was proven to be true, one might argue that it was too localized or too unique a subject to provide a helpful perspective on the LAPD's effort to shut California's borders. Viewed from a remove, however, the episode underscores how decisions made by one community's leaders can have consequences that cascade through the lives of people far from that community.

The mere fact that the rumor about Payne existed and the reality that it was invoked in a feud as deeply personal as the one between McCracken and French illustrates the widespread, lasting, and powerful presence the blockade occupied in the public psyche, even far from Los Angeles. The operation did not cause the Alturas newspaper feud or other already toxic situations it may have further poisoned, but it was a complicating, aggravating factor and perhaps even an accelerant for that deadly feud.

None of the blockade's consequences are more significant than the way it upended the already disrupted lives of thousands of migrants, and the added burden the operation placed on already strained taxpayers still grappling with recovery from the Depression were widely felt. Still, the blockade's wreckage spread far beyond Los Angeles and the migrants headed to the Golden State from America's Dust Bowl.

The blockade had even helped William J. Atkinson evade consequences for killing Joe Dillard, disorderly as Dillard might have been. It poisoned politics and community relations in Modoc County. It even destroyed John Langan's family and contributed to the bitterness of a heavily publicized, hotly contested child custody battle that all but certainly left an indelible mark on daughter Joan Langan's entire life. Additionally, similar blockades in other locales inspired by Los Angeles's unleashed their own cascading consequences on the many lives and communities they impacted.

---

The present is a fabric woven with the past's threads. Nobody should think straight lines run from 1936 Los Angeles through 2020 Minneapolis into 2021 Capitol Hill and beyond, just as no one should assume that the White Tom Joad and *Migrant Mother* of John Steinbeck and Dorothea Lange wholly capture the direst circumstances of the era. Hundreds of thousands, if not millions, of Black, Latinx, Asian, and indigenous people experienced some of the deepest despair that darkened the 1930s, while the Los Angeles Police Department under James Davis absolutely informs the racist policing that contributed to the deaths of people such as George Floyd and Breonna Taylor. Moreover, the racist history includes seeds planted well before Davis and even before California joined the Union.

As we unravel the Trump administration, 2020's summer of rage, the ever-expanding litany of abusive policing, the dehumanization of migrants pushed from foreign shores by climate calamity and then blocked at democracy's shores, the clearing of homeless camps and murders of houseless people, and the imbalance of pandemic recovery and relief, we find threads from Davis's border blockade and the people, forces, and events surrounding it.

Davis and Shaw were relative newcomers to Los Angeles, but that doesn't make their abuses alien to the city. Neither man corrupted the City of Angels. Ambitious, corrupt, and deplorable as they may have been, they were also tools of power. Their ambition was useful to Los Angeles's ruling circles. Davis protected and advanced the interests of the publishers, bankers, industrialists, commercial leaders, and real estate moguls who placed Shaw in office and positioned Davis to become chief; he seems to have been fully aware of how useful he was to those with influence. But he was no more an outsider bringing lawlessness to the state than were the migrants he cast as invading hordes. Two Gun Davis cannot be untangled from Los Angeles's ills. In turn, the city's ills cannot be unwoven from California's ills, nor can the Golden State's ills be unraveled from the ills of the United States.

Can evil ever truly be laid at any one individual's feet? If not, how do we address it? Whose responsibility is it to unravel the complications as best as possible? When whoever that is inevitably fails, how does the person fairly balance the sacrifices and compromises that must happen?

Homelessness is another reality that we must acknowledge, as is its increasing politicization. The COVID-19 pandemic and the economic disruption it caused intensified an existing housing crisis, and encampments of houseless people—one might call them modern Hoovervilles—have become increasingly visible throughout the country. In turn, they've stoked increasingly vitriolic reactions from neighbors, including in Los Angeles, land of the erstwhile border blockade.

Even before the pandemic, Joe Buscaino seemed to sense a political opportunity in homelessness's increased visibility and the bitter backlash against it. Now, as Los Angeles voters prepare to elect a new mayor, Buscaino clearly sees his aggressive focus on homelessness as crucial to persuading them to select him.

Buscaino launched his campaign in 2021 at an event at the Venice Beach Boardwalk. Theatrics one couldn't have credibly scripted followed. As Buscaino addressed his audience, a woman burst from the crowd holding a knife. Though the woman threatened to kill people in the crowd, she didn't, and she was arrested before causing significant injury to anyone but the arresting officer. Still, the woman's actions represented the perceived public safety crisis Buscaino would campaign upon. Fully aware that the boardwalk was a frequent flashpoint for conflicts between police and people experiencing homelessness, the mayoral candidate invoked those conflicts in the months to come, exploiting voters' fears of violent attack by unpredictable houseless individuals who may very well be in mental distress because of policy proposals such as bans on encampments of houseless people near schools.

Buscaino's campaign dovetails with frequent news stories about wannabe vigilantes torching homeless encampments and about dehumanizing sweeps, not just in Los Angeles but throughout the country. In places considered beacons of progressiveness, such as Portland, Oregon; San Francisco; and New York, civic leaders, business owners, and residents opine that homelessness hurts cities' quality of life, but they do not focus on the quality of the lives lived in tent camps, under overpasses, or bouncing between shelters, motel rooms, and old cars. They focus on their own quality of life as leaders, business owners, and residents who don't want to encounter the less comfortable lives of their unhoused neighbors.

The decades that followed the antivagrant dragnets and migrant-targeting state residency requirements have been rife with sit-lie ordinances, encampment sweeps, nuisance complaints, and private security patrols in tony neighborhoods and business districts. As we cope with deepening political discord and recover from the pandemic's weighty toll on public life, one wonders if we might better understand our relationship with our neighbors, our country, and one another by examining how we valued such relationships during the Great Depression.

Yes, James Edgar Davis played to newspapers to portray his blockade as a necessary response to an emergency (albeit an emergency defined on his own terms), and yes, it appears he frequently concocted the figures he used as evidence to claim the operation's success. The blockade was certainly just one of many controversial moments in a policing career that ended amid citywide scandal. The border blockade did not ultimately succeed. Tens of thousands of displaced people still came to California in 1936 and in the years that followed.

But the foregoing doesn't mean the blockade should be dismissed as a PR stunt. It was a real attempt by a man reveling in his reputation as a gun-loving authoritarian to circumvent constitutional protections, and it very well could have precipitated an armed nationwide crackdown on interstate travel. That the blockade occurred amid the incendiary political climate of 1930s America (and the world) only underscores just how much was at stake. Roosevelt did win reelection handily in 1936, but during that winter eighty-five years ago it was a distinct possibility that he might face a significant challenge from one of many demagogues vying for America's attention, even as events in Spain, Ethiopia, and China ignited the violent ideological battles about to set the world on fire.

As the events of January 6, 2021, most recently remind us, we often only understand how near we tread to catastrophe in those moments when we steer away from it. Only as waves crash and the water's surface breaks do we understand the turmoil in the darkness beneath. Just because documented, outright assaults at the LAPD's border checkpoints were relatively few (or were poorly documented) doesn't make the many seemingly petty or less overt abuses of power that did occur and that were documented any less significant. Similarly, just because insurrectionists who invaded the capitol in the waning days of the Trump administration hadn't killed Mike Pence, Nancy Pelosi, or Alexandria Ocasio-Cortez nor prevented Joe Biden from becoming president does not render untrue that they absolutely aimed to do so. Accepting reality means acknowledging that thousands of people attempted to violently overthrow American democracy and that very powerful people blessed them in their attempt. It also means realizing that in 1936 a police chief and the institutions that empowered him circumvented jurisdictional, legal, constitutional, and moral constraints in pursuit of their personal definitions of stability, even if they couldn't maintain their hold on power once they'd seized it.

The insurrection we witnessed happened. So did the "bum blockade." As we wade further into the future's uncertain seas, accepting such realities may be the only way to avoid sinking into the darkness beneath.

# NOTES

## Prologue: Here and There, Now and Then

*"didn't like the homeless"*: James Queally, "Eagle Rock Man Charged with Torching Homeless Encampment, Sparking Brush Fire in 2019," *Los Angeles Times*, March 31, 2021, https://www.latimes.com/california/story/2021-03-31/eagle-rock -man-charged-with-torching-homeless-encampment-sparking-fire.

## 1. The "Bum Blockade"

*"penniless itinerants"*: "Los Angeles Border Police Arrive Here," *Alturas Plaindealer and Modoc County Times*, February 5, 1936.

*"reserving our final judgment"*: "Los Angeles Border Police," *Alturas Plaindealer*.

*"instances when social workers"*: California State Relief Administration, *Transients in California* (San Francisco: California State Relief Administration, 1936), 245, via Internet Archive, https://archive.org/details/transientsincali00cali.

*"extremely hostile toward"*: California State Relief Commission, 254.

*"wild, mountainous country"*: Frank Sullivan, "French Charged with First Degree Murder," *Nevada State Journal* (Reno, NV), March 27, 1937.

*"[held] water by either"*: "Border Patrols Go into Action at Ports of Entry," *Reno Gazette-Journal*, February 5, 1936.

## Part I: Fuse

*"We're sorry, said the"*: John Steinbeck, *The Grapes of Wrath* (New York: Penguin, 2006; orig. publ. 1939), 14.

## 2. Children of the Golden West

*"the founding family"*: Rachel Young with Sara Gooch, "Bricks, Milk, and Vegetables: Ed Dorris," *Journal of the Modoc County Historical Society* 19 (1997): 19.

*commit themselves to four principles*: Bertha A. Briggs, "Founding of the Order of Native Daughters of the Golden West," Native Daughters of the Golden West, https://www.ndgw.org/about-us/founding-of-the-order/.

*"rare intelligence, discretion"*: "French-Payne Nuptials," *Alturas Plaindealer*, August 8, 1907.

*"highest compliment that"*: "French-Payne Nuptials," *Alturas Plaindealer*.

*"unquestionably its guiding force"*: Robert L. Sloss, "The Modoc Press," *Journal of the Modoc County Historical Society* 3 (1981): 18.

*"topped by a bronze bear"*: "Monument to Be Dedicated," *Sacramento Bee*, June 12, 1926.

*"It has been said"*: "Address of Col. Wm. Thompson at Dedication Exercises," *Alturas Plaindealer*, June 26, 1926.

*"The suprise [sic] Valley"*: Local News, *Alturas New Era*, June 19, 1912.

*"about as lively as a graveyard"*: Untitled front-page item, *Alturas New Era*, November 1, 1918.

*"Most of our citizens"*: *Alturas New Era*, November 1, 1918.

*"Sheriff Sharp and his wideawake deputy"*: "Sheriff Sharp Has Summer Round-Up," *Alturas Plaindealer*, August 6, 1926.

*"A sheriff should be"*: "Business Men Make Best Sheriffs," *Petaluma Argus-Courier*, August 27, 1926.

## 3. City of Dreams

*"the scum of the earth"*: Joseph Gerald Woods, "The Progressives and the Police: Urban Reform and the Professionalization of the Los Angeles Police" (PhD diss., University of California, Los Angeles, 1973), 210.

*"It is not our duty"*: Woods, 210.

*"pool halls, railroad yards"*: "Jail Threat to Force $2 Labor," *Los Angeles Record*, February 5, 1923.

*"Quiet and unobtrusive"*: A. M. Rochlen, "Jim Davis Man Who Can Wait," *Los Angeles Times*, February 24, 1926.

*"This appointment is such"*: "Captain James Davis Is Named to Succeed Heath; Will Take Office April 1," *Los Angeles Evening Express*, February 23, 1926.

*"Los Angeles' immaculate"*: "Cops' Trousers Must Not 'Bag,'" *Los Angeles Evening Express*, April 28, 1926.

*"look as well as"*: "Cops' Trousers," *Los Angeles Evening Express*.

*"We mean to see"*: "Spirits Frisky on 'Halloween,'" pt. 2, *Los Angeles Times*, November 1, 1933.

*"To make crime unpopular"*: Rochlen, "Jim Davis Man."

*"courageous"*: "What Sort of a Person Is This Chief of Police?," *Los Angeles Times*, August 1, 1926, part II, p. 1.

*"If it goes through"*: "What Sort of a Person," *Los Angeles Times*.

*"These narcotic addicts"*: "Stamping Out the Drug Habit in Los Angeles," *Los Angeles Times*, November 21, 1926.

*"I am determined to eliminate"*: "Stamping Out," *Los Angeles Times*.

*"suspicious characters"*: James Edgar Davis, *Annual Report of the Police Department, City of Los Angeles, California, for the Fiscal Year 1926–1927*, June 30, 1927, 5, via Internet Archive, https://archive.org/details/annualreportofpo1926losa/page /n9/mode/2up.

## 4. Regime Change

*"At that, however, Modoc"*: B.S.B., "Mainly Modoc," *Modoc County Times*, May 5, 1930.

*"Earlier economic setbacks"*: Leonard Leader, *Los Angeles and the Great Depression* (New York: Garland Publishing, 1991), 2.

*"Some may say to deport"*: "Alien Drive Speeds Up," *Los Angeles Times*, April 11, 1931.

*"The change in attitude"*: "Local Mexican Held in Jail for Investigation," *Alturas Plaindealer*, January 27, 1931.

*"As all know, the Modoc tribe"*: Colonel William Thompson, "Col. Thompson Denies Schonchin's Story," *Alturas Plaindealer*, January 27, 1931.

*"insult to the memory of"*: "The Peter Schonchin Story," *Alturas Plaindealer*, January 27, 1931.

*"employment mirage shimmering"*: A. Harris, "Employment Mirage Gives L.A. Problem," *Oakland Tribune*, November 21, 1931.

*"Davis will have no strings"*: "Davis Named Police Chief; Crime War On," *Los Angeles Illustrated Daily News*, August 10, 1933.

*"I am not defending lynching"*: "L.A. Officials, Citizens Comment on Lynching," *Los Angeles Daily News*, November 28, 1933.

*"The lynching symbolizes"*: "L.A. Officials, Citizens Comment," *Los Angeles Daily News*.

*"It was one of the rare occasions"*: Mary June Barton, "The Runaway Boy Who Became Our Chief of Police," *Los Angeles Times Sunday Magazine*, September 24, 1933, 19.

*"Physically, he might be"*: Barton, 3.

*"He is a self-educated man"*: Leon Lewis, "Memorandum on Conference Held This Morning with Mr. Armin Wittenberg and Chief of Police Davis," September 15, 1933, 2, Jewish Federation Council of Greater Los Angeles Community Relations Committee Records, California State University Northridge.

*"the Germans could not compete"*: Lewis, 1.

*"the anti-American purposes"*: Lewis, 1.

## Part II: Fuel

*"In 1933 America was"*: Carey McWilliams, *It Can Happen Here: Active Anti-Semitism in Los Angeles* (Los Angeles: American League Against War and Fascism and Jewish Anti-Nazi League of Southern California, 1935), 5.

## 5. Red Dust, Red Menace

*"Our cotton would be"*: Vera Ruth Woodall Criswell, interview by Stacey Jagels, *California Odyssey: The 1930s Migration to the Southern San Joaquin Valley*, February 24, 1981, tapes and transcript, 4:20:00, tape 2, side 2, transcript p. 21, California State College, Bakersfield, Oildale, CA.

*"You'd try to eat"*: Criswell, 21.

*"a fine example of"*: "Local Mention," *Conrad Independent*, Dec. 31, 1914.

*"Jackson to Victor"*: Claude McCracken, "Reporter Describes Plane Trip from Jackson to Victor," *Jackson's Hole Courier*, January 18, 1934.

*"There was no better"*: "Death Claims Noted Editor, Author and Pioneer," *Alturas Plaindealer*, May 30, 1934.

*"Davis did not become"*: Barton, "Runaway Boy," 3.

*"Americans are asleep"*: "Clubwomen's Help Asked in Safety Drive," *Hollywood Citizen-News*, March 1, 1934.

*"white spot on the map"*: Harry Carr, "The Lancer," *Los Angeles Times*, February 13, 1933.

*"the greatest danger at hand"*: "Clubwomen's Help Asked," *Hollywood Citizen-News*.

*"sat and dreamed a good deal"*: Louise Ward Watkins, diary entry, March 1, 1934, Louise Ward Watkins Papers, Huntington Library, San Marino, California.

*"threatening menace of radicalism"*: "Daughters of Golden West Continuing Intensive Program of Philanthropy," pt. 3, *Los Angeles Times*, January 13, 1935.

*"The police really take"*: Gordon Ray Young, "The Way Los Angeles Does It," *American Rifleman*, July 1936, 28.

*"However, permission to use"*: Young, 28.

*"The society women of California"*: J. B. Matthews and R. E. Shallcross, *Partners in Plunder: The Cost of Business Dictatorship* (New York: Covici Friede, 1935), 234.

## 6. State of Emergency

*"This is the most strategic point in"*: "Women View Communists' Propaganda," *Los Angeles Times*, October 26, 1934.

*"The numbers of people invading"*: "Chief Davis Sees Trouble in California Invasion," *San Pedro News-Pilot*, October 25, 1934.

*"This is not a social organization"*: Crete Cage, "Louise Ward Watkins Calls New Anti-Red Club Not Social but Belligerent," pt. 2, *Los Angeles Times*, December 6, 1934.

*"a very appropriate place"*: Cage, "Louise Ward Watkins Calls."

*"advancement of Americanism"*: Cage, "Louise Ward Watkins Calls."

*"every movement to reduce crime"*: "Wider Crime Control Urged," *Bakersfield Californian*, December 29, 1934.

*"While American-born Japanese"*: California Joint Immigration Committee, "Flood of 100,000 Asiatics," *Grizzly Bear*, January 1936, 2.

*"hundreds of thousands"*: "Red Rehearsals to Pave Way for Revolt Are Told," *Sacramento Bee*, March 23, 1935.

*"It is [the CPOA members']"*: Homer Cross to Leon L. Lewis, April 1, 1935, item CRC-1-17-22, Community Relations Committee Records, Jewish Federation Council of Greater Los Angeles, California State University, Northridge.

*might be "abused"*: Leon Lewis, memorandum, circa 1935, 1, item CRC-1-17-22, Community Relations Committee Records, Jewish Federation Council of Greater Los Angeles, California State University, Northridge.

*"and in fact any racketeer"*: Lewis, memorandum.

*"Before us is the sink"*: Herbert Hoover, "Responsibility of the Republican Party to the Nation," Sacramento, CA, March 22, 1935, transcribed in *Addresses upon the American Road, 1933–1938* (New York: Charles Scribner's Sons, 1938), 40.

*"Small businessmen have been"*: Hoover, "Responsibility of the Republican Party," 41.

## 7. Sunset

*"so menacing"*: "An Indigent Quarantine," pt. 2, *Los Angeles Times*, May 18, 1935.

*"indigent alien transient"*: California State Relief Commission, *Transients in California*, 245.

*"common refrain"*: Paul S. Taylor, *The Migrants and California's Future: The Trek to California, and the Trek in California*, Resettlement Administration, 1, MS 3580, folder 748, box 35, ACLU of Northern California Records, California Historical Society.

*"prison camp where undesirable"*: Minutes of the regular meeting of the City Council of the City of Los Angeles, January 7, 1936, no. 4118 (1935), 775, via the City of Los Angeles Archived Digital Vault, https://clkrep.lacity.org/oldcfidocs/.

*"The conditions affecting transients"*: M. H. Lewis, introduction to *Transients in California*, by California State Relief Commission, 11.

*"non-constituted resources"*: Lewis, 17.

*"No doubt seeds have"*: Lewis, 11.

*"Families scattered"*: "Unique Human Experiment in Camps Ended," *Daily Oklahoman*, February 4, 1936.

## Part III: Spark

*"Are these people riff-raff?"*: Taylor, *Migrants and California's Future*, 2.

## 8. The Gate Slams Shut

*"Tonight's story is a true story"*: *Calling All Cars*, episode 116, "Young Dillinger," featuring James Edgar Davis and Jesse Rosenquist, aired February 12, 1936, on Don Lee Network, https://anchor.fm/otr-calling-all-cars/episodes/Ep116--Young-Dillinger-eaq8qa.

*"foresight and civic-mindedness"*: *Calling All Cars*, "Young Dillinger."

*"what the migratory criminal problem"*: *Calling All Cars*, "Young Dillinger."

*"headquarters division"*: James Edgar Davis and Homer Bryan Cross, "Special Instructions," Office of the Chief of Police, Los Angeles Police Department, February 1, 1936, MS 3580, folder 748, box 35, ACLU of Northern California Records, California Historical Society.

*"Individual initiative is encouraged"*: Davis and Cross, 1.

*"vagrants wandering from place to place"*: Davis and Cross, 2.

*"[They] said they had"*: California State Relief Commission, *Transients in California*, 250.

*"I thought there was something"*: "Dorris to Have Border Patrol," *Klamath News*, February 6, 1936.

*"The officers boasted"*: California State Relief Commission, *Transients in California*, 252

*"If they can prove"*: Snoop, Street Gleaning, *Alturas Plaindealer*, February 5, 1936.

*"I wish to make my position clear"*: "Modoc Sheriff Says Local People Cannot Tolerate Restriction," *Alturas Plaindealer and Modoc County Times*, February 12, 1936.

*"In fact, Chief"*: "Modoc Sheriff Says," *Alturas Plaindealer*.

*"Insofar as the border blockade"*: "Modoc Sheriff Says Tourist Gate Is Open," *Sacramento Bee*, March 6, 1936.

*"that their rights as citizens"*: "Modoc Sheriff Says," *Sacramento Bee*.

*"If these itinerants are"*: "Los Angeles Border Police," *Alturas Plaindealer*.

*"Yet potentially all"*: "Los Angeles Border Police," *Alturas Plaindealer*.

*"Were Modoc County located"*: "Los Angeles Border Police," *Alturas Plaindealer*.

## 9. It Can Happen Here

*"tolerant, approachable people"*: Rose Marie Packard, "The Los Angeles Border Patrol," *Nation*, March 4, 1936, 292.

*"The inhabitants were very bitter"*: Packard, 292.

*"Los Angeles police adopt"*: "The 'Promised Land' Barred to 'Hoboes,'" Hearst Metrotone News footage, via YouTube, uploaded by danieljbmitchell, July 14, 2007, https://www.youtube.com/watch?v=zIZDMtRDCxI.

*"dumping ground for transients"*: "The 'Promised Land,'" Hearst Metrotone News.

*"The officers at this point"*: California State Relief Commission, *Transients in California*, 254.

*"looked like wealthy tourists"*: California State Relief Commission, 256.

*"They talked to all"*: California State Relief Commission, 256.

*"Los Angeles is facing"*: "Mayor Supports Chief," *Van Nuys News*, February 6, 1936.

*"shock troops"*: *Encyclopedia Brittanica*, s.v. "Horatius Cocles," last modified April 3, 2020, https://www.britannica.com/topic/Horatius-Cocles.

*"No one objects to"*: R. H. Henderson, "Just Between You and Me," *Calexico Chronicle*, February 5, 1936.

*"repugnant to the United States constitution"*: Ernest Besig to US Attorney H. H. McPike, February 6, 1936, MS 3580, folder 748, carton 35, ACLU of Northern California Records, California Historical Society.

*"street beggar class"*: Crete Cage, "Friday Morning Club Backs Drive to Halt Influx of Indigent Transients," pt. 2, *Los Angeles Times*, February 15, 1936.

*"Perhaps the greatest enthusiasm"*: Cage, "Friday Morning Club."

*"WHEREAS—large numbers of persons"*: Minutes of the Friday Morning Club, February 14, 1936, 27, mssFMC-76, Friday Morning Club records, Huntington Library, San Marino, California.

*"No one can tell"*: "Angels . . .," *Feather River Bulletin* (Quincy, CA), February 6, 1936.

*"The double purpose is"*: "Police War on Transients in California and Place Patrols on State Border," *Reno Evening Gazette*, February 4, 1936.

*"would greatly increase"*: "Davis Plans Radio Link with Border Blockade," *Los Angeles Times*, March 2, 1936.

*"for the best interests"*: Ted Le Berthon, "US to Probe Bum Blockade Suit Withdrawal," *Los Angeles Illustrated Daily News*.

*"I am not convinced"*: Le Berton, "US to Probe."

## 10. Backlash

*"professional hobo"*: Margaret Cochran Bristol, "Transients in Recent Reports," *Social Service Review* 10, no. 2 (June 1936): 314.

*"The police of the city"*: Ulysses S. Webb to Arthur Arnoll, February 18, 1936, reprinted in California State Relief Administration, *Transients in California*, appendix B.

*"our strutting Mussolini"*: Minutes of Los Angeles City Council, February 13, 1936, 477, via City of Los Angeles Archived Digital Vault, https://clkrep.lacity.org/oldcfidocs/.

*"damnable, absurd, and asinine"*: "Arizona Aroused by Patrol," *Hollywood Citizen News*, February 4, 1936.

*Let's Have More Outrages*: "Let's Have More Outrages" (editorial), *Los Angeles Times*, February 5, 1936.

*"it is a pretty well-established"*: "Let's Have More Outrages." *Los Angeles Times*.

*"That is a day"*: Claude McCracken, "GOP Is Not Worried About Human Rights," *Sacramento Bee*, March 25, 1936.

*"chain gang"*: Ada Sprague, "California's Border Holdups," *Morning Oregonian*, February 11, 1936.

*"'Transient Camp?'"*: "Martin Shuts Relief Camp; Views Aired," *Oregon Daily Journal*, January 14, 1936.

*"[Oregon] has enough misery"*: "Martin Fears Oregon Made Goat in Drive," *Klamath News*, February 6, 1936.

*"Certainly if California"*: "California's Ban on Transients," *Morning Oregonian*, February 7, 1936.

*"And if he persisted"*: "Detour on the Open Road," *Sunday Oregonian*, February 9, 1936.

*"blight on our civilization"*: Resolution 21140, Portland, Oregon, February 17, 1936, 2.

*"We are not going to let"*: United Press International, "Blockading of Borders Meets Defy by Sheriffs," *Sacramento Bee*.

*"It is a state problem"*: United Press International, "Blockading of Borders."

*"throwing indigents back"*: "Report All Beggars Is Plea," *Los Angeles Herald-Express*, February 6, 1936, quoted in *Interstate Migration: Hearings Before the Select Committee to Investigate the Interstate Migration of Destitute Citizens*, 76th Cong., vol. 7 (Washington, DC: Government Printing Office, 1940), 2965.

*"[Nevada] will not stand idly by"*: United Press International, "L.A. Blockade Is Attacked by 3 States," *Oakland Tribune*, February 5, 1936.

*Transient Backwash*: "Transient Backwash Is Viewed as Potential Threat to Old Pueblo," *Tucson Daily Citizen*, February 4, 1936.

*"Just where are you"*: Roy Raymond Colby to the Los Angeles Board of Police Commissioners, February 24, 1936, 3, Los Angeles City Archives.

## 11. Aftershock

*"These men are respectable"*: "Modoc Sheriff Repels Los Angeles Invasion," *Sacramento Bee*, March 12, 1936.

*"If I were sheriff"*: Rambling 'Round, *Alturas Plaindealer and Modoc County Times*, March 11, 1936.

*"Our main object is"*: Nolan Norgaard, "Martial Law in Southern Colorado," Associated Press, *Daily Sentinel* (Grand Junction, CO), April 19, 1936.

*"These states did not"*: Elisa Martia Alvarez Minoff, "Free to Move? The Law and Politics of Internal Migration in Twentieth-Century America," (PhD diss., Harvard University, 2013), 135.

*"Being alone in a strange city"*: Harry M. Nelson, "Up Goes the Bums' Blockade," *Sunday Journal and Star* (Lincoln, NE), December 20, 1936.

*"capable of distinguishing"*: "Ten Counties Map Drive Against Hobos," *Los Angeles Times*, Nov. 8, 1936.

## 12. Off Goes the Lid

*"Tonight about 6:30"*: "Editor, Fatally Wounded, Wires His Final Story," *Sacramento Bee*, March 26, 1937.

*"As her husband was"*: "Mrs. McCracken Attends Husband as His Nurse," *Nevada State Journal*, March 27, 1937.

*"The son of a bitch"*: People v. French, 12 Cal. 2d (February 27, 1939), https://scocal .stanford.edu/opinion/people-v-french-23632.

*"Counsel for appellant"*: French, 12 Cal. 2d.

*"blow the tower off"*: "Bombing Victim to Expose L.A. Vice," *Los Angeles Daily News*, January 15, 1938.

*"No member of"*: "His Men Can't Be Guilty, Says L.A. Police Chief," *San Francisco Examiner*, January 21, 1938.

*"contains much valuable information"*: Woods, "The Progressives and the Police," 584.

*"We went round and round"*: "Confidential" (memorandum), June 18, 1938, Los Angeles Times Records, Huntington Library, San Marino, California.

## 13. "Basic to Any Guarantee of Freedom"

*"chaining people to"*: Brief of Samuel Slaff, appellant, Fred F. Edwards v. California (October 1940), as quoted in *National Defense Migration: Hearings Before the H.R. Select Committee Investigating National Defense Migration*, 77th Cong., vol. 26 (Washington, DC: Government Printing Office, 1942), 9996.

*"set up immigration barriers"*: *National Defense Migration*, front matter.

*"The city of Los Angeles"*: Arlin E. Stockburger, opening remarks, *Interstate Migration*, 76th Cong., 2803.

## Conclusion: Attacking Democracy to Save Democracy

*"Regardless of its demagogic"*: McWilliams, *It Can Happen Here*, 31.

*William H. Parker*: Joe Domanick, *To Protect and Serve: The LAPD's Century of War in the City of Dreams* (New York: Pocket Books, 1995; orig. publ. 1994), 27.

*"But you will never"*: Colby to Los Angeles Board of Police Commissioners, 4.

# INDEX